ELDER VOICES

Critical Perspectives on Asian Pacific Americans Series

Critical Perspectives on Asian Pacific Americans aims to educate and inform readers regarding the Asian Pacific American experience and to critically examine key social, economic, psychological, cultural, and political issues. The series presents books that are theoretically engaging, comparative, and multidisciplinary, and works that reflect the contemporary concerns that are of critical importance to understanding and empowering Asian Pacific Americans.

Books in the Series:

1. Diana Ting Liu Wu, *Asian Pacific Americans in the Workplace* (1997)
2. Juanita Tamayo Lott, *Asian Americans: From Racial Category to Multiple Identities* (1998)
3. Jun Xing, *Asian America through the Lens: History, Representations, and Identity* (1998)
4. Pyong Gap Min and Rose Kim, editors, *Struggle for Ethnic Identity: Narratives by Asian American Professionals* (1999)
5. Wendy Ho, *In Her Mother's House: The Politics of Asian American Mother-Daughter Writing* (1999)
6. Deborah Woo, *Glass Ceilings and Asian Americans* (2000)
7. Patricia Wong Hall and Victor Hwang, editors, *Anti-Asian Violence in North America: Asian American and Asian Canadian Reflections on Hate, Healing and Resistance* (2001)
8. Pyong Gap Min and Jung Ha Kim, editors, *Religions in Asian America: Building Faith Communities* (2002)
9. Pyong Gap Min, editor, *The Second Generation: Ethnic Identity among Asian Americans* (2002)
10. Susie Lan Cassel, editor, *The Chinese in America: A History from the Gold Mountain to the New Millenium* (2002)
11. Sucheng Chan, editor, *Remapping Asian American History* (2003)
12. Monica Chiu, *Filthy Fictions: Asian American Literature by Women* (2004)
13. Him Mark Lai, *Becoming Chinese American: A History of Communities and Institutions* (2004)
14. Daniel F. Detzner, *Elder Voices: Southeast Asian Families in the United States* (2004)

Submission Guidelines:

Prospective authors of single or coauthored books and editors of anthologies should submit a letter of introduction, the manuscript, or a four- to ten-page proposal, a book outline, and a curriculum vitae. Please send your book manuscript or proposal packet to:

Critical Perspectives on Asian Pacific Americans Series
AltaMira Press
1630 North Main Street, #367
Walnut Creek, CA 94596

ELDER VOICES

Southeast Asian Families in the United States

DANIEL F. DETZNER

ALTAMIRA
PRESS
ALTAMIRA PRESS
A Division of Rowman and Littlefield Publishers, Inc.
Walnut Creek • Lanham • New York • Oxford

AltaMira Press
A division of Rowman & Littlefield Publishers, Inc.
1630 North Main Street, #367
Walnut Creek, CA 94596
www.altamirapress.com

Rowman & Littlefield Publishers, Inc.
A wholly owned subsidiary of The Rowman & Littlefield Publishing Group, Inc.
4501 Forbes Boulevard, Suite 200
Lanham, MD 20706

PO Box 317
Oxford
OX2 9RU, UK

British Library Cataloguing in Publication Information Available

Library of Congress Cataloging-in-Publication Data

Detzner, Daniel F.
  Elder voices : Southeast Asian families in the United States / Daniel
F. Detzner.
      p. cm. — (Critical perspectives on Asian Pacific Americans
series ; v. 14)
Includes bibliographical references (p. 197) and index.
  ISBN 0-7591-0576-6 (hardcover : alk. paper) — ISBN 0-7591-0577-4
(pbk. : alk. paper)
  1. Southeast Asian American families. I. Title. II. Series.

E184.S695D38 2004
305.895'073--dc22

                    2003022378

Printed in the United States of America

    ♾™ The paper used in this publication meets the minimum requirements of
American National Standard for Information Sciences—Permanence of Paper f(
Printed Library Materials, ANSI/NISO Z39.48–1992.

*This book is respectfully dedicated
to Xia Moua, the elders and their families, and to Florence Detzner*

When you enter a river, you go along the water flow, you go into the city according to the country. This saying is a tradition we used to tell our children long ago. It meant wherever you go, you must follow other people's ways. . . . If the river bends, you must bend with it.

Cheam, sixty-nine-year-old Cambodian man

CONTENTS

PREFACE

IN 1987 I PARTICIPATED in the first national conference on Southeast Asian elderly refugees when it was held in downtown St. Paul, the capitol city of Minnesota.[1] The conference was held in an upper-Midwestern state because the impact of the twelve-year Southeast Asian migration to the United States had a disproportionate impact on the state of Minnesota and its neighbor Wisconsin. The interest of conference planners in older refugees was embedded in larger concerns about the adjustment of families, the differential experiences of each generation, and the long-term complexities of adaptation. The presentation I prepared for the conference was focused on a comparison of the family issues confronting older immigrants and their families at the end of the nineteenth century with those confronting newcomers to the United States at the end of the twentieth century. I was invited to speak because of my interdisciplinary interests in family gerontology and the social history of immigrant groups and my earlier research on Irish and German immigrants in St. Paul (Detzner 1985). The conference planners assumed that historical and cross-cultural perspectives would be useful to the educators, social service professionals, and health care professionals at the conference who were struggling with the multilevel adjustment problems confronting immigrant families of the Southeast Asian diaspora.

My presentation linked the historical experiences of Irish and German immigrant families that came to St. Paul at the turn of the nineteenth century to what little was known at the time about Vietnamese, Cambodian, Lao, and Hmong elderly refugees who arrived after 1975. In preparing for the talk and while listen-

---

1. Growing Older in America: Issues of Aging in the Southeast Asian Refugee Community, October 15–16, 1987. Coordinated by the American Refugee Committee through a grant from the McKnight Foundation. Cosponsored by the Wilder Social Adjustment Refugee Program, Wilder Foundation, and the Minnesota State Refugee Program Office, St. Paul, Minnesota.

ing to other conference speakers, I was struck by the similarities between this group of newcomers and the German, Irish, and other immigrant families that arrived in Minnesota more than a century before them. Although dramatic historical and cultural differences separated these groups, the new immigrants inhabited the same neighborhoods and homes that previous immigrants had built, and they appeared to be confronting many similar family dilemmas. In these highly disparate immigrant groups and historical periods there was evidence of many parallel family adjustment problems, including disputes about language use, concerns about the undue influence of the host culture, conflict between generations, and uncertainty about how to parent in a foreign environment.

In a country whose cultural history is so inextricably linked to its immigrant roots, it surprised me that succeeding groups were unaware of the experiences of those who came earlier. My historical comparisons suggested that each new immigrant group had to rediscover and live through the same intergenerational struggles and family adjustment problems as their predecessors. There appeared to be almost no learned experience or common knowledge transmitted between immigrant groups arriving in different historical periods, in part, because common language proficiency was not shared across groups. I began to wonder whether the life experiences, adjustment problems, and family coping strategies of Southeast Asian families could be recorded and interpreted in such a way that their voices could be heard by succeeding generations of their own group and by other immigrant groups yet to arrive. Perhaps these collective immigrant voices could help us all to better understand the social and cultural roots of American family life, the recurring struggles of each new wave of migrants, and the complexities inherent in the adaptation process.

On the first day of the conference, Xia Moua, a seventy-one-year-old Hmong woman from the mountains of northern Laos, was assisted onto the stage wearing the brightly colored traditional clothing that she had been able to preserve in the passage. She courageously sat in front of a microphone for the first time in her life and told stories of her life experiences to a group of more than three hundred people. In her quiet and steady voice, she spoke of her family's war experience in Laos, their escape to Thailand, and their eventual resettlement in St. Paul. Nealcheng Thao, an intern at the American Refugee Committee, translated her Hmong words into English for an absolutely stunned audience. She described in detail the family's hardships, multiple losses, and tenacious resilience. At a time in her life when honor, respect, and deference were anticipated, this elderly woman was struggling with dramatic changes in the structure, culture, interactions, and identity of her family in a Midwestern state and western country she knew little about. Her powerful story and strong voice would never have been heard had the conference not invited her to tell it and had it not been translated for the audience. It was this courageous Hmong storyteller who inspired the decade-long series of research projects of which this book is a long-anticipated outcome.

The old woman's story included riveting tales of family terror, a dangerous escape across the Mekong River, years living in a Thai refugee camp, and the difficulties of adaptation to the cold weather and northern people of St. Paul. She demonstrated the dramatic power of an elder's life story and the insights that stories might bring to our understanding of immigrant life at an early stage in the resettlement process. These eloquent stories of family heartbreak, courage, and resilience demanded to be heard and preserved because of their intrinsic value to future generations and as documentation of the impact of war on families. Life history narratives of individual elderly refugees are valuable personal and family documents that preserve the historical experiences of the oldest generation.

The forty life histories of Southeast Asian elders gathered for this study collectively reveal personal perspectives on new immigrant family adaptation to American life at the end of the twentieth century. The stories preserved here are "Americanized" versions of the originals, translated into English and interpreted by the author to fit the chapters and categories developed for this book. If future generations of immigrants are able to access these narratives, it will require a significant degree of English language literacy. Ironically, many of the insights revealed by these narratives may have already been experienced or learned by acculturated immigrant readers; however, they may take comfort from knowing that others have passed this way before.

My interest in life histories as a method for understanding the complexities of a long life is embedded in the pedagogy I have developed to teach family gerontology courses. Students have been asked to write a life history of an elder as an assignment in my University of Minnesota course on families and aging since I first started teaching a version of it in 1975. For more than twenty years, I have written and spoken about the value of life history narratives as a method for encouraging healthy reminiscence and life review in elders and for helping students to understand the changing drama of individual development within family life (Detzner 1981). During that time, my students have written more than 1,100 life histories of elders.

Although I was experienced in the gathering of life histories and familiar with Asian perspectives on elders and families, I knew that undertaking a major life history project on elders from Southeast Asia would take years to complete. I had a long-term interest in cross-cultural gerontology, having studied elders and families in China and Japan. In 1992, I spent part of a sabbatical year in northeast

Thailand conducting research in three Hmong villages, a Thai village on the out-skirts of Bangkok, and Ban Vanai—the large camp on the Mekong River where many of the Hmong refugees in Minnesota lived before migration.

I knew that many formidable cultural, linguistic, and access barriers would challenge me throughout the research process, but I also thought that my inter-disciplinary background in American studies, cross-cultural research experiences in Asia, and family gerontology background helped to prepare me for these challenges. It was necessary to work on this project in stages, with observation, participation with elders in groups, and trust-building activities occurring simul-taneously with literature review and the planning of naturalistic research methods. The details of the methods I used, my own position within the research process, and the variety of studies that evolved from this project are described in the appendix, and those who are interested may wish to read it before beginning with chapter 1.

Since 1975, more than 1.2 million Southeast Asian people have fled to the United States seeking refuge from a decade of war and its long-term aftermath. From 1975 to 1995, refugees from Vietnam, Cambodia, and Laos were the largest group of legal immigrants and the fastest-growing ethnic minority popula-tion in the United States and Minnesota (Lee 1998; Martin and Midgley 1994; Spain 1999). Only a small percentage (1–2 percent) of forced migrants from Southeast Asia are chronologically "old" if we use the commonly accepted Ameri-can definition of sixty-five years or the United Nations definition of age sixty as the onset of late life. There are many problems with using chronological age to define the status of being an elder in these Southeast Asian groups, since "middle-aged" parents and grandparents in their forties are considered elders by the younger generation. After working long hours in the fields, receiving poor health care and nutrition, and experiencing the stress and trauma associated with war, escape, camp life, and relocation, a premature physiological aging in adults is not uncommon. Whatever their age or health status, elders who arrived with their adult children and grandchildren, and those who joined them later, were usually central figures in their extended kin network and key informants about the fami-ly's changing circumstances.

More than a quarter of a century has passed since the first Southeast Asian refugees arrived in this country, and by now many elders have left the world with-out recording their heroic tales of survival. Stories filled with horror and trau-matic events are best left to professional grief counselors, mental health professionals, and native healers; however, many others stories, filled with drama, cunning, and the powerful spirit of resilience, must be preserved and heard by a wider audience. Many elders have maintained their traditional family roles as storytellers and keepers of the past and can be encouraged to retell stories at family gatherings or special events usually reserved for insiders. Few elders have told their stories in a formal way so that outsiders can also hear them. Language barriers, family privacy, and social isolation have made it almost impossible for these voices to be heard outside the family.

The overall goal of this book is to understand the family life of Vietnamese, Cambodian, Lao, and Hmong refugees from the perspective of the oldest generation and other adults who are considered elders. This work focuses on male and female elders from four distinct cultural groups that migrated in large numbers after the U.S.-Vietnam conflict. Their stories are composed of complex family narratives, and our task will be to uncover the many ways in which the migration and resettlement processes are experienced. While each elder has a unique experience of family life before and after migration, collectively these informants also have had many similar experiences, and we intend to examine what is unique and common across groups. Although middle-generation parent and adolescent voices from all four cultural groups are also included in two chapters to add an intergenerational perspective, the oldest generation is the focal point for the study.

Because of their advanced age and formidable language barriers, elders often have difficulty making their voices heard. Despite the many barriers that separated us, I found that the elders we approached were eager to tell their stories and hopeful that their experiences and insights would be preserved as a legacy for their family. It is my hope that the articulate, albeit translated, voices of these elders will become more accessible to their descendants and to students, service providers, and scholars who are concerned with family, ethnicity, and aging.

I also hope that this study will contribute to methodological discussions about appropriate, culturally sensitive, and unobtrusive study of ethnic groups and immigrant populations by outsiders (Hirschman, Kasinitz, and DeWind 1999; McLoyd and Steinberg 1998; Foner, Rumbaut, and Gold 2000). According to Andrew Greeley (1974), writing on the process of ethnogenesis: "ethnic groups come into being in the United States and have a natural history" (297). The natural history approach utilized in this study draws on historical, ethnographic, and other qualitative techniques with roots in interdisciplinary fields such as American studies, social history, ethnic studies, family studies, social gerontology, and women's studies. Symbolic interaction and life course conceptual frameworks helped the researchers to organize and analyze the interactions between elders, families, and their social-cultural environments. A naturalistic approach is well suited to studying socially isolated elderly individuals with diverse cultural experiences and multiple language differences, since careful attention to the sensitivity of data-gathering methods is a basic premise of the approach and critical to a cultural outsider's ability to develop trust.

Life histories were selected as the primary naturalistic method of inquiry because they are attractive to elderly informants and because they yield rich insights into a multitude of family, community, and social interactions (Kenyon, Clark, and deVries 2001; Birren and Burren 1996). Collected during 1989 and 1990, the life histories included here are unique qualitative portraits through which families can be seen as they struggle with the impact of war, escape, refugee camp life, and resettlement in the United States. The life history interviews with elders enabled us to develop multiple insider perspectives on the dynamics of family life before and after migration. Detailed individual life history accounts provide rich narratives that can be analyzed across genders and cultural groups, providing insights into similarities and differences. Narratives of family life are embedded within the individual life histories, and when the narratives are analyzed across multiple informants, it is possible to develop tentative understandings about several important domains of family life. The life histories of forty insiders take on depth as well as breadth when combined with related research on Asian immigrant populations, participant-observation fieldwork, case studies, and in-depth group interviews conducted during 1995 and 1996 with Southeast Asian middle-aged parents and adolescent youth as part of a series of studies on Southeast Asian parenting (Detzner, Xiong, and Eliason 1999; Xiong, Detzner, and Rettig 2001; Xiong 1997, 2000). The appendix provides more detailed explanations of the methods, theories, and samples employed throughout the series of investigations I conducted with a number of graduate and undergraduate students, community leaders, and service providers during more than a decade of involvement in the Southeast Asian community.

To develop the broader context for the study, the first chapter outlines the research literature associated with issues of Southeast Asian elders and family migration and several case examples of ethnic-community development in the Twin Cities metropolitan area. The second chapter develops a broad context for the elderly participants and their families, focusing on cultural beliefs surrounding filial piety, sources of stress and distress as refugees, and their new lives in the upper Midwest. Chapters 3, 4, and 5 examine the elders' perceptions and reconstructions of their family stories, changing family structures, and divergence of family cultures. Using materials from three generations, chapter 6 addresses intergenerational conflict in family interactions, and chapter 7 examines the multiple family identities that have emerged in the new environment. Several recurring themes—including gender and generational conflict, the centrality of filial piety, the impact of multiple losses, and the resilience of elders and families—are integrated throughout these chapters. Case studies of specific elders' family lives and direct quotations of the informants' translated words document these themes and variations on them in individual stories and across cultural groups. In keeping with the critical perspectives focus of the AltaMira series, the final chapter directly addresses the implications of the study for research, theory, and practice, with an emphasis on state and national policies that affect immigrant elders and families.

An important observation that emerges from the entire project is the importance of diversity both within and between cultural groups. There are many obvious differences between Vietnamese, Cambodian, Lao, and Hmong elders, including language, social class, historical experience, and individual life experience. Within each cultural group there are also important differences between the young, middle, and older generations regarding adaptation, the maintenance of tradition, and changing roles of men and women. New arrivals are likely to have a perspective very different from that of their cultural peers who have been in the United States for several years. Many elders resist acculturation in the new context, hoping instead to return home or, at least, to maintain cultural continuity amidst so much that is strange. Members of the middle generation, conceptualized for this study as individuals between the ages of twenty and fifty, are often pulled between two cultures and frequently feel as if they do not fit well into either. They are financially responsible for both younger and older dependents yet vary significantly in their ability to manage the complexities of work and life in the new system. Adolescents and young adults who grew up in their homeland are often quite different culturally from their peers who were born in the camps or the United States (Portes 1996). Youth who were born outside their homeland are attracted to the freedom of American adolescent culture, trying desperately to fit in and to be accepted, yet forever destined to be different in appearance, family background, and cultural history than their Euro-American and other ethnic group peers.

Despite all these between- and within-group diversities, the elderly informants in this study had much in common at this stage of their lives, given their diminished status, current circumstances, and geographical location (Bicultural Training Partnership 1996). They were all forced from their homes by the same war within a few years of each other. Most spent a significant amount of time separated from family members while waiting for asylum in refugee camps, usually along the Mekong River on the northeast Thai border. For many different reasons, all the informants in this study found themselves living in the cold climate of the Twin Cities metropolitan area, in a relatively affluent upper-Midwestern state. Nearly all of the informants lived with very limited resources, a major language barrier, and families caught in the intergenerational tangle of adjustment at a time in their lives when stability, harmony, and respect had been anticipated.

The study is significant because it contributes to our limited understanding of the family life of Southeast Asian immigrants living in the United States and because it contributes to important methodological and interdisciplinary conversations about families, elders, ethnicity, and American society. This study is unique because it focuses on the seldom-heard voices of elders from four interconnected ethnic groups and it examines their accounts from a family level perspective. It critically evaluates the current policies and practices affecting refugee families and offers alternative perspectives to policy makers, service providers, resettlement workers, family life educators, and scholars.

The location of the study in Minnesota adds to its uniqueness, since voices from Midwestern heartland states are often neglected in immigration research because of the large populations in New York, Los Angeles, San Francisco, and Miami. The few other books using a life history or narrative approach to study Southeast Asian refugees are focused on smaller numbers of accounts from middle-aged adults or youth, and most such studies were conducted in California, where the largest number of Southeast Asians reside. Nazli Kibria's (1993) book using life histories examines Vietnamese families in Philadelphia. Kibria's book addresses resettlement issues at the family level rather than from an exclusively individual, psychological, or macrosocial perspective. Rather than examine only one group, as does most research on immigrants and refugees, the present work addresses the commonalties of family experience across four cultural groups that have experienced similar displacement.

The interdisciplinary nature of the study suggests that many different types of readers might find it useful. Students in undergraduate and graduate courses that address issues of immigration, intergenerational relations, and ethnicity will find information of interest here. Practitioners who work in the field with refugee populations—including social workers, health providers, resettlement workers, teachers, and family life educators—should find insights helpful in their work. I am hopeful that Southeast Asians who read the book will find a respectful treatment of their elders' perspectives and a mirror held to their own family experiences. Any insensitivities or misunderstandings that arise are entirely the result of my own inability to understand the complex lives and meanings of the elders. I apologize for the limitations of my understanding and hope that the voices of the elders will speak louder than my words.

ACKNOWLEDGMENTS

THIS BOOK IS THE CULMINATION of two investigations entitled Southeast Asian Families with Elders (SAFE) and Helping Youth Succeed (HYS) that were designed to study the memories, perceptions, and constructed meanings that Southeast Asian elders, parents, and adolescents have developed to explain the changes and current realities of their individual and family lives.

The research team for the SAFE project at various stages of the data gathering and interpretation process included Jane Bennett, Carol Elde, Sara Fogarty, Punnary Koy, Jennifer Inthisone, Peter Inthisone, Roger Light, Mai Ly, Annette Lynch, Doaunkgamol (Vechbunyongratana) Sakulnmarka, Mary Seabloom, Chantha Sok, Khiem Thai, Phuong Thai, Thong Thao, Bee Vang, and Poonsuk Wachwithan. Community leaders from five different elder groups asked to remain anonymous, however, their insights and influence on this work is present and visible throughout the manuscript. I am indebted to each of them for trusting me and for teaching me at each step in the research process.

The HYS project included an even broader array of community resources that guided the focus group data gathering and the curriculum development project. My first order of thanks goes to Dr. Blong Xiong, currently a faculty member in the General College, University of Minnesota. Our work together on the HYS and subsequent projects has enriched my understanding of Southeast Asian families and communities in more ways than I can recount. He has been a genuine colleague and cultural guide to me throughout our eight years of work together. I am also indebted to Patricia Eliason, Assistant Director of the Commanding English program, General College, University of Minnesota for her deep understanding of bicultural family life and for her gifted writing talents.

The community advisory committee for the HYS project and their affiliation at the time of their participation: Shirley Barber, Ramsey County Extension Service, University of Minnesota Extension Service; Claire Chang, Resources for Child Caring; Kim Dettmer, Southeast Asian Community Coalition for Youth and Families; Robin Murie, Commanding English Program, General College, University of Minnesota; Doaunkgamol (Vechbunyongratana) Sakulnmarka, Dakota County Extension Service, University of Minnesota Extension Service.

The names and affiliations of persons from the community who helped us to conduct the focus groups with middle generation parents and adolescents from the four cultural groups included: Anh Hoang, Community-University Health Care Center, Minneapolis; Khao Insixiengmay, Lao Parent-Teacher Association, Minneapolis; Seam Lat, United Cambodian Association of Minnesota (UCAM), St. Paul, Mayly Lochungvu, Northside Family Connections, Minneapolis; Vuthy Pril, United Cambodian Association of Minnesota (UCAM), St. Paul; Khambay Sivongsay, Burnsville High School, Burnsville, Minnesota; Danh Truong, Vietnamese Social Services of Minnesota, Minneapolis; and Phia Xiong, Winona State University, Winona, Minnesota.

We were fortunate to attract several talented graduate and undergraduate students to this research project. They included: Ciloue Chang Stuart, a doctoral student in Family Social Science, University of Minnesota; Jeff Temple, an undergraduate student in History, University of Minnesota; Beng Xiong, an undergraduate student in Family Social Science, University of Minnesota; Michelle Gross, an undergraduate student in Family Social Science, University of Minnesota. Although he did not work on the project, Ross Roholt a graduate student in the School of Social Work provided me with a good bit of humor and a regular reminder about the importance of its completion. Kevin Green created digital versions of the family trees.

We learned a great deal about Southeast Asian families and intergenerational relationships from the field-testing of the family stories in all four of the ethnic communities. These field tests were conducted with the help and cooperation of the following individuals and nonprofit agencies. At the Cambodian site: Vuthy Pril, United Cambodian Association of Minnesota (UCAM). At the Hmong sites, Roxy Foster, Minnesota Parenting Association; Kao Lee, Cleveland Junior High School; Chue Chao Thao, St. Paul Hmong Alliance Church; and Vang Xiong, Cleveland Junior High School. At the Lao sites: Montha Phetsavang, University of Minnesota Extension Service, Dakota County; Doaunkgamol (Vechbunyongratana) Sakulnmarka, University of Minnesota Extension Service, Dakota County; Khan Keo Sayachack, University of Minnesota Extension Service, Dakota County. At the Vietnamese sites: Hoa Young, St. Paul City Mayor's Office; and Kim-Vu Friesen, Minneapolis Public Schools.

The University of Minnesota Translation/Interpretation Services office provided valuable services as interpreters and translators of the curriculum into the four Southeast Asian languages. We are indebted to Larry Bogoslaw and Dr. Bruce Downing, Minnesota Translation Laboratory for their assistance in developing a highly skilled multicultural team of professional translators to work with us. They included Cambodian translators: Chamreun Tan, Ramsey County Human Services and Noeurng Ourn, Regions Hospital, and United Cambodian Association. Hmong translators: Muaj Lo, University of Minnesota Medical School and Soua Yang, Minneapolis Public Schools. Lao translators: Dr. Khamchanh Phanthavong, Lao Parent and Teacher Association, and Banlang Phommasouvanh, Minneapolis Public Schools. Vietnamese translators: Van Michalek, University of Minnesota Medical School and Henry Mai, Independent Translator/Interpreter.

The development of a videotape of six family stories would not have been possible without the in-kind and community support provided by Ange Wong, Executive Director of Asian Media Access—a highly successful producer of film and video by members of the Asian American community.

Funding for these two projects was provided by grants from the Agricultural Experiment Station, University of Minnesota; the University of Minnesota Extension Service; the College of Human Ecology and the Family Social Science department, University of Minnesota; and the Minnesota Department of Human Services, the Refugee Service Section, Child Welfare Services to Asian and Amerasian Refugee Youth Program; the Center on Aging, University of Minnesota; and the Undergraduate Research Opportunities Program, University of Minnesota.

I wish to acknowledge the continuing contributions of several valued colleagues here in the Family Social Science department and the College of Human Ecology at the University of Minnesota who have encouraged and supported me through the long gestation of this project. Dr. Hal Grotevant is the department head that everyone wishes they had. He knows and understands my work, creates a positive environment where the work can be done, and brags about the work when it is completed. Dr. Paul Rosenblatt is a colleague and friend who tells me and others the truth, even when we do not want to hear it. His own work in the study of cross-cultural families has made important contributions to our understanding and his productivity and range of interests is a continuing inspiration to me. Dr. Mary Heltsley was the dean of the college during much of the time this work was underway. She encouraged the work, praised the integration of research-teaching-outreach, and made important decisions that positively affected my career at several important stages. I am proud to consider her a mentor. My close friend and colleague Tom Skovholt encouraged me every step of the way around many turns at St. Paul's Lake Como.

I am very grateful to Dr. Gina Masequesmay, Assistant Professor of Asian American Studies at California State University at Northridge. She read the entire manuscript with great care and made many helpful suggestions that improved the quality of the book. Her understanding of the complexities of ethnic identity formation had an important impact on the rewriting of chapter 7.

Special acknowledgement to the contributions of all the informants and research participants whose names we cannot recognize in writing due to confidentiality. The forty elders, thirty-six parents, and forty-two adolescents from the Vietnamese, Cambodian, Lao, and Hmong communities contributed their stories and experiences to this project in hopes that they would provide a broader understanding of the intergenerational dynamics occurring in families during the early years after arrival. Although the stories were sometimes painful to tell or hear, they are the real experiences of real people struggling to adapt to new contexts and circumstances. They provide insights, not only into their own diverse families, but also to the processes that occur in other immigrant families as well. I have been enormously enriched and humbled by their willingness to tell these stories to me and to others who have worked with us.

My hope is that tolerance for the difficulties of the resettlement process and a better understanding of the complexities of adjustment will be the long-term outcome of these efforts. My other hope is that the words of the men and women informants will speak louder than my words and that they will see reflected in the pages that follow a helpful synthesis of their experiences in this country. To the extent that this does not occur, it is a consequence of my own limitations as a researcher and cultural interpreter. I apologize for any misinterpretations and mistakes that have entered into the text and hope that the body of the work will do justice to the resilience and tenacity of these most recent newcomers.

Finally, I am grateful to my immediate family Althea, Jessica Clare, and Toni for listening to my enthusiastic re-telling of these stories over the years. They have lived with and learned about these elders and their families and have come to understand the multilevel meanings of filial piety. After reading every word of several drafts of the manuscript my mother, Florence Detzner, became my most consistent source of encouragement. It is to her and the elders who shared their stories with me that this book is respectfully dedicated.

If the River Bends: Forced Migration to the Midwest   I

A
T THE TURN OF THE MILLENNIUM, the number of worldwide refugees exceeded twenty million persons—cumulatively representing the largest forced relocation in human history. An estimated twenty million more persons were internally displaced within their own countries as a consequence of civil war, ethnic conflict, famine, or natural disaster. Countless other immigrants were on the move across borders in search of economic opportunity and a better life for their extended families. The radical transformations occurring in the home, family, and cultural lives of these millions are rarely examined because the dramatic ecological changes occurring over time are difficult to conceptualize or generalize about. The lives and perceptions of a small number of informants with similar migration experiences can, however, provide a glimpse into the changes in family life of four cultural groups as they try to "bend with the river."

The natural relationship between humans and their near environment is never more apparent than when families are forced to migrate from their home, way of life, and familiar context. Refugees forced from their homes because they are in harm's way are also forced into a radical reorganization of their families in unfamiliar and sometimes hostile environments. The most direct impact of forced displacement falls on those who must leave their land, home, extended kin network, village, and homeland; however, it appears from the narratives of the elders that the impact varies across generations and genders. Most adult refugees are simultaneously confronted by multiple losses, economic hardship, and an uncertain future as they struggle to establish equilibrium in a completely different environment. Homeostasis is difficult for families to achieve because the migration experience has an unsettling and differential effect on each contemporaneous generation, and the effects are experienced by succeeding generations. Within the larger context, many elders consider the economic prosperity and freedom of the United States to be mixed blessings because they often create new and different types of stress in families already burdened by the internal tensions caused by the simultaneous desire for continuity and change (Kibria 1993).

Adaptation to family and environmental change is a universal experience of immigrant families. Each migrating person who chooses or is forced to leave is typically pushed out by a crisis situation at home or pulled out by the hopes of economic opportunity and education for children. Some leave because the climate has changed both politically and literally, as in Sudan, Somalia, and Ethiopia. Ancient ethnic or religious conflicts force others out, as in the former Yugoslavia and Soviet Union, Ireland, Israel/Palestine, and Afghanistan. Each year many more Cuban, Haitian, Chinese, and Mexican migrants pursue improved economic circumstances and hope for their family's future by migrating across the porous borders of the United States.

After the U.S.-Vietnam conflict, many thousands of Vietnamese people risked death in small fishing boats to avoid political persecution, fear, and insecurity in their homeland. An elderly Vietnamese widow interviewed for the study, Nu, was unable to escape with her two daughters because she lacked the funds required to bribe the government officers who processed emigration documents. She recounted her experience: "I didn't have money to give to them, so I had to find some other ways. I sold everything that I owned to get some money for my daughters, so they could escape. Even though my heart was full of sadness when I sent my daughters away, I knew they might die in the ocean. Because of their future, I had to take a chance and send them to the open sea to find their freedom."

Families who choose to migrate in an orderly fashion and those who are forced to abruptly leave dangerous situations confront different challenges in the process of migration. Cambodian, Hmong, and Laotian elders tell harrowing escape stories with forest bandits seeking to rob them, Vietnamese soldiers pursuing them across the Mekong River, and Thai border guards demanding bribes for admission to refugee camps. Mao, an elderly Hmong woman we interviewed, described how difficult the journey was for her and for thousands of other escapees from Laos. Having traveled by foot for days through difficult terrain she reached the Mekong River:

> We do not have any [rubber] tubes so we carry from the jungle bamboos for two days before we reach the Mekong River. We drill holes through the bamboo and tie the bamboo around our armpit then we go into the water. . . . [T]he bamboo floats so that your arms are free to pedal with your feet in a walking motion. . . . [J]ust when we approach the Thai border, the Thai people bring a boat for us. We tell

the Thai that we will not be needing their boat. The Thai pull us up to the boat by the arms. We reach the other side of the riverbank. Whatever money that we have, the Thai take them all.

Following one or more escape attempts, those who were successful often had to endure several years of ambiguity in crowded camps with no assurance of permanent relocation. Some adults left home alone seeking to establish a new home base where other family members could find refuge in an orderly fashion. Thousands of unaccompanied minors who came alone were Amerasian youths whose fathers were American soldiers in Vietnam and whose mothers were shamed for their offspring (Martin 1987). Most Southeast Asians, including the informants in this study, came to the United States in small family groups, often leaving behind many other members of their extended families. Following the pattern of previous immigrant groups, one or more family members established a home and employment foundation and gradually sponsored other family members. Elders report that extended families were sometimes separated during transit, with some members remaining at home, some languishing in camps, and others relocated to one or more asylum countries. Five of the forty escape stories told by our informants include family separations that occurred during the leave-taking. Chong, an elderly Hmong male, explains how his family was separated during their escape from northern Laos: "When we came to a town, they left us four there because I was sick and couldn't catch up with them. . . . Some of my children had died and some already left me behind. So I feel sad about myself, and heartbroken. That's why I decided to leave, even when I was not strong enough to drag my wife and my daughter-in-law and her son across the river."

Individuals and families who find a safe haven confront predictable resettlement issues, including the immediate need for food, shelter, and clothing and the longer-term need for language training, work skills, and family assistance services. Beyond the humanitarian support of asylum governments and the financial support of sponsoring agencies are the broader issues of acceptance and tolerance in the host community. The hosts' ability to integrate strangers into an established social, economic, and political structure and their willingness to share resources and living environments are what make a new place feel welcoming. In some asylum countries and regions within countries, there are strong pressures for rapid assimilation and the submerging of native culture and language. Evidence of assimilation may include conversion to the predominant religion; changes in hair, clothing, and food preferences; and the loss of skill in the ethnic group's language. In extreme cases, a reactive group nativism erupts, making it difficult for an ethnic group to maintain its language, as with German usage in the United States after

World War I (Detzner 1985) or the Japanese internment during World War II (Takaki 1993). Some individuals and groups in host societies are overtly hostile to foreigners, xenophobic, and resentful that crisis situations in other regions have somehow become the responsibility of their country or local community. Covert discrimination in employment, housing, and education affects the quality of life for immigrant families for several generations after migration. In the post-9/11 environment, these nativist, xenophobic, and racist tendencies within American society are clearly rising, as the fear of foreign terrorists grips the nation.

The younger generation often finds it easier to adapt because they are not as rooted in the traditions, language, history, and place that nurtured the older generation (Portes 1996). Their adaptability in the new context is continuously challenged, however, by daily life in multigenerational families managing several stages of cultural adaptation and development simultaneously. Cultural and developmental ambiguity is often the focus of generational conflict in these families, as the elders seek to retain tradition while their grandchildren introduce Western values, behaviors, and ideas into the household.

Families forced to migrate are composed of survivors; however, not all members thrive in the new environment. Successful adjustment depends on, among other things, the ability of migrants to establish support networks in the host society (Portes 1995). Successfully relocated extended families become a magnet for other family members and an important source of information, contacts, and financial support. Formal support services in the host community are often necessary to supplement family support, but they also threaten pride, established family relationships, and independence. Often formal services are not culturally sensitive, the providers lack workers with language skills and ethnic knowledge, and they foster misunderstandings, despite good intentions (Gelfand 1982). This is especially true in the early years of a population's migration. Host nations and social service agencies often make the mistaken assumption that all extended immigrant families are able and willing to take care of elders (Sokolovsky 1990a).

Whatever the reasons for relocation, whether it is across international borders or within the country, the amount of time in transition, and the ultimate destination, the economic consequences of forced migration typically include several generations of economic hardship. Families typically reestablish economic independence within a few years after arrival; however, it may take some families several generations to achieve self-sufficiency (Roberts 1995). Between 1980 and 1990 individuals in all four Southeast Asian groups discussed here improved their economic circumstances the longer that they were in the United States (Bureau of the Census 1990/8). During the prosperous years of the 1990s, similar patterns of improvement occurred. Not all immigrants become economically successful over time. Poverty and a lack of resources in contiguous asylum countries and the camps they reluctantly host means that below-subsistence living circumstances confront escapees from the beginning. Political refugees, who are vulnerable in their native lands, leave the insecurity of home only to achieve insecurity at another level in the country of first asylum. Adjustment to the lower economic levels in resettlement countries is likely to be more difficult for immigrants who were prosperous at home. The relative affluence of resettlement countries means, however, that even poor immigrant families have clean running water, electricity, and refrigeration, unthinkable luxuries in many rural villages and refugee camps.

The difficulties and losses associated with giving up a home, an extended kin network, and an economic livelihood are long lasting. In some families there are horrible collective memories of murder, starvation, struggle, and rape. Virtually every Cambodian family that survived the forced migration during the Pol Pot regime has stories of family terror. In subsequent chapters, we will see more clearly how the death and separation of families significantly alters their structure, culture, interactions, and identity. For those who are most seriously affected, the symptoms of traumatic stress include recurring nightmares and night sweats, paranoia, hyperalertness, obsessive hatred of the perpetrators, an inability to concentrate, extreme sadness, and clinical depression. There is evidence that posttraumatic stress affects not only individuals but also entire families brought back repeatedly to the ultimate moments of horror in their history.

First-asylum countries such as Thailand, Malaysia, and Hong Kong face difficult international and internal issues of their own when considering whether and how to assist political refugees. In addition to the immediate financial resources needed for humanitarian relief, first-asylum host countries also must pay the psychological and political costs of focusing their very limited resources on a problem created by others, while their own pressing domestic problems go unattended. The economic and political burdens associated with refugee in-migration partially explain why sixty-two countries have not signed the 1951 United Nations Convention and/or the 1967 Protocol Relating To the Status of Refugees and why an alarming number of countries that have signed are pushing back persons seeking political asylum.

Southeast Asian Migration to the United States

Within these broad historical and international contexts, the forced migration of Southeast Asians was an extraordinary occurrence because its dramatic inception was covered on U.S. television during the final days of April 1975. As frightened Vietnamese clerks, attachés, and others affiliated with America's presence in Vietnam climbed from the American embassy roof to board helicopters, the mass migration of more than 1.2 million Southeast Asian people to the United States was underway. The beginning of the Vietnamese diaspora was an embarrassing end to an ill-fated attempt by the United States government to create political change in a part of the world it did not fully understand. Postwar feelings of guilt generated a sense of obligation in many Americans to those whose lives had been most directly affected by the decade-long intrusion. There was an unprecedented call for Americans to commit to the financial and social obligations of sponsorship for individuals and families they had never seen before. Thousands of American citizens, often through church groups and nonprofit organizations, sponsored the resettlement of families from camps in northern and eastern Thailand. Although thousands of Southeast Asians resettled in other Asian countries, as well as in Australia, Canada, and France, the vast majority came to the United States. From 1975 to 1995, Southeast Asians were the largest group of legal immigrants or refugees admitted into the country. From 1980 to 1990, they were the fastest-growing ethnic group in the United States (Lee 1998; Martin and Midgley 1994). It is impossible to know the exact number who lived in the United States before 1980 because the census data were gathered under the undifferentiated "Asian-Pacific Islander" category. Individuals from specific Asian countries such as Laos and Cambodia and those from ethnic groups like the Hmong and Chinese Vietnamese are not visible in these data. The 1980 census indicates approximately 320,000 Southeast Asians (Burmese, Vietnamese, Cambodian, Lao, and Lao-Hmong and other hill tribes) were living in the United States. By 1990, the number of Southeast Asians living in the United States had grown to over one million, and a strong case could be made for a significant undercount.

Unlike most previous immigrant groups, Southeast Asians arrived in the United States rather suddenly, between 1975 and 1980. There were efforts made to place these newcomers in all regions of the country; however, a few states resettled most of them. In 1990, when the years of heaviest migration were over, California had by far the largest number, with approximately 456,310 Southeast Asians. The next largest numbers in order were located in Texas, Washington, Minnesota, Massachusetts, Virginia, Pennsylvania, New York, Wisconsin, and Florida. Eight of those top ten states are likely candidates for large resettlement populations because they are among the most populous states. Minnesota with the fourth-highest and Wisconsin with the ninth-highest rank are the anomalous states, since they are among the top recipients yet rank toward the middle in population base. When the citizen-to-refugee ratio is calculated it reveals the comparative impact of refugee populations on the host state. From this perspective, Minnesota and Wisconsin rank at or near the top among the states most significantly affected by the forced migration of Southeast Asians.

The anomaly of these two upper-Midwestern states is visually dramatic if you imagine a map of the United States with the ten largest recipient states shaded. Minnesota and Wisconsin are all alone in the middle of the country, while the highest levels of resettlement occurred on the west coast, in the south, and along the eastern seaboard. Considering the tropical climate in Southeast Asia, it is easy to understand the pull toward the hot sunny valleys of California, the humid fishing towns along the gulf coast, and lush vegetable farms and citrus groves of Florida. But what was the pull toward the upper-Midwestern states, particularly Minnesota, whose reputation as the "icebox of the nation" is carefully guarded by the natives so as to discourage too many newcomers from moving there?

In all large-scale population movements there are both "push" and "pull" factors that influence the movement of groups away from or toward a particular place. The "pulls" toward Minnesota include the early leadership of social service and relief agencies like Catholic Charities, Lutheran Social Services, and the International Institute of Minnesota (Sherlock 1987; Mason 1981). Hundreds of Minnesota parishes and synagogues participated in the relief effort, with thousands of families volunteering to assist as sponsors. When I am asked at community talks and conference presentations "Why did they come here?" I always reply, "Because we invited them." In a state with a liberal tradition and a favorite son named Hubert Humphrey whose chance at the presidency was marred by President Johnson's escalation of the war, there were plenty of guilty people and good intentions to go around. Minnesota and Wisconsin share similar liberal traditions, prosperity, and low unemployment rates. Both states are known for their excellent educational systems, social services, and relatively low crime rates, and, with the possible exception of the cold winter months, both states have a high quality of life. Many newcomers were pulled toward the Midwest because government "family reunification" policies encouraged previously resettled family members to sponsor close relatives. An unknown number left the states where they first resettled after a few months or years and moved to Minnesota or Wisconsin in a secondary migration.

The "push" factors include U.S. policies that encouraged distribution of refugees across states and regions so that the economic "burden" would be broadly shared. Some were pushed from initial places of resettlement because they could not find enough work to support their families; because they heard there were more opportunities in the Midwest; or because sponsors exploited them or pressured them to make a religious conversion. Undoubtedly, many left Minnesota and Wisconsin for other states too, but the net in-migration appeared to many observers and field workers as considerable. By 1990, there were considerably more than the 36,506 Southeast Asians counted by the census in Minnesota and 23,027 in Wisconsin. The Minnesota Refugee and Immigration Assistance Office estimated the actual number of Southeast Asians in 1990 at 56,000, with at least 10,000 Hmong people not counted. Four of the top ten cities in the country for Hmong resettlement were located in Minnesota and Wisconsin, with the Twin Cities ranking a close second to Fresno, California, for the largest number of Hmong. By the mid-1990s, St. Paul contained the largest urban population of Hmong people of any city in the world.

The migration into Minnesota was quite steady between the years of 1979 and 1993, with approximately 1,500 to 2,500 official new arrivals each year. Three years were exceptional: 1979, when 3,817 arrived; 1980, when 6,457 arrived; and 1981, when 3,296 arrived. In all, more than 13,500 new arrivals came to Minnesota during those three years. Most of them came to the Twin Cities metropolitan area, with the Hmong coming especially to St. Paul, straining the volunteers and resettlement agencies seeking to help them. High fertility rates in the Hmong population increased their numbers significantly after the initial years of resettlement.

This was quite a demographic leap for a city and a state with predominately German, Scandinavian, and Irish ethnic backgrounds. Although there were southern and eastern Europeans living in identifiable ethnic neighborhoods throughout Minneapolis and St. Paul during the early decades of the twentieth century, and many languages spoken on the street, there were almost no Asians and very few residents from non-European cultures. In 1980, approximately 5 percent of Minnesota's population was nonwhite (Adams and Van Drasek 1993). Like the rest of the country, the state has become increasingly diverse during the past two decades as a consequence of immigration; however, the state's capitol city is unlikely to ever compete with San Francisco, Chicago, Miami, or New York for ethnic diversity. Indeed, the Minneapolis–St. Paul metropolitan area is not ranked in the top fourteen metropolitan areas with large numbers of Asians–Pacific Islanders in the 2000 census (Bureau of the Census 2000). Small numbers of earlier Asian immigrants from China, Japan, and the Philippine Islands means that the overall numbers are comparatively small, but they also suggest how much adjustment needed to occur on the part of the newcomers and their hosts when the Southeast Asians started to arrive in large numbers. By the year 2000, the census had accounted for 41,800 Hmong, 18,824 Vietnamese, 9,940 Laotians, and 5,530 Cambodians living in Minnesota. With another 33,791 Hmong living in Wisconsin, the two states combined had more Hmong than California or any other two states combined.

Indeed the setting that these groups found themselves in was more than a little confusing to the newcomers, and they were confusing to the host community as well. During the early years, little was known about the cultures, languages, and family practices of the new groups by the staff working in resettlement, social service, and health care agencies. The Hmong were the least understood of the four groups and soon became the largest Southeast Asian group in Minnesota. In 1979 and 1980, when the influx of newcomers was greatest and calls to the University of Minnesota for information were a daily event, a small group of faculty working with the Center for Urban and Regional Affairs developed the center for Southeast Asian Refugee Studies (SARS).[1] This small center focused on developing and disseminating a collection of research and background materials on the new groups. In addition, it sponsored national conferences and conducted research. SARS eventually developed a broad collection of materials on Southeast Asians, especially the Hmong; it published an internationally distributed research newsletter; and it published occasional papers and bibliographies. As the state became even more diverse and African refugees increased in number and visibility in the state, the center broadened its mission, became more inclusive, and changed its name to the Refugee Studies Center. The research collection is now located in the University of Minnesota's Immigration History Research Center, which can be accessed at www.umn.edu/ihrc/news.htm.

An early difficulty that many citizens in the host cities experienced was distinguishing between the four cultural groups. People understood why the Vietnamese were leaving their country; however, few understood the Hmong population or why they were arriving in such large numbers in Minnesota and Wisconsin. Their origins in the mountains of northern Laos, slash-and-burn agricultural practices, animist spiritual beliefs, and clan-based family structure made them dramatically different from the Norwegian bachelor farmers of Minnesota made famous by Garrison Keillor's *Prairie Home Companion* program on National Public Radio. After a few years and numerous newspaper and television stories, many Minnesotans assumed that all the Asians they saw were Hmong, since the Hmong were the most numerous and visible in the media. The tendency to lump the four groups together as if they were one was troublesome to community leaders, especially since the memories of conflict between groups and factions were still fresh in their minds. In fact, as new arrivals continued to join those who had been here for a number of years, the diversity *within* each cultural group became even greater. Within ten years of the first arrivals, it was hard to say what it meant to be a Southeast Asian "refugee," since there were many different variations within groups and between groups and individuals at diverse stages of adaptation. Many of those who arrived in the early years disliked the label "refugee" after they had become integrated into some segments of the new society. The diversity within and across groups was stratified according to gender, generation, and recency of arrival. With each year bringing new arrivals and high birthrates in some groups, a multiplicity of Vietnamese American, Hmong American, Cambodian American, and Lao American identities emerged.

Comparing some of the differences between groups is relatively simple, since the patterns are consistent, especially in the realm of economics. In every measure of economic well-being at the time of the interviews, the Vietnamese were better off and the Hmong were worse off than the Lao and Cambodians (Bureau of the Census 1990/2). In addition to differences in background, education level before arrival, and previous economic circumstance, the high birthrate of the Hmong partially explains the economic differences. Hmong men and women continued to value the large families that were important to economic survival when they were farmers in the highlands. The fertility rate of Hmong women living in Minnesota was quite high, with almost 60 percent of the women between 25 and 34 having five or more children, whereas almost no Vietnamese women in that age group reported having that many children (Bureau of the Census 1990/3). As a consequence of this high birthrate, more than 60 percent of Minnesota's 1990 Hmong population was under the age of 17 and the median age of Hmong people as a whole was 12.4 years. By comparison, only 32 percent of the Minnesota Vietnamese were under 17, while all four groups had a median age of 24.5 years (Bureau of the Census, 1990/4). By the 2000 census, there had been little change in the age distribution of the Hmong in Minnesota. More than 62 percent of the Hmong were age 19 or under and the median age was 15.9 years. In comparison, the Minnesota Vietnamese population's median age in 2000 was 29.4 years and the Minnesota white population's median age was 37 years (Bureau of the Census 2000). Because the Hmong are the largest Southeast Asian group, their young age has important consequences for the St. Paul school district, in which Hmong students compose 31 percent of the enrollment, with approximately 1,000 Hmong students in each of the K-12 grades (Leslie 2002).

At the other end of the life course, the number and percentage of the Southeast Asian "elderly" population living in Minnesota is comparatively small. Most persons in Southeast Asian cultures are considered "elders" by age 45; however, we have already pointed out the problems with using a specific chronological age to define "elder." At the time we conducted the interviews in 1990, approximately 14.3 percent of Vietnamese were over 45; for the Cambodians 11.7 percent; for the Lao 10.7 percent; and for the Hmong only 8.8 percent. Between 1 and 2 percent of the people in all four groups were over the age of 65, the traditional chronological marker of old age in the United States (Bureau of the Census

1990/4). In the 2000 census, many of these same patterns were present. For example, 13 percent of the Hmong population was over 40, and 2.2 percent of Hmong women and 1.3 percent of the men were over age 60 (Bureau of the Census 2000).

An important difference between the four groups is reflected in their household composition. For example, between 1990 and 1995 only 11.1 percent of Vietnamese households had seven or more persons, while 43.4 percent of Hmong families lived in such households (Bureau of the Census 1990/5). By the year 2000, only 8 percent of the Vietnamese lived in households with seven or more persons, while 48 percent of the Hmong lived in such households. In comparison, only 2 percent of Minnesota's entire population lived in households with more than seven members. Hmong families lived in a household that averaged 6.13 persons, while Vietnamese families lived in a household that averaged 3.42 persons (Bureau of the Census 2000). Home ownership rates reveal a similar disparity, with the 1990 census data indicating that 14.4 percent of the Hmong owned the home they occupied compared to 43.4 percent of the Vietnamese (Bureau of the Census, 1990/1996). More than three times as many Hmong (14.2 percent) reported that they spoke no English at home, compared to 4 percent of the Vietnamese (Bureau of the Census 1990/7). Almost half of the Hmong reported in 1990 that they had household incomes below $15,000, while fewer than 20 percent of the Vietnamese had incomes below that level. Although Cambodians ($10,885) had a slightly lower median family income than the Hmong ($11,934), the Vietnamese ($26,614) had more than double the poverty-level incomes of the other three groups. The Hmong were by far the lowest in per capita income ($2,540) compared to the Cambodians ($4,639), the Lao ($5,776), and the Vietnamese ($8,423). More than two-thirds of Minnesota's Hmong population was living below the poverty level in 1990 (Bureau of the Census, 1990/1998).

The point here is not to make comparisons that show one group to be superior or inferior to others but rather to demonstrate the dramatically different experiences of the groups using some common indicators of economic well-being. Although the Cambodian and Lao groups fell statistically between the Vietnamese and Hmong in almost every economic and social well-being category, their historical experiences were quite different. The Cambodian families, in particular, were stricken by the ever-present memories of the Pol Pot holocaust. During the early years of resettlement all four groups had their own struggles, collective histories, and identities to reconstruct without much help from peers outside their families or from ethnic organizations. The evolution of distinct ethnic identities is discussed in more detail in chapter 7; however, it is important to point out here how vibrant the communities became where these new immigrants lived and conducted their business.

In only a few years, each of the groups began to develop a visible cultural presence in the Twin Cities area. As the groups grew in size they congregated in public housing projects; they developed shops, markets, and restaurants; and they sometimes clashed with their hosts. The development of diverse ethnic communities in Minnesota and the Twin Cities during the 1980s and 1990s is worthy of a book-length treatment by itself. A few examples here will illustrate the variety of ways in which the host and immigrant communities interacted with each other as new ethnic organizations and cultural identities emerged.

Developing Ethnic Communities in Minnesota

From 1975 to 2000 the growth of the Southeast Asian population and the development of its ethnic communities could almost be measured horizontally by the growth of Asian businesses along University Avenue, the main east-west business thoroughfare between St. Paul and Minneapolis. The St. Paul *Pioneer Press,* in a front-page article called "University Avenue the 'Asian Main Street'" (May 30, 1999), illustrated this growth with a full-page map detailing the dozens of new business and ethnic organizations that made their home on the busy thoroughfare. At the east end of the avenue in St. Paul is the Minnesota State Capitol building and associated state office buildings; at the west end in Minneapolis is the University of Minnesota campus, the Hubert H. Humphrey Metrodome sports arena, and downtown Minneapolis. Just north of the capitol building in St. Paul the heart of the Hmong community is located on a hill in the Mt. Airy/McDonnough public housing complex, where several thousand families make their homes. Nearby neighborhoods on both sides of University Avenue and the East Side neighborhood east of the 35E freeway are ethnically mixed, with a predominance of Southeast Asians, especially the Hmong.

In his comparative study of Vietnamese and Russian refugees, Gold (1992) points out that the growth of ethnic businesses and organizations serves multiple purposes in the development of an ethnic community. First, ethnic entrepreneurs utilize resources from their communities and families to compete with more well-established mainstream businesses. By offering goods and services, they provide a public good to the larger community; they also provide employment for family, friends, and new arrivals with limited language skills. In the case of University Avenue, the new business development revitalized a shabby and run-down part of the city and brought positive visibility to Southeast Asian groups. Such examples demonstrate that ethnic solidarity and adaptation are not mutually exclusive concepts but rather mutually reinforcing.

The first Southeast Asian businesses along University Avenue were small restaurants seeking to attract nearby residents with familiar foods and aromas and drawing the state capitol crowd with the newest ethnic food. After a few years other businesses, social service agencies, and mutual assistance associations serving the Asian community sprang up farther west of the capitol. New establishments included video stores, grocery stores, auto repair shops, the Asian-American Press, the *Hmong Times*, a jewelry store, churches, and more restaurants. Today there are several Asian businesses on almost every block of University Avenue from the midway point between the Twin Cities all the way to the capitol—a distance of several miles. Evidence of the integration of Southeast Asians into the social, economic, and political fabric of the community is also revealed by the growth of ethnic organizations in the area. An Asian American Business Association began in the 1980s to help local businesses get started by focusing on capacity-building and community improvement activities. Although not every business in the 2000–2001 Hmong American Yellow Pages is owned by Asians, there are ninety pages of listings and advertisements. The Directory of Asian American Community Organizations in the Twin Cities (1995) listed 116 nonprofit organizations that were serving the needs of the Asian American community. The 2001 Directory of Nonprofit Organizations of Color in Minnesota takes sixty pages to list all the organizations serving Asian Americans in the state, outnumbered only by the better-established African American/African organizations. Many of the Asian American nonprofits are located on or near the University Avenue corridor.

Mutual Assistance Associations

It did not take long for leaders in the Southeast Asian communities, like leaders of immigrant groups preceding them, to form mutual help associations to improve the social and economic circumstances of their people. At first, associations were formed to bring dispersed members of the ethnic group together to socialize and celebrate important holidays. Later the groups became more formalized into a number of mutual assistance associations (MAA). Like the Lutheran Brotherhood of an earlier time, these groups were developed to insure members against the unexpected expenses of death or illness or to loan money for a good cause or a business start-up. There were at least thirty-seven such organizations in the Twin Cities in 1987 (Sherlock 1987). Many of the groups were eligible for grants from state and federal governments and foundations to develop programs for women and children, English language education, chemical dependency prevention, runaway youth, and early parent education, as well as other programs. Unable to sort through the competing applications, funding agencies were frustrated by competing proposals from multiple MAAs, sometimes from the same cultural group. Several coalitions of MAAs were formed to provide a common voice, but after a few years, when funding ran out, the coalitions died.

Each cultural group used its mutual assistance associations to obtain funding, to teach about and negotiate the American system, to train emerging community leaders, and to provide social and financial support to its constituents. There were numerous internal political squabbles within and between groups, and struggles for power and leadership as well. Although internal dissension is not a wise survival strategy for new immigrant groups, it is a sign of vitality and ethnic identity development within emerging new communities.

Hmong New Year Celebrations

Although all four groups celebrate the new year at different times of the year, the Hmong celebration in the fall is always the largest and most visible in the Twin Cities. During the Thanksgiving holiday weekend in November the Hmong mutual assistance associations and other affiliated groups rent the downtown St. Paul Xcel Energy Center, formerly the Civic Center, to celebrate Hmong life and culture. Hmong people from all over the country, especially Wisconsin and California, flock to St. Paul for the biggest celebration in the nation. The celebration is as much about the presence of a large community of Hmong people in such an unlikely place as it is about the new year. A great deal of food is prepared and eaten. Adolescent boys and girls participate in the traditional ball toss ritual, in which they are supposed to meet their future spouses. There is a Hmong Teen of the Year contest with ten male and female finalists. Young children and teenage girls wearing traditional clothing dance on stage to the delight of the parents and grandparents in the audience. At night, there is a teen dance with rock music and the Hmong American kids in jeans. Inevitably there is a photograph in the two major newspapers of a young girl in brilliantly colorful traditional clothing.

The bicultural nature of the new year celebration is revealed in many subtle ways through the new year clothing that is constructed by elders for their grandchildren (Lynch, Detzner, and Eicher 1996). In a study combining participant observation of Hmong youth and the life histories of elders we found that the "traditional" clothing worn by the young girls for the new year's celebration was really an intergenerational cross-cultural construction of traditional designs using many American materials. Thus, as the grandmothers lovingly constructed the most important piece of clothing of the year for their grandchildren, they were also combining the old with the new in a symbolic linking of the Hmong past with their granddaughters' Hmong American future. We concluded that "Hmong

American New Year's dress is thus a rich medium used by both wearers and designers to express a myriad of feeling related to attempting to balance the desire to remain tethered to the past with the equally strong desire to be in step with contemporary reality" (Lynch, Detzner, and Eicher 1995, 8).

Building Buddhist Temples

The growth of small businesses, strong mutual assistance associations, and the annual celebration of the new year are visible indicators of emerging ethnic communities and the development of social capital. The construction of the Vietnamese Buddhist temple just north of St. Paul on Highway 36 in the early 1980s was a daily reminder to thousands of commuters that these newest immigrants were planning to stay. Many Southeast Asians consider themselves to be Buddhists, including many who have "officially" converted to Christianity and those practicing ancestor worship and animism. Even if these immigrants do not formally practice the Buddha's way, the cultural framework and worldview of the predominant Southeast Asian religion has a pervasive influence on their values. To provide a place for the Vietnamese community to practice its beliefs, the Vietnamese Buddhist Association purchased the building that became the centerpiece of the new temple. Volunteers from the Vietnamese community did all of the work to remodel the building into a beautiful temple. Slowly, brick by brick, the Asian style roofline became apparent, and when the new Buddha statue was first installed, the entire community turned out to celebrate with monks who came all the way from California. The physical presence of the temple is important to the community because it is a place to meditate and reflect, to light incense before the wall with names and photographs of deceased friends and relatives, and to put oneself back at home again, if only for a few hours. Besides being a powerful symbol to the Vietnamese and the American communities, the temple serves as a place of solace, repose, and continuity, especially for the elders. They value the temple most highly because its presence suggests that important elements of Vietnamese culture will remain with their descendants. The temple was built for the same reason that the nineteenth-century German-Catholic immigrants in St. Paul built churches and schools before building their own homes. They wanted a place where the sounds and smells of the Old World could be re-created and where children would learn to respect the values and traditions of their culture.

At about the same time the Vietnamese Buddhist temple was built, the Cambodian's Buddhist Society built its own temple at a farm it bought outside of Hampton, Minnesota, a small town about thirty miles south of the Twin Cities. The large family gatherings at the temple, the monks in saffron robes, and the smell of incense were concerns to some residents of the local rural community. There were uncertainties about the types of activities going on at the temple and a great deal of suspicion. After several meetings, the townsfolk were reassured and some even went to the temple to observe the family activities and religious rituals.

The building of the temples is a source of pride to the ethnic communities and a visible reminder of the growing presence of newcomers. Although the newcomers are very different from the European immigrants who built their places of worship in the same communities more than a century before, their need to rebuild traditional religious practices in their new homes emerged from a similar human need for spiritual and cultural continuity.

Culture Clashes

Building ethnic communities is more than the building of new temples, businesses, and mutual assistance associations. Inevitably, members of the new communities clashed with the laws, traditions, and practices of the host communities. There were countless minor conflicts and a few major ones between the hosts and these newly forming ethnic communities. A few examples illustrate how easily misunderstandings can occur. One Southeast Asian man was arrested for having caught hundreds of fish in one of the local city lakes. He had never heard of a fishing license and had no concept of a limit on the catching of fish. A Hmong man who was stopped from hunting squirrels in the city with a twenty-two-caliber rifle was unaware that it was illegal to shoot a gun in the city. Many kids in school complained that their peers made fun of their limited English or called them names like "gook" or "chink." Children were told to go back to China, an odd challenge to children born in the United States who were citizens by birth.

Many of the traditional practices and simple survival issues of the newcomers seemed alien to those who looked at the world through Western eyes. When the Hmong began arriving in large numbers during the late 1970s, there were Twin Cities televised news reports on Hmong families who slaughtered pigs and chickens in their garages or back yards for important feasts and ceremonial holidays. At a 1995 national education conference in St. Paul, a young Hmong woman who had just completed medical school told the story of how her resourceful family lured pigeons into their high-rise apartment building by opening the windows and scattering corn on the floor and tables. When several birds entered, the family quickly closed the windows and dined that evening on freshly caught fowl. Countless other encounters and experiences like these caused consternation to those who did not understand the newcomers.

Conflicts between newcomers and their hosts are often the result of cultural misunderstandings or differences in perspective. Conflicts or misunderstandings within families about social practices, official rules, and laws can disturb the internal harmony and balance of a family system. Not knowing what is expected, or having some family members who know and some who do not know, are recurring sources of stress for individuals and families. Several examples indicate that not all parents and adolescents in the new ethnic communities were aware of the serious consequences that can result from law-breaking.

More serious misunderstandings and criminal behaviors resulted in the loss of juvenile lives. One tragic case involved two young Hmong boys who stole a car for a joy ride. When pursued by police, they sped away until the car crashed. When the kids fled the crash scene, a suburban police officer who had never fired his weapon in more than twenty years on the force panicked, thinking he saw a gun in the hand of one of the boys. He fired at the boy and killed him instantly. The bullet went through the body of the first youth and into the body of the second, killing him as well. No weapon was found.

In a second incident, two Hmong boys intended to rob a food cooperative near the St. Paul campus of the University of Minnesota. When they pulled their weapon on the store clerk, they did not realize that an off-duty police officer hired by the co-op was watching from the next room. When he surprised the kids with his presence and weapon, the boy with the gun panicked and aimed it at the police officer. The boy was shot dead. The other boy fled. These are two of many incidents that indicate that the growing presence of Southeast Asians was sometimes perceived as threatening, especially when juvenile boys were involved.

There were other indicators that not everything was harmonious between these newly developing ethnic communities and their hosts. The growth of gang activity among adolescent youth was a phenomenon completely unexpected by families and by the larger community as well. The "model minority" stereotype of Asian youth suggested that they were quiet and respectful to adults. They were good students and they worked very hard to succeed. Like other immigrant groups, they valued education highly and did well in school because their parents expected them to and they had an obligation to make their family proud. The wearing of gang colors and gangster clothing and organized criminal activities frightened Southeast Asian families even more than it did the larger community. According to the Minnesota Gang Strike Force, there were at least twenty-two Southeast Asian gangs operating in Minnesota and Wisconsin by the mid-1990s. Kids as young as thirteen were becoming members and there were several girl gangs as well. Groups with names like the Vietnamese "Nasty Boys," the Cambodian "Night Creepers," the Lao "Lost Boys," and the Hmong "Asian Mafia Crips" became highly visible as drive-by shootings, fire bombings, and other criminal activities repeatedly made the evening newscasts. Although not all of them can be attributed to Asian gangs, in one month there were twenty-seven drive-by shootings in the Twin Cities area—a virtual shoot-out in a state with historically low crime rates.

Although some people mistakenly assumed that any public gathering of Asian kids was evidence of gang activity, research shows that problems in families create the climate for gang membership. The classic research on the formation of gangs suggests that youth join gangs to re-create a family structure and a sense of belonging that they do not have at home or in the larger community (Whyte 1943; Wooden 1995). In many ways, the existence of gangs shows the naturally evolving problems that families have reestablishing themselves in the new environment and the failure of the host community to make a place for adolescents who have no choice about who they are or where they grow up. Later we will examine in more depth the perceptions of elders, middle-aged adults, and adolescents about what is happening in families as parental authority erodes. For now we mention the development of Asian youth gangs as evidence of ethnic community development, in this case with negative implications for families and the community.

The Science Museum of Minnesota's Hmong Exhibit

Despite negative publicity and growing tensions, the Hmong community continued to develop its positive image. The major science museum in St. Paul decided to take down its long-standing Mayan Indian exhibit and to install a Hmong exhibit in its place in the early 1990s. Several trips by science museum staff were made to Thailand and Laos to gather artifacts and photos; clothing and textiles were borrowed and purchased from local families; and a Hmong house was reconstructed inside the museum as a focal point for the exhibit. The grand opening of the exhibit brought out many Hmong elders and younger leaders in the community. A strong representation of state and local government office holders indicated that the Hmong had arrived, not only as a source of cultural study at the museum, but as a political force as well.

Curators of the exhibit tell stories of elder Hmong women coming to visit the museum with a group of young children. Often they sat on the floor or on the small bench near the hearth and explained to the children in Hmong how they used to cook, what the utensils were used for, and how they made a certain dish. One woman simply sat in the corner for a long time with tears running down her face. The house became a place to teach Hmong kids about the past, a place to remember quietly, and a source of continuity to those thousands who had lived many years in houses just like the one the community pointed to with such pride.

Community Vegetable Gardens and the Farmers' Market

The powerful desire for continuity led many Southeast Asians to re-create a small-scale version of the farm life and open markets of their homelands in the Twin Cities. In the late 1970s and early 1980s, Southeast Asian gardeners began growing vegetables for their tables and the farmers' markets using many vacant lots within the cities. Along Hiawatha Avenue, the connecting route between the international airport and downtown Minneapolis, there was a long stretch of open land that had been cleared in the 1960s in hopes of expanding the highway or building light rail transit. The Hiawatha Avenue corridor became, for several years, a haven for hundreds of small plots for Southeast Asian gardeners. On a hot summer evening you could walk down the street and see many extended families working in the fields, wearing the traditional Vietnamese pointed straw hat to block the sun, and imagine what it must have been like for these farmers back at home. This subsistence farming within the city was an impressive sign of hard work, ingenuity, continuity, and the growing visibility of developing ethnic communities.

These small family plots were an early manifestation of a major contribution Southeast Asian farming skills have brought to the larger community. For years, the Minneapolis farmers' market struggled because of its difficult-to-reach location under an intersection of highways on the north side of the city. Few people came to shop and few truck farmers found it worth the effort. The influx of new farmers from Southeast Asia revitalized the market in Minneapolis, and soon a new market emerged in St. Paul. Beautiful vegetables, handicrafts, *pandau* (story cloth quilting), and other creations of the handwork of the newcomers found their way to the market. Rather quickly the markets became much more cosmopolitan places to visit; the vegetables were good, and there were unusual ones not seen before in Minnesota. Some of the early arrivals saved enough money to purchase land in outlying areas of Dakota County, contiguous to the metropolitan area and on the edge of the agricultural hinterlands. Truck farms were established and entire families came out to work on the weekend. At the annual Farm Family Recognition event held at the University of Minnesota in the spring of 2000, one of the honorees was a Hmong man who had managed to send his five children to college from the family's labor on a small truck farm in Dakota County. Many of the vegetables grown by Southeast Asians made their way into the new markets and cooperative food stores, and the Twin Cities became a healthier and more interesting place to live.

Making a Home

Many other examples of ethnic community development and segmented assimilation in the Twin Cities could be cited, including two Asian newspapers, several Hmong television and radio programs, a Hmong website, a Hmong cultural center, cultural groups within schools and colleges, the Asian Business Directory, and the election of the first Hmong person to the St. Paul school board and the city council. In 2002, Mee Moua, a lawyer and community advocate from the East Side of St. Paul, was elected in a special election to a state Senate seat, the first Hmong person in the United States elected to a state legislature. Cy Thao was elected later that year to the state House of Representatives. Mai Neng Moua edited *Bamboo among the Oaks* (2002), the first book of contemporary creative writing by Hmong American authors, which was unveiled at a large gala event at the Minnesota Historical Society.

When a relatively small state attempts to resettle tens of thousands of refugees from four distinct cultural groups, the efforts become highly visible in ways that are perceived as both positive and negative by the hosts and the newcomers. The Twin Cities, especially St. Paul, became a kind of naturally evolving experiment in how a well-established social system, largely white and European based, would integrate its new neighbors into the fabric of the community.

When a state like Minnesota agrees to accept international refugees in large numbers it is agreeing, in effect, to accelerate the diversification of the state. The state agrees to share resources and to make room for the newcomers within the larger community. There is an understanding that it takes time to adjust to the new environment and that, after an unspecified period of time, "adjustment" is expected to have occurred. Host communities assume an obligation to help the newcomers and expect that each ethnic group will contribute its talents to the improvement of the larger community. Ethnic businesses and nonprofit organizations will develop to employ and serve the community and eventually the new immigrants will begin to feel at home.

This is an old American story, told here with new voices. In the case of the forty elder informants, the story is told primarily from the perspective of the developing family system in the midst of crisis. Before we focus on the elders' stories, it is useful to examine what we know about Southeast Asian immigrant families and the multiple stresses they confront in their long journey to find a safe place and build a new home.

Note

1. Glenn Hendricks, Bruce Downing, Amos Deinard, and Timothy Dunnigan were the early leaders of SARS.

The Stressful Lives of Southeast Asian Elders 2

THE IMPACT OF WAR on elders and their families can be compared to the dropping of a boulder into the placid waters of a large lake. After the shock of the initial impact, a series of waves form concentric circles that expand landward, ultimately engulfing the entire body of water and all that it touches in overlapping swells. Long after the direct impact, the waters remain unsettled.

A single mortar shell dropping out of the night sky engulfs the lone Laotian fishermen casting his nets in the calm backwaters of the Mekong River. A large extended family is forever altered by his death and the multiple stresses of forced migration that follow. An uncountable number of men, women, and children were similarly affected by the conflicts in Southeast Asia and their series of successive waves. The impact of these conflicts continues to be felt today by thousands of children who were not alive when the bombs were falling but who spent their childhood years in crowded refugee camps and their adolescence in disrupted stress-filled families. Many adult survivors with posttraumatic stress continue to hear the bombs exploding even though the skies have long since become silent. Other unsettling waves from the conflict continue to engulf the thousands of Vietnamese peasants and American soldiers scarred by agent orange, the Cambodian farmers and their children who lost limbs from exploding land mines hidden by Pol Pot forces, and the Lao and Hmong elders struggling to maintain their family identity after relocation thousands of kilometers from home.

Many official statements and symbolic gestures have been made to declare the U.S.-Vietnam conflict over since the United States's withdrawal from the roof of the Saigon embassy in April 1975. These gestures include belated welcome home parades for American veterans, amnesty for draft resistors, Maya Lin's sacred wall monument to the fallen American soldiers, the 1989 inaugural address of President Bush, the election of a president who opposed the U.S.-Vietnam conflict, a three-day reading of more than fifty-eight thousand names of deceased American soldiers, and the first official postwar visit to Vietnam by a U.S. president, made by Clinton in the last days of his presidency. Despite efforts to put the war behind them, millions of families on all sides of this multinational conflict continue to experience the long-term impact of the war. Like concentric waves on disturbed water, the war continues to agitate, surround, and engulf, and to create ripples in succeeding generations.

The Decline of Filial Piety

We are beginning to understand the stressful internal and external pressures affecting elders and their multigenerational families when they are forced to migrate under duress to a dramatically different sociocultural environment (Liu and Fernandez 1988; Rumbaut 2000). We know that in the years immediately after the war Southeast Asians were one of the fastest-growing and poorest ethnic minority groups in the United States (Rottman and Meredith 1982) and that they share many similar values and traditions with other Asian cultural groups. Traditional Asian families are patriarchal, authoritarian, and organized around the elders in a strict hierarchy. Their cultural traditions and family practices are rooted in the basic values and diverse beliefs of Confucianism, Buddhism, animism, and ancestor worship. Values and beliefs arising from this heritage include a strong sense of family identity, a belief that current situations are influenced by past events (karma), an acceptance of life as suffering, a desire to avoid conflict, an emphasis on self-discipline, a focus on educational achievement, and respect for authority (Lee and Lu 1989; Kinzie 1989).

Filial piety is a central organizing principle of Asian philosophical and spiritual values and traditions. It is expressed as respect for age and authority in family relationships and it extends beyond the family to include teachers, community leaders, government officials, and others in positions of authority. All family members, both living and deceased, are arranged hierarchically by generation and gender into a network of obligation and authority. Threads of continuity connect the family with ancestral generations, define its associations in the larger community, and determine the patterns of family relationships in the future. The continued practice of filial piety through ancestor worship is important to the broad definition of the family as relationships extend forward and backward in time. As the forces of relocation alter the long-established filial piety practices of Southeast Asian families, the worldview of elders is seriously threatened. A loss of continuity in the tightly woven web of family, culture, and history means a loss of the group identity that gives structure and meaning to life (Boenlien 1987).

Within the obligations of filial piety, a tension between generations is inherent. Through the upheavals of war, escape, and resettlement, the tensions between generations and value systems became more acute. As each generation seeks to fulfill its divergent obligations, filial piety is the primary arena in which these intergenerational tensions and value differences unfold. The traditions of piety emphasize reverence for the past, maintaining the culture, and devotion to elders at a time when younger family members are focused on the future, adaptation to Western culture, and new freedoms.

Even before the "official" 1975 conclusion of the U.S.-Vietnam conflict and the forced migration to the West, the traditional Southeast Asian family practices of filial piety were already being challenged from two directions (Henkin and Nguyen 1981). The influence of Western individualism challenged family-oriented Eastern values during the French colonial era and, later, during the war years. Since 1975, the challenges to families have come from the Vietnamese, Lao, and Cambodian governments, which established more centralized power over the allegiances of families (Henkin and Nguyen 1981). During the last several decades, young people in Southeast Asia have encountered conflicting values, changing governments, and revised demands for loyalty as national schools taught youth to serve the country first, thus weakening primary allegiance to the extended family.

Many of the most important values and traditions of Southeast Asian elders have their roots in Chinese culture and the centuries-old beliefs of Confucianism. Sih (1961), Maxwell and Silverman (1970), and Yu (1983) have examined filial piety within the context of Eastern and Western cultures. Sih (1961) describes the central importance of filial piety within Chinese culture as "loyalty, respect, and devotion to parents. It represents one of the basic social and religious concepts of the Chinese people. It is considered *the virtue of all virtues* and the soul of Chinese culture" (18; emphasis mine). Yu (1983) defines the obligations of Chinese youth and adults to their elderly parents as fourfold: caring for parents' health needs, placing their financial security above that of all other family members, providing them with a family living space, and demonstrating to them continuing respect and unquestioning obedience. An important dimension of filial piety is deference, which Maxwell and Silverman (1970) define as "a type of behavior that is intended to convey respect and appreciation on the part of one person or persons for another. This is a broad category of acts in the course of which younger people indicate they hold old people in esteem by communicating to them a sense of integrity and worth" (96).

Elders and middle-aged informants in our studies believed that the young no longer maintained traditional filial piety obligations in the ways that were expected. Because filial piety is central to the family's structure, culture, interactions, and identity, a significant unifier of family life has been diminished and family stress has been increased (Seabloom 1991; Parker 1996).

Multiple Sources of Stress

The decline of filial piety was an important source of stress to elders as well as to youth, who reported that they could not fulfill the very high expectations of their parents and grandparents. The decline of filial piety in the new context is very important; however, it is only one of the many stressful circumstances confronting families that have resettled in the United States. These common and recurring stresses help to explain the context of daily life for elders and their families in the United States.

Having left places where they held high status, elders now confronted cultural and social isolation, loneliness, intergenerational conflict, and language barriers (Coleman 1980). Gozdziak (1988) identifies intergenerational tensions as an important family problem confronting Southeast Asian elderly refugees. Lum (1983) points out that elders have greater needs and diminished status in their new homes. In a study of elderly refugees in Illinois, the Office of Refugee Resettlement identified the most common problems: multiple losses (friends, status, power, authority, respect), isolation, difficulties accepting change, depression, and a lack of English language skills (Northwest Educational Cooperative 1987). Another study identified problems confronting elders in the United States as isolation, homesickness, intergenerational conflict, fear of death far from ancestors, fear of rejection, lack of language skills, and depression (Refugee Reports 1987).

Economic deprivation is a recurring source of stress for almost all refugee populations after resettlement. A 1990 survey of Minnesota's Southeast Asian elders reported that they were overwhelmingly poor, with 87 percent living below poverty level compared to 12 percent of elders in the general population. In addition, many lacked significant family roles (Chase 1990). A multicultural survey of new immigrant groups in Minnesota by the St. Paul Foundation (Sherlock 1987) revealed that elderly Southeast Asians, especially Cambodians, were particularly vulnerable to depression due to multiple traumas, the uncertainties of their lives, and the stresses of resettlement.

Van Arsdale and Skartvedt (1987) found that older Vietnamese, Cambodian, and Laotian resettled males had severely disrupted family lives, intergenerational family conflicts, and a perception of diminished respect within the family. Yee (1986) discovered that older refugees were more depressed than younger cohorts and had more difficulty adjusting. As younger family members assimilate to some elements of the new culture, older persons experience a loss of continuity. Efforts to preserve traditional values, traditional practices, and cultural continuity are often rejected by the younger generations, especially adolescents (Weinstein-Shr and Henkin 1991).

A significant body of research was conducted on Vietnamese elders and their families during the 1980s. Elderly homebound Vietnamese were the least knowledgeable about social services and least likely to use them compared to African American and Hispanic elderly, primarily due to language barriers (Berkowitz 1989). In Lynch and Do's (1986) study 77 percent of the Vietnamese elders had minimal English language skills. As a result, they experienced feelings of loneliness, helplessness, uselessness, emptiness, fear, and isolation. Although one-third lived with an adult child, 83 percent did not discuss their feelings or problems with the adult child. Despite this stark reality, Vietnamese families believe that parent–adult child relationships are important and that adult children should be the primary means of support to family elders (Prendergast 1985). The greatest difficulty of Vietnamese elders who resettled in Great Britain came from the erosion of the traditional family and their perception of themselves as a burden rather than a resource to the family (Refugee Action 1987). Although the Vietnamese are generally rated higher on most indicators of social and economic integration, Vietnamese women felt less control over their lives and more helplessness than other refugee populations (Yee 1989).

After the first decade of resettlement in Minnesota the problems of adaptation continued to include language and literacy difficulties, isolation, intergenerational conflict, employment and education difficulties, financial security, depression, homesickness, and physical and mental health problems (Minnesota Department of Health and Human Services 1988; Refugee Reports 1987). Scholars have begun to understand the connection between the ability to learn a language and depression for new immigrants (Bertrand 1992; Mouanoutoua 1989). Those who know enough English can tell their stories and verbalize their grief with service providers and other outsiders. Those with some English language facility are more likely to become involved in social and educational programs, decreasing their likelihood of isolation and depression (Bertrand 1992).

Among the Southeast Asian refugees interviewed by Yang and North (1988), the most commonly cited problems after resettlement included: intergenerational conflicts, drug abuse, delinquency and youth gangs, marital and cultural adjustment, and mental health problems. Intergenerational conflict and marital problems are issues within the family, while the others are directly linked to family relationships and identity. According to Lin (1986) the primary sources of stress include: loss and grief, social isolation, status inconsistency, traumatic experiences, "culture shock" and adjustment to new lifestyles, acculturation, accelerated modernization, and minority status. We shall examine Lin's categories in more detail as they apply to the experiences of the informants in our study.

Loss and Grief

It is important to distinguish between the unique experiences of elders who are forced to leave their homes and immigrants who leave voluntarily. Although both groups experience significant stress as a consequence of relocation, it is generally agreed that refugees have much more difficulty with adjustment and integration. The "refugee experience" is defined as "the accumulation of demands, changes, transitions, hardships, ambiguities, crisis and all that goes together to act as stressor events for these refugees" (Anderson n.d., 2). Despite divergent socioeconomic and cultural backgrounds, refugees are said to "encounter similar kinds of adaptational difficulties and develop certain types of problems" (Lin 1986, 61).

Using the life histories from this study, Parker (1996) discovered similar loss and grief experiences as Lin (1986). Unlike voluntary immigrants, who leave their homeland in a planned way, refugees leave home because of well-founded fear for their lives and their family's future. Their leave-taking often occurs suddenly, with little time for the liquidation of assets and with only the belongings that can be carried on their backs. During the escape and the months or years spent in refugee camps, the few personal possessions they bring with them are often stolen, lost, or bartered away. Many arrive in the United States with only the clothes on their bodies and a few personal belongings. The losses of businesses, farms, animals, and homes are important because these tangible assets were the source of income, status, and a way of life. Cherished objects such as photographs of deceased family members, traditional clothing, family heirlooms, and other valuable objects, once lost, cannot be replaced (Hoskins 1998). These material losses are an ongoing source of discontinuity and continue to be grieved years after departure.

A major source of grief is the interpersonal relationships and family ties that have been broken. Many elderly informants report the loss of their ancestral burial grounds, an important source of family continuity stretching back hundreds of years. In some cases, members of the family were left behind, lost during the escape and sojourn in the camps, or are simply missing in action. Almost one-third of the forty elders we interviewed could not declare their marital status, since their spouses were missing, their whereabouts unknown and fates uncertain. Scholars in the family field (Boss 1991) argue that this ambiguous type of loss, when the status of a close family member is unknown, is the most difficult, since one cannot move beyond grief with uncertainty lingering. The physical absence and psychological presence of a family member means that the family continues to hope and despair at the same time. In addition to absent family members, many lifelong friends who created a support network are no longer available.

Closely connected to long-term stress associated with the loss of interpersonal relationships and social networks is the loss of family members and other loved ones through death. More than two million Southeast Asians are estimated to have died during the years of the U.S.-Vietnam conflict and its aftermath. Many were lost at sea as the Vietnamese boat people floundered and sank off the coast of Malaysia or in the South China Sea. Others were lost in the jungles or in the muddy waters of the Mekong River as thousands of refugees walked and swam toward an uncertain future. Pol Pot's Khmer Rouge extremists in Cambodia murdered more than one million. The unsympathetic communist Pathet Lao group in Laos forced many thousands of American-supporting Hmong to flee. The victorious North Vietnamese soldiers and government officials "reeducated" many South Vietnamese who were thought to be sympathetic to the United States. A continuing source of undiminished grief for elders comes from the death of family members, their inability to properly bury and respect the dead as revered ancestors, and their inability to grieve the losses with family (Parker 1996).

In families organized around structured hierarchical relationships, gender- and age-based roles, and strict rules about the status and position of widows and widowers, the death of a spouse or elder means a radical reorganization of the family system. Difficult enough to accomplish within a supportive environment, reorganizing family roles becomes even more difficult in families undergoing many simultaneous transitions. In families in which several members have died, reorganizing is even more problematic. Some of the elders we interviewed, especially Hmong and Cambodians, had lost many members of their extended families. One Cambodian elder we interviewed had lost eight of her nine siblings and seven of her eight children during the Pol Pot reign of terror (see Touch's family tree and resiliency story in chapter 3). At the time of the interviews she lived in the United States separated from her only remaining child, a son who attended college in another city.

The farm, the village, the food, and the way of life in a tropical climate are significant memories that adults frequently reminisce about when they are together. A poignant example occurred during fieldwork with Hmong elders when a group visited the local nature conservatory, a glass-enclosed building where many tropical plants and palm trees grow. The elders were very excited to see, touch, smell, and tell me about the various plants and how they are used as food, medicine, or tools in their homelands. They were delighted to be in a famil-

iar tropical environment that brought back happy memories of life before resettlement.

Social Isolation and Status Inconsistency

Socially isolating factors creating stress for elders include their lack of language
skills and education, the government's policy to disperse refugees, the difficulties
of finding employment, the high crime rates in low-income neighborhoods, and
the high mobility rates inherent in the initial stages of resettlement. Several factors
interfere with elders' efforts to reestablish cultural and social networks in the host
society. There is a tendency toward mutual suspicion among many Southeast
Asians, caused by memories of wartime trauma, that prevents many refugees from
reaching out to one another. Living with fear and distrust of their own people,
other ethnic groups, and people in the host society promotes social isolation at a
time when reestablishing a supportive network and community integration should
be a high priority.

The dichotomous position of refugees caught between an emotional attach-
ment to and desire to return to their own culture and the need to integrate into
the larger society also encourages social isolation. Feeling betwixt and between
two cultures often means that they feel part of neither. Despite the distrust, fears,
and liminal position of elders, Gold (1992) shows that viable ethnic communities
develop over time, providing social capital resources to families and evidence of
powerful resiliency.

It is not uncommon for people crossing cultural boundaries to experience
discrepancies between their identity and their actual social position in the host
society. These discrepancies contribute to their sense of deprivation, insecurity,
and stress. Some elders, especially in the Vietnamese community, had professional
positions in their home country as doctors, lawyers, teachers, and businesspeople.
They had high levels of education, respect from the community, and relatively
high incomes. In the United States, their education, knowledge, and skills are not
recognized, so they are forced to seek work in low-wage unskilled jobs. Only a
few of the forty elders in this study were formally employed outside their homes.

The elders we interviewed all believed that loss of status within the family
was an important consequence of their migration to the United States. Rather
than holding positions of honor in the family and community, they expressed
concern about children and grandchildren not respecting them in the way that
the filial piety concept requires. Although many families seek ways to involve and
honor elders, most of the time and energy of the younger generations is focused
on education, integration, and making a living. Instead of enjoying high status,

elders often perceive themselves on the family's periphery, a source of conflict and a burden to younger generations.

An Accumulation of Traumatic Experiences

Psychological and physical trauma often affects health in a delayed and recurrent manner. Posttraumatic stress is present in many adult refugees who experienced frightening escapes, brutality in the camps, rape, and torture. Many lived for years with a powerful fear of persecution, imprisonment, and the stark realities of death.

Many of the elders were traumatized by their escape and the difficult life in the camps. Lynellyn Long (1993), in her work on the Ban Vanai camp in Thailand, where many Hmong were detained, examines the systems for managing detained refugees as political, economic, and legal constructions. During a short visit to Ban Vanai in 1992, I witnessed firsthand the unsanitary conditions, United Nations food relief, and absence of productive work for the few thousand Hmong refugees remaining in the camp during its final months before closure. Poverty, disenfranchisement, alienation, fear, and dependency on international organizations for basic assistance were the stressful realities of daily life (Long 1993; Mortland 1987). Mollica and Jalbert (1989) suggest that the crowded, demoralizing conditions of the camp and the lack of physical safety promoted the development of mental illness.

Stressful conditions prior to resettlement have inevitable effects on the subsequent interactions of individuals within families, the ethnic community, and the host community (Long 1993). Southeast Asian elders living in the Twin Cities who participated in a social adjustment program reported experiencing an average of 4.4 traumatic events, including witnessing the death of family members, the destruction of home and possessions, and systematic torture. Of the participants, 41 percent presented themselves for treatment of physical health problems; 33 percent for problems with family functioning; 29 percent for social and emotional health problems; and 22 percent for a variety of other health-related problems (Robinson 1987). Most participants presented multiple overlapping problems and countless others avoided presenting their problems to strangers who were not family members.

Given the extensive trauma experienced by many refugees, "successful adaptation" can be defined only in relative terms. Lum (1983) argues that elderly Indochinese refugees who left the camps are placed in a position of "quadruple jeopardy" upon arrival in the United States because they are simultaneously poor, minority, old, and non–English speaking.

The Cambodian and Hmong populations were the most traumatized groups among the Southeast Asians who migrated. After being forced from their homes, businesses, and daily lives in Phnom Phen by the brutal Khmer Rouge troops, urban Cambodian families were forced to work in the fields and live off the land. Many starved to death or were beaten and tortured by very young soldiers who thought of themselves as the vanguard of purification in a corrupted Cambodian society. Almost all of the Cambodian and Hmong elders in our research described dangerous escapes and traumatic experiences that caused them to have difficulty sleeping at night, recurring nightmares, intrusive thoughts, flashbacks, physical ailments, depression, and other classic symptoms of posttraumatic stress. Because few have experience with or trust in the psychological services available in the West, most are unable to utilize resources that may help them to heal. Many Southeast Asian adults were treated in culturally sensitive ways at one of the first Centers for the Victims of Torture in the world, established during the 1980s on the University of Minnesota campus. Others sought help from shamans and other traditional healers.

The Hmong fought in cooperation with American troops in the so-called secret war in Laos. They rescued American pilots who were shot down by the North Vietnamese, they harassed supply carriers along the Ho Chi Minh trail, and they served as loyal allies for many years. In return, the Vietnamese and the communist Pathet Lao troops raided their villages, forcing them to repeatedly move their families and entire villages to maintain a safe distance. After the American withdrawal from Saigon, the Hmong who had fought with the American soldiers were no longer safe in Laos. Yet there was no mass evacuation as in Saigon. The Hmong had to hide in the forests and flee through the jungles toward Thailand, where they often spent years seeking refuge in the United States, as promised by the CIA. As a hill tribe people that lived in small villages at one thousand or more meters above sea level, the Hmong were ill prepared for life in a modern Western society. Their continuing difficulties with adjustment are, in part, the result of trauma and the enormous distance they have traveled both geographically and psychologically to reach a safe haven in the United States.

Culture Shock and Accelerated Modernization

Not knowing the cultural messages and norms of the host society, refugees often find themselves in highly stressful situations (Garza and Guerrero 1974; Spradley and Phillips 1972). The contrast between Eastern and Western ways of understanding and living in the world is sharply focused in the early years after resettlement. For example, the Hmong people had little understanding of American social and cultural norms, even though the men had worked and fought with American soldiers and CIA operatives in Laos. To move from remote mountain villages, inaccessible for months during the rainy season, to the modern urban setting of St. Paul, accessible even during a January blizzard, is an experience that stretches our understanding of the term "culture shock." Although many newcomers were initially shocked by the cultural contrasts, many others gradually learned the new ways, found employment, learned English, and built a new, but very different, life.

Unlike the assimilation, amalgamation, and melting pot theories of accultura-tion, the ethnogenesis theory rejects the simplistic notion of the United States as a place where culture is inevitably lost and everyone blends in (Greeley 1974). Instead, ethnogenesis points to the complex diversity that exists within and between immigrant populations as they develop their own sense of ethnic identity that is different from the hosts' stereotyped perceptions and the traditional identi-ties of the immigrants' homeland. Ethnogenesis explains the complexities and conflicts within families and ethnic communities as a function of the multiple identities that each new wave of newcomers brings with it. Ethnogenesis also sug-gests that acculturation is bidirectional, with the host culture changing at the same time that it influences the new immigrants.

The cultural differences between men and women who have been living in the United States for a decade or more and those who have recently arrived means that each new cohort has quite different expectations of family, friends, and the host society. Between the oldest, middle, and youngest generations there are sig-nificant differences in adaptation to American ways and acceptance of native cul-tures. The oldest generation, in its desire for continuity, often resists cultural change, while the youngest generation, in its desire for acceptance, embraces it. The middle generation, with adult experience in both cultures and responsibility to care for both the old and the young generations, is truly caught betwixt and between. When all three generations are living in the same extended-family house-hold, as was the case for many of the elderly informants in our studies, the diverse levels of acculturation are a recurring source of stress within families (Detzner 1992).

Closely associated with the stresses of acculturation and the processes of eth-nogenesis are the multiple effects of accelerated modernization. Elders from small or remote villages are faced not only with drastic differences between rural and urban environments but also with the dramatic impact of modernization and the accelerated pace of change in their everyday lives. Modernization theorists like Cowgill (1986) point to the stressful consequences of urbanization and industri-alization for almost every aspect of family life, including the diminished status of elders. The process of modernization usually occurs over many decades, with several generations involved in a series of transitions. The informants in our study, however, did not have many years to adapt. Many were forced to move quickly, without knowing an ultimate destination. Some found themselves outside the region of their village for the first time in their lives and then flown to a technologically advanced city in the northern part of the United States before they even realized where they were.

The family is an important crucible in which the stresses of accelerated modernization are played out. Each new group of arrivals learned how to use modern electrical appliances and taken-for-granted services such as grocery stores, buses, and bank accounts. While modern tools and services simplified and improved the families' quality of life, they also changed drastically the ways in which the families had typically lived together and associated with one another. For example, no one will question the value of the modern telephone as an effective means of communication between family members; however, the phone often became a source of conflict between adults and adolescents (see case 10: "Why is calling a boy on the phone a big deal?" in chapter 6).

The speed of change is frightening to many adults and another source of continuing stress. During the early years of Hmong resettlement in St. Paul, there were recurring examples of young adult males who died inexplicably in their sleep. Dr. Yang Dao asserts that the stresses associated with acculturation, rapid modernization, and multiple losses overwhelmed some of the middle-generation men. In recent years, there have been far fewer reports of these unexplained deaths as the Hmong population established itself in Minnesota (Yang 1996).

Minority Status

Upon arrival in the United States, all Southeast Asian immigrants found themselves with a dubious new status as unwilling members of an ethnic minority group. As such, many experienced for the first time overt and covert acts of discrimination as a continuing and unexpected source of stress in their lives. Except for the Hmong, a small ethnic hill tribe minority in Laos (and several other Asian countries), and the Chinese Vietnamese, the refugees who arrived in the United States had not experienced life as an ethnic minority. They were unprepared for racial and ethnic slurs, stereotyping, and discrimination. Unlike parents in other American ethnic groups with a long history in the country, Southeast Asian elders did not know how to prepare their adult children or grandchildren for prejudice and discrimination. Nor did the adults understand why so many educated Americans had little or no understanding of the war that forced them here or the cultures they were trying to maintain. The confusion of many Americans about why so many Southeast Asian refugees rather suddenly appeared in their midst was puzzling to many elders, since they viewed themselves as victims of the "American war" in their homelands, supporters of the anticommunist conflict, and patriots of the highest order. Their deeply rooted cultural practice of welcoming guests with great respect and affection was not always their everyday experience on the street, although sponsoring families and resettlement organizations extended a much-appreciated hand of support. These mixed messages from the host society often created confusion, misunderstandings, frustration, and ongoing stress.

Sources of Distress

These multiple sources of stress cumulatively influence the mental health of elders and their families. Lin (1986) reports that an accumulation of stress may manifest itself as physical and psychological pain with behavioral symptoms of anxiety and depression, somatic complaints, and marital conflict. Depression in older refugees is a not-too-surprising consequence of their multiple losses, social isolation, reduced roles, and diminished social status. Feelings of hopelessness are compounded by the ever-present sense of ambiguity and limnality inherent in their displaced lives. Pressures to change, culture shock, and the pervasiveness of modernization can become overwhelming. The continuing emphasis on adjustment, adaptation, and rapid acculturation, when added to the normative physical problems associated with aging and the nonnormative effects of trauma, create conditions for recurring depression and anxiety. Some degree of mental illness may be present in 20 to 80 percent of all refugees (Minnesota Department of Health and Human Services 1988).

On a traditional psychological depression scale, older Hmong adults were found to have more symptoms of depression than younger adults (Mouanoutoua 1989). In a sample of 123 Hmong, depression was negatively related to education and Hmong women were more depressed than the men (Mouanoutoua 1989). Depression was not related significantly to the length of stay in the United States or the amount of social support; however, the quality of support *and* overall life satisfaction was a significant predictor of depression (Mouanoutoua 1989).

Social workers rated depression as a problem in more than 90 percent of the Southeast Asians who participated in a social adjustment program; anxiety and worry were evident in nearly 90 percent of the cases; language barriers occurred in slightly less than 90 percent of the participants; and hopelessness and isolation were present in three-fourths of the group (Robinson 1987). An earlier study documented severe depression and psychosomatic complaints in almost 80 percent of the Southeast Asian clients between the ages of five and sixty-four (Fox 1984).

Somatization is a widely reported phenomenon among refugee populations and other survivors of trauma and a physical manifestation of severe stress that has been viewed by some as an alternative to depression (Westermeyer, Neider, and Vang 1987; Minnesota Department of Health and Human Services 1988; Rozee and Van Boemel 1989). Southeast Asian elders experienced a greater proportion of physical health problems than other ethnic elders in a Chicago study (Yu, Fugita, Prohaska, and Liu 1988). Sutherland and associates (1983) discovered that 17 percent of the Southeast Asian elders who were treated at the Mayo Clinic had been referred for psychosomatic problems or psychiatric disorders. Two explanations for the perceived somatizing or hypochondriacal tendencies in Southeast Asian displaced people are their traditional values emphasizing interpersonal harmony and avoidance of direct expression of negative feelings. Health beliefs are components of cultures that can affect how distress and dysphoria are experienced, interpreted, and expressed (Kleinman 1976). Many Asian adults believe in psychosomatic unity, and regard both physical and psychological symptoms as signs of physiological disharmony. In many cases, refugees are not familiar with the concept and profession of mental health care, and the discussion of anything but physical symptoms may seem irrelevant to them. Language barriers between family members and health professionals can severely impede communication and treatment, despite the best intentions of all parties (Fadiman 1997).

Married couples experiencing the stresses of relocation may be desperately in need of mutual support; however, they are often so exhausted and vulnerable to their own distress that they are unable to sustain emotional support for each other. "Anger can be easily displaced, and a spouse is often the most convenient target for such a displacement" (Lin 1986, 66). Furthermore, the multiple demands of family life in the new country, the difficulties experienced by other family members, and the breakdown of extended family systems are additional factors that may weaken married couples' ability to support one another. Although there are no hard data to support the claim, many elders and community leaders report a dramatic increase in separations and divorce among married couples, a situation that is virtually unheard of in their homelands.

The literature on refugees and the stresses they experience is filled with references to problems that families face across generations. There appear to be large gaps between the experiences of elders, middle-aged parents, and their adolescent children that are, in many cases, almost insurmountable. The differences between generations are probably inherent in families across cultural groups; however, the stressful circumstances of war, forced migration, and cultural adjustment in a new context exacerbate these differences and make family life an arena in which conflicts are a reality of everyday life. In Western-oriented theories of family relations, conflict is viewed as a useful method for directly addressing normative problems, the stress of daily life, and the diverse developmental agendas of each generation (Sprey 1979). Addressing problems between generations may be particularly difficult in Southeast Asian families because the dictates of filial piety prohibit direct confrontations and negative communications with elders.

Direct or overt conflict is considered disrespectful and shameful in Southeast Asian families and it is to be avoided. As a consequence, the adjustment problems and differences that each generation confronts in daily life cannot be talked about, argued through, or resolved very easily; family rules do not allow for freewheeling disagreements and discussions. Nevertheless, the discussion groups with parents and adolescents we conducted and later research conducted by Xiong (2000) with Hmong families reveal a considerable degree of overt conflict between parents and their children.

To avoid the stress of direct confrontation, there is more often a quiet truce between generations and a large number of issues and problems that cannot be discussed. Many of these losses, conflicts, and stresses are dramatically revealed in the stories that elders tell about their family lives in the following chapter.

Family Stories of Elders 3

Introduction

THE ELDERS WE INTERVIEWED were generally quite eager to tell stories of what had happened to their families before, during, and after the war. The family stories were composed of intertwined individual life stories, constructions of reality based on the experiences and perceptions the storytellers were willing to tell an outsider. The forty stories of these elders often provide rich narrative details revealing the traumatic impact of war and the stresses of resettlement on families. Although every family has a collective story, each individual within a family may have a different version of the story or, in some cases, a different story altogether, depending on his or her age, gender, position within the family, and experiences. Careful analysis of stories and narrative fragments from the life history interviews reveal common themes, dominant motifs, and recurring metaphors (McAdams 1993; Kenyon, Clark, and deVries 2001). Stories, themes, motifs, and metaphors that recur across several life histories and cultural groups can be grouped together, tentatively named, and reanalyzed for common and discordant elements. The family stories of the forty Southeast Asian elders in this study reveal four recurring themes: separation, loss, conflict, and resiliency. These themes are broadly represented in the research literature on refugees and at-risk families, but here they are told from the unique viewpoints of the oldest generation.

The attempt to understand the meanings of life for immigrant families using narratives can be traced to Thomas and Znaniecki's classic sociological work, *The Polish Peasant in Europe and America* (1918–1920), and Hess and Handel's *Family Worlds* (1959). There is a tradition of life history and narrative research in many other disciplines, including social history, oral history, gerontology, anthropology, literary studies, American studies, and women's studies. More recently, the *Journal of Narrative and Life History*, the annual *The Narrative Study of Lives*, and the new *Narrative Inquiry* have included many selections that focus on narratives as a means to study family processes and interactions (see, for example, Gleason and Melzi 1997; Stavans 1996; Apter 1993; Bennett and Detzner 1997).

Family narratives are emerging as an important new qualitative way of knowing and categorizing families. They complement well-established quantitative marital and family typologies that reveal patterns of family interactions. The important outcomes of these classification schemes are assessment instruments that predict marital or family functioning. Such schemes help to conceptually simplify the structure and interactions of complex family systems, thus providing opportunities for intervention. Examples of frequently cited typologies include Fitzpatrick's (1977) couple-oriented typology that defines marital dyads as traditional, separates, and independents; Kantor and Lehr's (1976) open, closed, and random family types; and Olson, Russell, and Sprenkle's (1979) circumplex model of cohesion and adaptability in a family system.

In cross-cultural research, families are categorized according to structure, stage of the life cycle, controls, and functions; they may also be categorized according to some classical types, such as the polyandrous Toda family, the matrilineal Hopi family, the polygynous Baganda family, the Chinese familism system, and the minimal family of the kibbutzim (Queen, Habenstein, and Quadagno 1985). Cross-cultural typologies can be developed from the kinship lineage system, marital pattern, historical period, ethnicity, or generations living in the household. The family story typology developed for this cross-cultural study is based on a qualitative approach in which a pattern of feeling, motives, and life experiences are grouped around a particular locus of concern or dominant theme in an elderly informant's family story (Hess and Handel 1959). The dominant themes demonstrate a recurring fundamental view of reality or a persistent issue or concern. For the purposes of this study the dominant family themes are revealed in the informant's narrative, especially his or her discussion of the family lineage.

Constructing a family tree is a useful technique to establish rapport with informants and to initiate interviews about the extended family's story from the perspective of the elder. The shared constructing of a family tree enables researchers and informants to develop a structure or map of the family that elicits many richly detailed stories about family life. Case-by-case analysis reveals important differences between families with different dominant themes. While developing the family tree, interviewers elicited information about the elder's family history, its changing structure, and the elder's personal experience of the war and resettlement. Constructing a general overview of the family's organizational structure helped to locate the interview and the interviewers within the family's changing geography and membership. Memories of distant births, deaths, and other family events were sometimes dim, the painful memories left untold and the chronology often uncertain. In some cases, significant events were simply recalled as occurring prior to or after other important events, without reference to a specific year. Much was left unsaid. Discrepancies in stories sometimes appeared in consecutive interviews with the same individual. There were gaps in some family trees where the fate of a missing family member was unknown. Although details were sometimes fragmentary, dates and ages not always known, and locations uncertain, the process of constructing the family tree often elicited lengthy storytelling by informants with rich details about the extended family. The family tree and life history interviews revealed dominant or recurring themes in each case that could be classified into one of the four family story categories: separation, loss, conflict, and resiliency.

A subsample of eight elderly informants was selected from the original forty for deeper analysis. A male and female were selected from each of the four Southeast Asian cultures and each of the four family story classifications. They were selected because their narratives were particularly rich, their family trees particularly revealing, and their stories generally representative of the major themes and stories of other informants.

All of the four themes have overlapping dimensions. Separated families are characterized by stories that emphasize the fragmentation of family systems over the course of many years. Many elders have family members scattered in various countries and continents. In one study, 96 percent of Southeast Asian refugees reported that they were separated from some family members (Rottman and Meredith 1982). In a needs assessment survey of Hmong households, 87 percent were concerned about being separated from family members (Meredith and Cramer 1979). Lost families are characterized by stories about the loss of land, homes, status, culture, and loved ones. Separation from family members is an ambiguous loss (Boss 1991). The magnitude of losses experienced by members of these groups has been previously discussed and well documented (Parker 1996; Bishop 1985; Boyer 1991; Downing, Egli, and O'Connor 1988; Hayes 1984, 1987; Northwest Educational Cooperative 1987; Robinson 1987; Yeung 1988). Conflicted families are more difficult to characterize because cultural norms discourage overt conflict in relationships and its discussion, especially with outsiders. Nevertheless, conflicts over role changes, Eastern and Western values, and generational differences are dominant themes in the narratives classified as conflicted (Detzner 1992). Although resilient families may also have experienced separation, loss, and conflict, the narratives consistently reveal the theme of successful adaptation to vast and rapid change in almost every domain of daily life. Having faced enormous difficulties and challenges over many years, resilient elders and their families are skilled in "survival" strategies (Boyer 1991). Family survival rather than the achievement of individual goals was a high value in the Vietnamese and Laotian refugee households that were interviewed in a small Midwestern town (Benson 1989). Resilient elders tell stories of reconstructed families with a positive outlook on the future; elders retain some degree of status, and each generation has learned to blend Eastern and Western values. Resilience is indicative of the families' ability to integrate the social capital of their ethnic community with the limited resources available to them in the host community (Zhou and Bankston 1998).

Family Separation Stories

The eight elders whose major family story theme was separation experienced widespread fragmentation of their extended family systems over many years. Family members were separated when the husband or father left to fight in the war; when he was incarcerated after defeat or capture; during the process of escape and refugee camp internment; and during the resettlement process. A sixty-nine-year-old Laotian woman named Dam explained what dominates her thoughts as she reflects on separation from family members: "when my family was together like my children and my husband, how happy we were. Now I live alone and it's sad." The following two case examples reveal some of the dynamics in families whose stories are classified as separated.

"The war makes them go from one place to another"

Luot is a seventy-six-year-old Cambodian man who was living with his second wife and youngest daughter at the time of the interviews. Another daughter lives in California with her eight children; and a son lives in the metropolitan area with his wife and six children. At the time of the interview, three other adult children remained in Cambodia and three others were "in the border" of Thailand. Luot finally arrived in the United States in 1985 after years of running, first from the Khmer Rouge, then from the Vietnamese invaders, and then from camp to camp along the Thai border. The only possessions he brought with him were an ax and a knife. The ax was later stolen but he still shows off the knife that he used for cutting bamboo trees and making baskets as a young man.

As a young boy he was free to run and play with his seven siblings and the other children who lived nearby. It was always easy to find many relatives to play with: "Since I can remember . . . the family and relatives lived around each other. My parents had two grandchildren who were living in [the household] and when they were living in Battambong they had many grandchildren."[1]

When he was seventeen, Luot wanted to become a monk and study at the

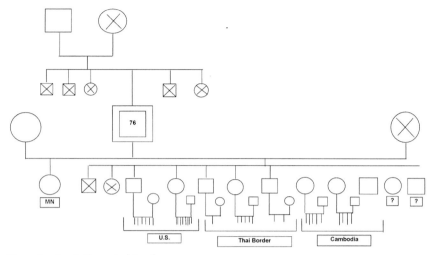

Figure 1.   Luot's Separated Family

temple; however, his parents asked him not to go because there were two younger siblings at home and they needed him to help out. Describing himself and his siblings, he said, "One became a monk, one plowing, and me who did everything from cooking, making grains, etc." At eighteen, his parents arranged a marriage for him. The young couple lived with his parents until their first child was born, when they built their own house. Over the course of years, they had twelve children; however, one died from an allergic reaction, and an anti–Khmer Rouge faction called "Near-Ra-Da" killed another. At the time of the interview, his brothers, sisters, and first wife were not living. "All are dead, there is only me left. They were sick and died because of starvation during the Khmer Rouge. . . . My wife died when the Vietnamese came in."

Not knowing what else to do and unable to assess the imminence of danger brought by Pol Pot's forces, he continued farming when the Khmer Rouge took over the country in 1975. As the explosions and gunfire moved closer, he moved the family along with the cows and oxen. "We just moved away again and again until we are in Battambong. There I made a house, day and night so that we could live happily." Luot had just completed the house when Battambong was invaded and his family was forced to leave again. "Everyone left. Whoever stayed they killed them all. We just went, and stayed wherever we wanted. . . . Afterwards when they went around and saw that you lived there, they told you to move somewhere else. If they did tell you to move, then you set up and stayed there. . . . [T]hey used us to plow the soil or whatever. . . . We just did what they said."

During this time, Luot's extended family was separated. Some had food to eat while others did not. He lived with his wife, a daughter, and a grandchild. When the Vietnamese invaded and the Khmer Rouge retreated in 1979, Luot's family was able to escape during the confusion. There were about twenty people in his family who left together, including children and small grandchildren. Fighting surrounded them wherever they went, with the Khmer Rouge on one side, the Ra-Pa freedom fighters on another, the Vietnamese on another, and buried land mines everywhere.

Eventually they were able to reach Thailand's Kaw-E-Dang camp, after leaving two children and their families behind in the Site 2 camp. During the year or so he lived there, Luot remarried, and his new wife gave birth to a daughter. Some of his extended family was moved to another camp. Luot and his spouse, their infant child, and a grandchild were moved to camp Sra-Keo for one and a half years and then back to Kaw-E-Dang. This time they stayed in Kaw-E-Dang for two years until they were released to Trong-Seat, a place where refugees were sent to school in anticipation of resettlement. From there, the four of them were sent to the Philippines for six months prior to their final arrival in the United States.

Now living in the northern part of the middle of the United States, Luot has few responsibilities at home and very little contact with most of his grandchildren. He does try to teach those of his grandchildren who live nearby how to live a good life. When they are not being serious about their schoolwork, sometimes he hits them out of frustration. "I hit them and it hurts. They play too much. When I see them play, that's not a good thing. I tell them to get some paper and start writing." His primary worries at this stage of life are not having enough money and concern for the adult children and grandchildren left behind in Cambodia. He thinks constantly about the fact that they do not have enough food to eat and about his inability to help them.

"After my husband died, I went to work"

Dam is a sixty-nine-year-old Lao woman who was born in a southern Lao village. When she was a child, her family's home was located in the middle of a village that was surrounded by fruit trees. The family also had land it farmed close to the Mekong River. When Dam was seven, her father became ill and died. Her family continued to live in the village while her mother worked as a weaver to support Dam's brother and two sisters. Although neither Dam nor her sisters attended school, her brother was sent to school in Vientiane, the capitol city. She stayed home to help her mother and sisters until she married at the age of eighteen.

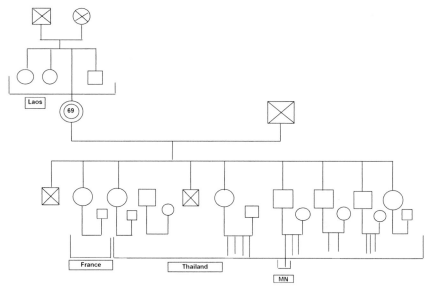

Figure 2.   Dam's Separated Family

For the first four or five years of their marriage, Dam and her husband Noukeo lived near her mother in a house of their own. Her husband worked as a doctor for the Laotian army and they moved to Moung Mune for seven years, to Moung Kong for three years, and finally to the village where she was born. During these years, she had ten children—four daughters and six sons. Although Dam was unwilling to get into the details, opposition forces killed her husband and one son.

The death of her husband meant that she was no longer able to stay home with the children. "After my husband died I went to work and I had some money to support my family. . . . I have to work to earn some money to buy clothes for my children." As the war expanded, Dam worked for the army from 1960 until 1975. At the end of the war, she planned to escape to Thailand because there were no jobs for her or her adult children, who were trying to support families of their own. She stayed with a cousin for several nights and was able to obtain assistance for the escape to Thailand. With a nephew and her daughter, she walked through the jungle for a long time before reaching the Mekong River. It rained throughout the journey. One of her children was already in the Thai refugee camp. Another daughter joined them later; eventually she resettled in France with her husband. Dam stayed in Thailand for three years in the Ouboune camp. Although she had shelter and food, she was often afraid of the burglars at night.

Dam arrived in the United States in 1980 and was initially resettled in Boston. When she learned that one of her relatives was in Minnesota, she asked her American sponsor for permission to move there. At the time of the interviews, she lived in a suburb of Minneapolis with her granddaughter. Although eight of her children are living and she has many grandchildren, she has few relatives in the United States. With most of her children remaining in Laos or Thailand, she would like to return to Laos, but does not know how she would support herself if she did. "Even though my children are back there, I'm afraid they would not be able to support me." Her work now includes cleaning house, managing meager family finances, and passing on cultural traditions and values to the younger generation.

She keeps most of her feelings of loneliness and sadness to herself. When she thinks about the past, she fondly remembers being in the temple with her friends. "We helped the monks because they were building a temple. I think of how much fun I had when I was young."

Family Loss Stories

Eight of the elders' families are classified as having loss stories because they are filled with a bewildering array of nonnormative loss experiences extending along the life course. A sixty-year-old Cambodian woman named Sally revealed a common feeling of elders about the nontangible, but very real, loss of filial piety by grandchildren and the decline of parents' and elders' authority:

> The feeling of insecurity is always in me. I'm afraid that they might not be what I want them to be because in this country the children are very unpredictable. . . . I just pray that my children will study hard and be good. I no longer have the authority to tell them what to do. . . . If they do something wrong, I just give them advice. If they listen then it is good. . . . I don't like to talk too much, because the more you talk the less respect they have toward you.

A sixty-five-year-old widowed Hmong man named Xi Chao explained what it was like for him to have lost his role as the economic provider for the family: "We Hmong never had a history of dependency on welfare or other people. Now . . . most of the older people are dependent on welfare, because we didn't have any education and can't go to work. However, most of the younger people who had [a] little education, they [are] already working and don't depend on welfare."

Multiple deaths, traumatic experiences, and tangible and nontangible losses characterize these powerful family stories. To illustrate, five of Xi Chao's twelve children have died, as well as his first wife and one of five grandchildren. In addition, only two out of his seven siblings are still alive. He constantly thinks of the past and misses the life he had in his homeland. He mourns the loss of a place for large traditional gatherings and the loss of economic self-sufficiency that once allowed him to provide for his family's needs. Xi Chao has experienced a loss of status since coming to the United States and he is frustrated that the law and police in the United States seem to have more authority over his family than he does. He explained:

> I come to this country and the new systems were different from our system. So now we can't really control our children to do what we think is best for them. When we think about this situation, it hurts our feelings and sometimes it makes us feel like useless parents. If we tried to stop them of what they did, sometime they call the police to arrest us and said that we were wrong. I don't know why. We only teach them to be a good person and we're still wrong to the law. So when we think of it, it hurts our feelings very deeply.

The fifty-eight-year-old Hmong woman named Mai whose family story is illustrated below had many family members murdered in the war. As a child Mai witnessed her mother and one of her sisters being blown up as they stepped on a land mine. She had fourteen siblings, nine of whom are deceased. One is missing. Her husband is dead, as well as five of her eight children. With the death of her husband and children, leaving behind many relatives, she escaped to a refugee camp. Mai currently lives with her sixteen-year-old son in St. Paul. Her two living daughters are married and live in Denver with her four granddaughters. Mai expressed her feelings of loss in this way: "when I thought about each time [a family member died] I felt so lonely and helpless."

"I stay home all the time and now I feel like they put me in jail"

Xi Chao is a sixty-five-year-old Hmong man whose family has suffered multiple losses. He currently lives with his son, his daughter-in-law, and their children. His wife lives nearby in another house with a daughter, her husband, and their children. They live in separate residences because the public housing authority will not allow the extended family to live together in one small apartment and because both of the grandparents are needed as baby-sitters in different adult children's households. Other clan members live nearby, but Xi Chao does not see them very often for family dinners or celebrations because there is inadequate

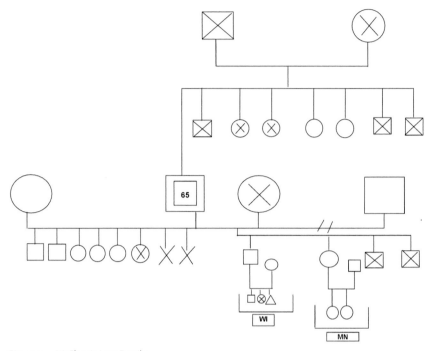

Figure 3.   Xi Chao's Lost Family

space for large gatherings, everyone is too busy, and there is not enough money to afford the food for large gatherings.

The loss of Xi Chao's father when the boy was five or six meant that his carefree childhood came to an abrupt halt. Shortly after his father's death, the entire village moved to a new location and he became "a farm boy who goes to work in the field every day and never had time to play." He evaluated his economic circumstances in his early years as middle class because he was not dependent on anyone and had a lot of horses, cows, and buffaloes. Over the years, Xi Chao and his first wife had eight children.

During World War II, Xi Chao became a soldier for the French army and later, during the Indo-Chinese conflict, he fought under the leadership of the famous Hmong General Vang Pao. During these war years, he spent most of his time separated from the family. Even after he was wounded, he continued to serve in the military as a cook. Because of his long absences due to military service, he ultimately lost his roles as husband and father in the family. As the U.S.-Vietnam conflict diminished in the early 1970s, additional losses mounted; two close nephews were killed in defense of the home village. It became impossible for Xi Chao's family to remain in one place for any length of time as the fighting with the Vietnamese came closer to his village. Eventually Vietnamese soldiers captured his family and many village members; they were imprisoned for five or six months before they escaped to Thailand. Because he was too weak to escape with other family members, Xi Chao was left behind to cross the Mekong later with his wife, daughter-in-law, and grandson. "I cut five or six long bamboo and tie it together for two persons and tie the other bamboo for another person. This is how we cross the river. I take the lead and tie them behind me."

Eventually they arrived safely in the United States but he was heartbroken to have left some family members behind. In addition to the two children with whom he and his wife are currently living, their youngest son lives in the United States. Two or three of his daughters and two sons died in Laos or Thailand. One of them died of sickness in childhood; however, the other deaths occurred as a result of the war and escape.

Once proud of his freedom and independence as a self-sufficient Hmong man, at the time of the interview, Xi Chao depended on a $300 monthly government supplemental security income subsidy. He misses his country, his land, the way he used to dress, and the opportunity to work: "The older [people] come here and couldn't learn anything and have to stay home. We elderly face a lot of loneliness and homesickness." He contrasts the self-sufficiency he knew in his home village with the helplessness he experiences now: "When I think about all these freedoms [in Laos], I feel very sad and heartbroken. . . . The country in Laos is . . . not like this country that you had to be educated to be able to work. In Laos every penny that you earn is yours, you don't have to pay tax, rent, and other things. Everything around you is free to use, because Mother Nature provides it." Xi Chao's current income is inadequate to pay the family's bills, so he never buys new clothing, and he "couldn't afford to buy fruit from the store to eat. So when I think of it, I want to cry and don't know what to do."

In addition to the loss of family closeness and the separation caused by the relocation, Xi Chao believes the Hmong children of today have lost respect for their parents and elders. Comparing the past to the present, he recalls, "In those days, they listen to their parents but now they don't care much about what their parent say."

"Over here, nothing I have is mine"

Mai is a fifty-eight-year-old Hmong woman who grew up in a mountain valley in northern Laos. Her grandfather was a leader in the village and their home was a gathering place for many important meetings and ceremonies. Together, her grandfather and father built a longhouse with enough room for the two families to live at opposite ends. Both her grandparents and parents were farmers in the surrounding hills and, as a small child, she helped with the household chores while the adults and male children were in the fields. "In Lao, I had so many things to do," including feeding the animals, caring for younger siblings, gathering wood, carrying water, and preparing rice by removing the seed coatings through grinding. She remembers that the responsibilities for work were clear: "there were no rules . . . everybody just knows what to do." The physically demanding nature of farmwork and scarce resources encouraged communal practices of reciprocity. "In our community we always help one another . . . you go to my farm today and help me and the next day I go to your farm and help you."

Mai was born in the middle of fifteen children, although only she and four (or five) of her brothers survived the devastation that came with the war. Because of the death of her older brothers and sisters, she acquired many new responsibilities for the family's care at a very young age. Mai was about ten years old when she escaped death while witnessing the death of her mother and sister. She and her father stood near the door of a hut as her sister stepped on a Vietnamese mine, cutting her in half at the waist as she "broke into small pieces." Mai's mother fell on top of the hole, and although her body "was like it had been chopped by an ax," Mai and her father carried the remains home for the funeral. She stayed with her family long after her mother's death, taking care of her younger siblings until a younger sister was old enough to cook and care for the family.

Among other factors, a young women's suitability as a marriage partner was based on how hard she worked; rough hands were a sign of a hard worker and they meant that she was not lazy. Mai remembers: "Men would secretly scan across the field to see who worked the hardest." At sixteen or seventeen she married and went with her husband Xao to live with his parents in another village. She imagined that her married life would be much the same as life in her father's house. For several years, they farmed and she was happy because she believed that he would take care of her forever. However, after they had been married for a few years, Xao joined the army and "he left me to take care of our kids alone. When I thought of it, I was more mad than happy." Life was hard with her husband gone and the family was very poor. Mai worked long hours in the fields until sunset. Anything needed for the eight children's well-being was obtained by selling animals. She describes her feelings: "During this time I was most worried about whether or not my kids would be healthy. Usually, they were all very sick. It cost a lot of money to put them on medication and to perform rituals for their well being." As the children grew older, Mai worried less about their health.

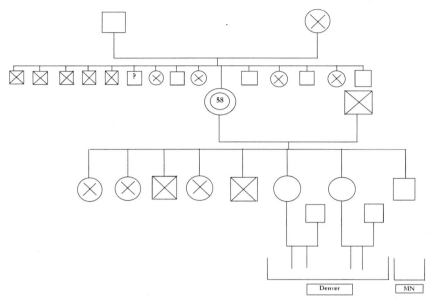

Figure 4.   Mai's Lost Family

When she was able to purchase a cow, it eased the burden of carrying the crops home from the fields every day. After obtaining the cow, "the only thing that I carried to the farm and back was my baby."

Of Mai and Xao's eight children, only three were still living at the time of the interviews. With the exception of one child who died shortly after birth, "I just remember that it was during the time everybody was fleeing from Laos that my kids began to pass away. We ran from place to place. Ever since the Vietnam War, my life has been downward. We didn't know what to do. Finally, we surrendered to the Vietnamese in Vas Vias. We stayed with the Vietnamese in Vas Vias for a long time." When many relatives were forced to go to Vietnam, Xao attempted to escape. Mai learned of his death in 1976 when she made her way with her remaining children to a village near the Thai border.

With her relatives in Vietnam and her husband dead, she did not know what to do. Her children were still quite small. She was frightened, surrounded by people she did not know, and she feared betrayal. Life in the refugee camp was not much better. "I was not even allowed to go and gather wood for fire." Her children longed to follow her brother-in-law to America: "They didn't want to stay in Thailand and suffer anymore." After a year in the camp, Mai decided to come to the United States, reasoning that "our country is ruined."

She arrived in Denver in 1983. Although other Hmong people were there, she had no relatives living in the area. After five years in Denver, she moved to Minnesota to be closer to relatives. At the time of the interview Mai lived with her sixteen-year-old son in St. Paul. Her younger daughter is married and living in Denver with two daughters of her own. Although the oldest daughter came with Mai to St. Paul, she returned to Denver to marry. She has two daughters. The only other family member living in the United States is Mai's brother-in-law.

At the time of the interview, Mai was waiting for her son to grow up and get married. "Only at that time will I be able to know whether or not they will take care of me. If he decides to marry someone who will come to love me and live with me then I can say that I have hope for him. Right now, I don't know because he doesn't have a girlfriend yet." In her current circumstances Mai has "nothing to do. . . . I just wait every month for money. If I was still young, I would not want to stay on welfare, I would rather work and get money every two weeks."

Although she remembers the sadness of the past as well as the happiness, Mai is nostalgic about her life before marriage. "I still remember my life as a single. Sometimes I wish I can be like that again. I want to be young forever. I wish that I can stay young forever and not die. I wish I could be reincarnated to be a baby again." The next time her life will be better. "If I can do that, I want to go to school and be someone. That way I can have a light job and earn a lot of money." Everything that she had in Laos was earned through hard work, but "over here nothing that I have is mine. I am very confused." She has literally lost almost everything of importance to her. She has no job; no house, land, or animals to care for; no husband; and few living relatives near to her.

Family Conflict Stories

Stories told by the elder in the four families classified as conflicted often involve disagreements about who is supposed to be fulfilling what role(s). The decline of filial piety practices and changing gender roles are recurring issues that cause conflict.

Parents report conflict over the disobedience of a son, confrontations with U.S. laws and school officials, the loss of humility of the young, and many inter-generational disagreements. A Lao elder woman named Bane explained the inter-generational and cultural conflicts between parents and children as she spoke about her daughter: "She can listen or not, but as long as she doesn't talk back. In my head I love her very much, that's why I discipline her. I don't want her to be a bad person. I want her to be like a Laos lady."

Conflict stories are characterized by ongoing disagreements and friction between family members. A Vietnamese woman named Ngo begins her conflict story when she was twenty-four and still living in Vietnam. When she met a man with compatible birth signs whom she wanted to marry, she met with disapproval from his parents. She explained:

> My father came from northern Vietnam and my mother was from southern Vietnam. Because of the discrimination between northern and southern at that time, my parents-in-law, who were southern Vietnamese, didn't like me that much. Secondly, I was very skinny, my parents-in-law were afraid that I might not be able to have children. We had to wait for seven years before we finally got married.

Unfortunately, she had difficulty during pregnancies and had three miscarriages. After Ngo relocated to the United States her husband could not find work. This created considerable conflict and adjustment issues between them, since they had been relatively wealthy in Vietnam.

Sith is a Laotian man whose conflict story is revealing. He has five children, three living in the United States, and two in Laos. He cannot afford to sponsor the remaining two adult children and their families to come to the United States. Because most of Sith's adult life was spent in the army, he was rarely at home with his family. At the time of the interview, he saw his children infrequently. Because he and his wife separated after their arrival in the United States, the family had not had a complete family gathering since their arrival almost ten years before.

"I might go back to her someday when I am better"

Sith is about fifty-eight years old and a member of a family with considerable internal conflict. He arrived in the United States in 1980 with his wife and several children. Since separating from his wife, he has lived alone in a sparsely furnished basement apartment in a small older home. Three of his five children live in the United States, one in California and the other two in the metropolitan area near where he lives. Two remain in Laos.

As a career soldier in the Laotian nationalist army, Sith spent most of his adult life living away from his wife and children. His life history is filled with the increasing responsibilities of his career, the movement of troops, and his various command positions. Immediately after marriage, he lived with his new wife for only seven days before returning to the military base. His wife lived with her parents for the next seventeen years, during which time he visited when possible; however, all of his children were born while he was away from home. Sith remem-

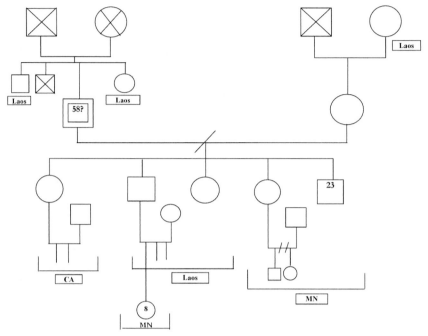

Figure 5.   Sith's Conflicted Family

bers leaving his three-month-old son and not returning until the son was more than three years old: "I reached down for his arm and he would not let me touch him. I felt like crying because I wasn't there during all those times, now he doesn't recognize me."

In 1969, Sith built his own house and, for the first time, lived with his wife and children, who were by then eighteen, seventeen, fifteen, fourteen, and eleven years of age. After the communist Pathet Lao government took over the country in 1975, he was sent to a reeducation camp, where, from 1976 to 1986, he was fed very little and forced to do hard labor. Later, he escaped with his wife and seven-year-old granddaughter, leaving behind a son and daughter in Laos.

As a child, Sith lost his father at age three and worked in the fields with the rest of his family starting at about age seven. They were very poor but were taught deference to elders. "You must put your hand like in a prayer and ask, 'How are you?' When an elder sits you must not walk right before them. You must say, 'Excuse me I'm going to pass by you' and bow your head." He thinks that in the United States the children respect the elders less than they did in Laos and that they are losing important aspects of their heritage, including reverence for the monks and the ability to speak the Lao language. The changes he perceives in the family as a consequence of relocation cause him sadness and anger and create conflict between the generations. "The children are growing up in America and when they see the monks they don't know who it is and I've seen a lot of that. . . . When the elders are sitting they just walk by. When they go to school they eat American food and they don't like Laos food at home. The children look like Laotians, but they have the American culture."

He does not have much to do each day. "I just walk around, I read and if I feel uncomfortable, I go to sleep." If he feels all right he goes twice a week to the YMCA, where there is a Laotian elders program. Although he does occasionally feel lonely, most of the time he is glad that "there's no one to bother me." His two nearby children visit about once a month. "They come by car and we talk. They would buy some fruits and stuff for me. Sometimes they spend the night and then go back." He talks with them by telephone approximately three times each week.

His wife lives nearby with friends. They do not visit and do not get together with the children. The separation was at his request. "It's me. I wanted to live alone since I got here. . . . I like it living alone because I don't want to fight with my children or argue." Sith elaborates on the conflict: "In every marriage there's a fight. I could not stand it when my wife argued with me. It's just me that's the problem. I might go back to her someday when I am better."

"My parents-in-law hurt my feelings"

Ngo was the oldest child in a Vietnamese family of thirteen children, five boys and eight girls. She came to the United States in 1983 after a seven-day stay in Thailand. At the time of the interview, she was fifty-one years old and living with her husband and son while her elderly parents lived with a younger sister in the same high-rise apartment building. A brother lived alone nearby. Despite the proximity, Ngo had little contact with her parents, and she was no longer speaking to her sister because the sister was dating a married man. Ngo had few friends because she was younger than most of the Vietnamese elders who lived in the apartment building.

Ngo was born in Cambodia. At age two she was sent with her younger sister to live with her maternal grandparents in South Vietnam because her parents had too many children to care for and many business responsibilities. At age five she moved back to her parents' house and began school. As the oldest daughter, she became primary caretaker of an ever-growing number of younger siblings. Her responsibilities increased every year as her mother had new babies almost annu-

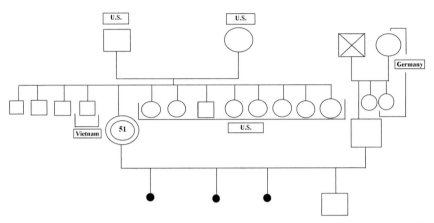

Figure 6.   Ngo's Conflicted Family

ally. An early instance of childhood conflict is still remembered after many years because it demonstrates both the authority of her father and the responsibilities of the oldest child: "One incident, my father bought me a small chick and my brother also had a small chick. But his chick wasn't as nice as mine. So he wanted to exchange his chick for mine; but I refused and he picked up my chick and threw my chick down to the floor. My father got so mad and punished me instead of my brother."

Parent-child conflict is a recurring theme in her narrative. Ngo reveals the multiple-layered nature of parent-child conflict in the United States:

> Children have too much freedom. For example, parents aren't allowed to punish their kids with sticks. In Vietnam, children respect their elders, but not in the U.S. I knew a friend who had a teenage daughter. His daughter didn't study hard; she went out with her boyfriend every day. So her father punished his daughter by hitting her with a stick. His daughter went to tell her counselor at school that her father abused her. So finally, the agency moved the daughter from the father and put her into a foster home. Her father is very depressed now.

A story similar to this was told by many of the elders we interviewed, revealing not only the conflict between generations but also the conflict with the U.S. legal and social service systems.

At age seventeen, Ngo moved to Saigon to continue schooling and manage her own fleet of twelve taxis. When she failed her college entrance exam due to overwork, she quit, returned to her parents' home, and became a teacher. She contributed to the family income while her parents' economic status went downhill as their business selling silver, household appliances, shoes, and other goods declined. Ngo taught French and math in an elementary school and took accounting classes at night. One of her happiest memories was the conclusion of a successful business deal that made a very large profit, enabling her to give a substantial gift of money to her parents.

When Ngo was eighteen, young men began courting her, but none of their birth signs were compatible with hers, so they could not marry. When she was twenty-four she met a man named Nguyen with a compatible birth sign; however, his parents did not approve of her.

> We had to wait for seven years before we finally got married. Within those seven years, many other men came to ask me to marry them. Sometimes, I felt so angry at my husband's family, I was thinking of marrying someone else instead. The men who came to ask me to marry were very well educated. I was planning to marry one of those men, but the signs didn't match mine. I didn't like my husband's family that much. They were so strict. Even though I was so in love with him, but my parents-in-law hurt my feelings. A mother-in-law from the north side is usually very difficult. The daughter-in-law has to serve her mother-in-law like a servant.

Today the mother-in-law lives in Germany and, despite previous conflict, Ngo continues to send her money every month as required by tradition and the expectations of filial piety.

While waiting to marry Ngo built up her business buying and selling land and renting part of her house to Americans. When Nguyen's parents finally allowed the marriage, their son was thirty-five and quite ill and she was thirty-one years old. Ngo defines herself as "a clever lady who could do well in business." After marriage she continued in real estate to support the household while her husband went back to school to study accounting. During the war her husband lost his job and he remained unemployed during the communist rule that followed. After three miscarriages, a trip to France to correct a blockage in her fallopian tubes, and a year of strict Buddhist religious observance, Ngo produced her only child, a son. She also raised the two sons of her sister because her sister was too ill to care for them. When Ngo and her husband first came to the United States, they rented a small room with no heat in exchange for baby-sitting. Her husband has been able to find only part-time employment doing assembly work.

Ngo remembers their difficulty finding work. "I didn't speak English, I couldn't find a job. For example, my husband studied accounting for one year but he wasn't able to find a job because they said he didn't have enough experience. I don't like to receive welfare benefits. I tried to find a job to support my family, but I couldn't."

Because they were relatively prosperous in Vietnam from her business ventures and have lost all of their wealth, Ngo said, "some days when I wake up I feel very depressed." The biggest problem she confronts is "we can't speak English well, [so] we cannot start our own business as in Vietnam. I'm getting old now. I can't do things as younger people do." She and her husband are able to survive on his limited income in addition to the welfare benefits she receives. Currently, she does a variety of housekeeping and family chores to keep herself busy.

> Sometimes I wash clothes by hand and I exercise. Then I prepare food. I go shopping. I take a walk around the university with my husband. Around 10:00 a.m. I sew clothes. Because my heart is enlarged, I can't overwork. If whoever needs my help, I do my best to help them. At home, I help my son with his studies. It usually takes three to four hours for each visit, so by the end of the day, I'm very tired. . . . [T]he only wish I have is my son. I wish he will be successful in the future. We escaped Vietnam because of our son's future. Otherwise we would have stayed in Vietnam.

Family Resiliency Stories

The elders' stories classified as resilient are filled with efforts to balance the individualism, materialism, and the relative equality of American family life with their own more group-oriented, hierarchical family structure. Twenty of forty elders' family stories were classified as resilient, composing the largest group of recurring themes across cultural groups. These stories demonstrate the enormous flexibility, hardiness, strength, and tenacity of the elders who survived, and sometimes even thrived, amidst great adversity. Despite separation, loss, and conflict, these elders and their families refused to be victimized by the war and their experiences as refugees. The resilient elders' stories include a hopeful outlook on the future, despite the hardships they have endured.

While in Vietnam, Bich worked for an international peace commission and he had the opportunity to travel to the United States for training. He had the advantage of being familiar with the United States when he resettled and is one of only two informants who are fluent in English. Bich's reunited family is comparatively intact. All of his nine children are living in the United States. Four of the children live in California and five are living in Minnesota. Education is an important value to Bich and his family; two sons-in-law have master's degrees and four children have college degrees or were in college at the time of the interview. Although he is somewhat unhappy that he cannot provide economically for his family in the United States, Bich nevertheless has important roles in the family as a leader and teacher of morality and culture. His family still treats him with respect, and that makes him happy. Bich illustrates this point by saying, "although I'm not king but still being treated like king."

The resiliency that is consistently revealed in Touch's life history narrative was evident long before she was forced to leave Cambodia. Her life prior to marriage was relatively easy; however, her husband's early death left her with eight young children to support alone. This occurred at a time when resources were becoming scarcer for everyone and her youngest children needed care. Touch began cooking in restaurants and eventually opened a restaurant with her cousin. When conditions in the country began to change for the worse in the mid-1970s, she moved to a safer location and opened another restaurant with a son. When life became dangerous again, Touch escaped Cambodia with her youngest son, who was seven years old at the time. Although she expected that her other seven children would soon follow them, they were all killed. Touch explains how she has managed to survive such a difficult life in terms of the only family member she had left, her son: "[Sometimes] I can't sleep. I just sit there watching his face while he is asleep. When I see his face I think about my other [deceased] children. I keep myself alive because of my son. I don't want him to be alone. We've been through a lot of hardship together. You're happy here only if you have family with you."

"Things change. I'm no longer the king"

Bich is a sixty-nine-year-old Vietnamese man with a family resiliency story who worked in the American embassy in Saigon before the U.S. soldiers left in 1975. Bich is a Vietnamese citizen of Chinese ethnicity who came from a fairly wealthy family that provided him with an excellent education in the French school system of Vietnam. Because of his involvement with the United States government and his connections, he was able to leave with all nine of his children, several of their spouses, and some grandchildren in the first wave of escapees. Currently, four of his children live in California while he and his wife live in a large two-story St. Paul house with their other five children, three of the children's spouses, and three grandchildren. Throughout his life Bich has used his education, intelligence, and personal charm to obtain a series of good jobs that provided well for his family.

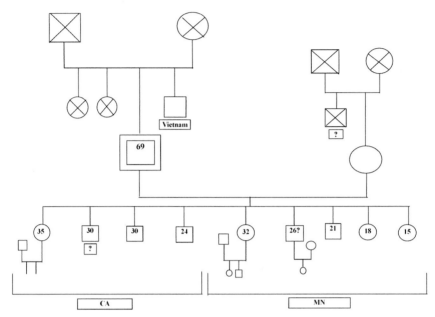

Figure 7.   Bich's Resilient Family

Although he is happy with his family's adjustment in the United States, Bich observes many negative relationships in the households of other Vietnamese people he knows. "In my house the kids are trained to serve tea to the guests and bow to elders. But not in other houses, because in here [the United States] they do not teach children how to serve tea to the guest. I feel sorry. But over here, difference. . . . The kids are happy to live in the U.S. but their parents not happy."

He is also concerned about the way that Vietnamese and American elders are treated in the United States, although he continues to have important roles in his own family and community as moral leader, teacher, financial planner, and teacher.

> The children say that the U.S. is a man's paradise. But when you come here, it's different. Elder people used to have respect back in their country. Children, even those who are grown up, would seek advice from them. But now it's no more. The elders don't feel like kings anymore. . . . In my family, the children must be respectful to the elders and polite to the guests. They must bow their heads, greet the elders, and they must serve tea to the guests in the proper way. The children

must speak Vietnamese at home. When they are at home they are Viet-namese and when they leave home, they are Americans.

When asked what his hopes were for his children's and grandchildren's future his first response was traditional:

> The oldest child must listen to their parent. The younger should listen to the older brother or sister so they can be a brother and sister and live very close together. So they will get along with other people around them. Another message that I would like to leave to everyone, I don't want people to have long hair, wear a shirt and pants that was cut into small pieces. . . . I[I]n other words, don't become punks or thieves.

The importance of adaptability to changing circumstances is central to Bich's thinking and a theme that runs throughout his resilient life story. He attended French schools in Vietnam; moved from North to South Vietnam when it seemed politically expedient; and now, as an immigrant, lives with his intact family in the United States. Although he has pragmatically declared himself to be a Christian, he continues to practice the ancestor worship that is central to his spiritual and family belief system. He expresses some confusion about his children's and grandchildren's future, but ultimately he wants them to adapt to life in the United States without losing the most important parts of Vietnamese culture: "I sing a song of Vietnamese history for my children to remind them about Vietnam. Usually the kids that are not very good children at home, will later hold better positions since they are more Americanized. So I don't know how I want my children. In order to be successful, you have to be more like American."

"We've been through a lot of hardship together"

Touch was born in 1925 and lived in the capital of Phnom Penh, where her father worked arranging trips for the prince. There were two houses on the family estate, one for her oldest brother and his family, and another shared by her parents, an aunt, and six of the ten children in the family. Three other siblings were married and lived elsewhere with their families. At the age of ten, Touch attended school, where she learned both the French and Khmer languages. She especially liked swimming, rope climbing, and participating in other physical activities held before and after school each day. Although her parents were very strict, her life as a child was comparatively easy. "[O]ther children whose parents were poor . . . could not concentrate on just studying. Me I did not need to worry about a thing except studying." Although Touch may have had few worries, as the oldest girl, "my parents put me in charge of everybody in the house." She kept track of who

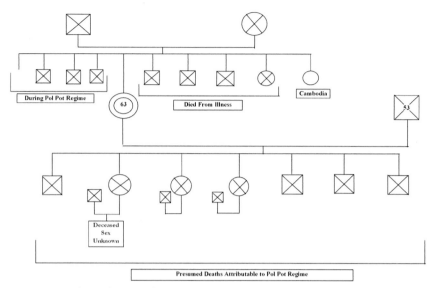

Figure 8.   Touch's Resilient Family

would be home for dinner and made sure that there was enough food for everyone. In addition, she had responsibility for tutoring her siblings: "if they would
not study because they were lazy then I punished them. That was why they were
afraid of me."

Her parents arranged her marriage to Kim in 1945 and, because her spouse's
parents were deceased, they lived with Touch's parents until the birth of their first
child. Before the birth of her son, Touch's household responsibilities continued
to include caring for her younger siblings in addition to outside work as a second
grade teacher. Touch and Kim had seven children living at the time of her husband's death from heart disease in 1971. After his death, "I used my retirement
money and child support to feed my family. I was very worried because I never
worked hard before. . . . I was scared about taking care of the children by myself."
She became a cook and co-owner with her cousin of a restaurant in Phnom Penh.
As the takeover of the capitol by the Khmer Rouge became more imminent, and
at the urging of her children, she left them behind and moved to Ream for safety.
She opened a restaurant business there with one of her sons. "I was thinking that
if the business went well, I was going to buy a lot and build a house there. After
that my children could come to stay with me." Her life changed dramatically and
in an unanticipated direction in April 1975, when ships arrived to help residents
escape the invasion of the Khmer Rouge. With her young son of seven, she
boarded the ship for an unknown destination, leaving her older son behind to

take care of the restaurant. He intended to meet them on a later ship. "I did not protest. I just let him stay. I did not know what to say. I could not think." All six children left behind were killed during the Pol Pot terrors. Four of her brothers died of starvation during the regime.

For twenty days Touch and her son traveled amid uncertainty and hopelessness on the open sea to Malaysia, where they were refused refuge. After replenishing its supplies of food, water, and medicine, the boat traveled to a base in the Philippines, where the refugees stayed for several weeks while waiting for an airplane to the United States. Touch arrived in California with her son in May 1975. An acquaintance secured sponsorships for them in Chicago, although they stayed there only three months. After discovering that the sponsor's brother was taking their welfare and food stamp benefits and giving her only fifty dollars a month, Touch and her son moved back to California. She made arrangements to stay with an acquaintance whom she had met on the ship and his wife. Although he invited Touch to "stay with him since he did not have a mother and he loved me like a mother," her living situation became worse. She worked as a nanny until she hurt her back lifting a child. Her son delivered newspapers. They "used both of us like their servants. I stayed there until I could not stand them anymore."

Touch called a friend in Minnesota and moved once again with her young son. They worked together supporting themselves for eight years before receiving general assistance and Medicare benefits. Her son is now attending college about 150 miles away from home. His success in school is very important to Touch's future, since it will help him to get a job and enable him to take care of her as she gets older. She is looking forward to her son's future so that she doesn't "have to depend on strangers anymore." Currently, she is unemployed and living in an apartment with several others, sharing a room with a cousin to save expenses. The apartment is very crowded because one of Touch's friends provides child care during the day for children in the community. "Sometimes I clean the house after the parents take their children home. My friend sometimes she's very exhausted by the time the children are gone. . . . [W]hen we have dirty laundry I wash them by hand." Touch tries to keep busy working on anything that she can so that she will feel tired and sleep at night.

Touch hopes soon to have enough money to rent an apartment of her own.

> I learn to cope with my problems by reading the Buddhist bible and thinking about what the bible says. . . . Whenever I can't sleep I read the bible so that I don't have to think about my children. It helps me to fall asleep by reading the bible. Sometimes I talk to my roommate. But I don't talk to a lot of people because the more I talk, the more I remember, and I just want to forget about it.

Although her life is filled with tragedies that would overwhelm most people, Touch continues to live and contribute to the well-being of her only remaining son. Her resilient attitude allows her to have hope for the future amidst her sorrow and grief.

Theoretical Implications

Collectively, the family stories of these eight elders reflect the disruption of traditional ways, a loss of continuity, and family adaptability in unfamiliar environments. The family trees and narrative histories reveal how dramatic the impact of war has been on the extended families' structure, culture, interactions, and identity. Almost every story includes some elements of the separation, loss, conflict, and resilience narrative themes, suggesting a similarity of perceptions and family experiences even when one of the themes is predominant.

The men's stories are revealing. Sith's story is dominated by his service in the Laotian army, long separations from his family, and unnamed conflicts that now separate and isolate family members in their new environment. Luot remembers his parent's household as supportive and close-knit, while his own family's life was dominated by war, repeated separations, insecurity, fear, and death. Xi Chao's family story begins with the loss of his father at an early age and continues with many additional losses in the fighting and his escape. The loss of land, home, work, and self-sufficiency makes him feel worthless and without a place in his final years. Bich experiences some loss of respect and position in his new environment; however, his intact family has learned the lessons he taught about filial piety and the importance of adaptability. To survive in the United States he encourages his children and grandchildren to adopt a bicultural lifestyle.

The women's narratives expand on these themes and add new ones of their own. Although Dam had ten children, only one of them lives in the United States. Her life course and family structure were dramatically altered by the death of her husband and migration; she now lives separated from almost everyone she cares about. Mai feels that she has lost almost everything as a result of the war and migration. She waits patiently for her only remaining son to marry so that she will have family to care for her in her final years. Ngo's life was filled with conflict before migration and after. She lives with resentments and anger toward her mother-in-law but still sends her money every month as a sign of her respect. Despite the loss of almost her entire family, Touch tries to look forward rather than at the past so that she can be the family that her only living son needs as he makes his way in the United States.

The family stories embedded in these eight cases can be viewed through the dual lenses of the continuity (Atchley 1989) and ecosystems theories (Bronfenbrenner 1979; Bubolz and Sontag 1992). The loss of continuity, the fear of this loss, and the effort to reestablish it within their families is a consistent and dominant theme in the lives of all the informants examined here. The desire for continuity often revolves around reestablishing family connections severed by the war and relocation process, especially the reunification with family members who were left behind or resettled elsewhere. As nominal heads of the household, the men consider it their responsibility to maintain the integrity of the group; however, this cannot be accomplished with some members of the family system scattered on two or more continents. The attempt to perpetuate the age-old expectations of respect, reverence, and devotion within the family is a natural way that these older men seek to maintain their power, control, and position in the hierarchy of the family and community. With the possible exception of Bich, the resilient Vietnamese man, these elders have lost important roles—their positions as head of the household, their status as breadwinner, and their authority as disciplinarian, moral leader, and teacher of the young. They frequently discuss this loss of continuity in terms of their feelings of uselessness and sadness. The women, despite multiple losses, find some measure of comfort and continuity in home and child care responsibilities, despite the separations and losses they have experienced.

The loss of continuity can be extended to the loss of *place* in an ecosystemic context that is familiar and that gives structure and meaning to life. These eight elders have left behind their homes, land, animals, ancestral graveyards, living family members, work, daily routines, familiar languages, and cultural symbols. As a consequence of relocation to the new environment, elders who were once considered the source of important information and advice by their families and communities are now in a situation in which they must ask their children and grandchildren to help them with the simplest task.

While elder status in their homelands brought prestige, support, respect, and deference, these elders tell stories about being uprooted from their rightful place in a well-balanced ecosystem and transplanted to foreign soil. At every level of the new ecosystem important elements are missing. These missing elements promote mental health because they give structure and meaning to daily life, and they establish an important place for the elders within their families and community.

Although it may be possible to uproot a tree and successfully plant it elsewhere, it is much more difficult to transplant an old tree because the roots are so deeply embedded in the soil. The tree may be able to survive in a different soil and climatic zone but it will flourish only with the greatest difficulty. Many of the family stories we have heard and will hear in subsequent chapters are testimony to the difficulties of transplanted survival and the radical changes that were made to adapt in the new soil and very different climate.

Note

1. All quotations come from the translated transcripts of the life history interviews. Thirty-eight of the forty elders were interviewed in their native languages and two were conducted in English. The interviews were tape recorded and translated by the native speaking co-interviewer shortly after the interviews were conducted.

Changing Family Structures 4

Introduction

IMMIGRATION IS A LIFELONG PROCESS that dramatically changes the everyday lives of migrants and the long-term structure of their families. According to McGoldrick (1982), the process of migration is so disruptive in itself that we could say it adds an entire extra stage to the life cycle of families who must negotiate it. The adjustment to a new culture and way of life is not a single event, but a prolonged developmental process of adjustment that affects family members differently, depending on their individual and family development stage during the transition (Carter and McGoldrick 1988). The developmental transition is complex for each generation; however, it seems especially difficult for the elderly informants in our study because they have already lived the majority of their adult lives in a completely different environment with deeply rooted expectations for how the family should be organized.

Separation of families severely disrupts the developmental continuity of lives and the ways that families are organized. In the previous chapter we saw how the impact of migration can be graphically displayed in family trees. These structures have missing parts and empty holes where family members have died or disappeared. Reestablishing family life is difficult with members missing; moreover, economic constraints, overwhelming grief, and conflict sometimes made it impossible to reconstruct the family in the new world. The relationships and roles of elders within families were altered by the war, the refugee experience, and resettlement in the West. We saw several examples in the previous chapter. Sith, Luot, and Xi Chao had few significant roles or responsibilities in the family or community, in contrast to their previous positions as head of the family and primary breadwinner. Sith, the Laotian soldier, was estranged from his wife and had distant relationships with his adult children because he was an absent father and husband during long periods of fighting the war. Luot's frustration with his grandchildren sometimes resulted in his hitting the children, a behavior that seeks to maintain his position of power over them. Xi Chao's loss of power in the family is an important theme in his life history and a source of great sadness and despair. Only Bich, the Vietnamese man, appeared to have retained some degree of power in his family because he relinquished his role as "king." Although Bich laments the overwhelming influences of the new environment on children and the diminishing filial piety he observes in other families, his satisfaction with life in the United States is a consequence of his family's resilience in a radically different environment. The women's narratives in the previous chapter are filled with the consequences of many changes in their family's structure. Husbands died, children were killed or left behind, and the women had to fend for themselves in alien and dangerous environments. Despite their losses and grief, many of the women increased their importance, power, and influence by assuming new roles and responsibilities within the remnants of their resettled families.

Before resettlement, Southeast Asian families were structured around a belief in the hierarchical nature of all family relationships inherent in the Confucian filial piety concept. Adult male and female roles were organized according to age, gender, and relationship, so that women learned early that they must respect and obey the wishes of their parents, older brothers, husbands, and in-laws, while men learned to respect their parents, especially the father and other male elders. Children were taught to be respectful to everyone in authority and to all those who were older than they. The unequal authority of elders, husbands, mothers-in-law, and older brothers often created fear in those with less power, especially girls and women. Many elders in this study say that Southeast Asian family structures are undergoing considerable change in the new environment, creating instability and uncertainty about the future This finding is consistent with those of Bishop (1985), who found that the distribution of power, authority, and control in the organization and structure of Hmong family relationships has rapidly changed since arrival in the United States.

According to LaRossa (1984), all family groups have a social structure and network of relationships with a power and role structure. One way to understand these structures in families is to examine the life history narratives for discussions of family relationships, authority, and roles. For example, in a few words a Vietnamese woman illustrated how the absolute authority traditionally exercised by older males has changed in the new context. According to Ngo, the reason is that in the United States: "Children have too much freedom." To understand the structure in Southeast Asian families, we will examine changes in elders' roles, family relationships, and power as they are revealed in the life history narratives.

Elders' Roles

A useful way to understand the changing structure of the elders' families is to examine the types and number of individual roles they currently perform compared to their roles in the past and to those of other, similarly situated groups. This comparison is also an indicator of the change in status of elders. Roles are defined using Linton's (1936) classic definition, which links appropriate individual behaviors to a particular position or status in a family, community, or social structure. Nye (1976) uses Linton's definitional link between roles and status to analyze role structures within family systems, and George (1980) uses this definition in her study of role transitions in old age. An individual's roles are usually good indicators of her or his power, status, and authority within a group. A loss of roles suggests a loss of function, responsibility, and authority, while an increase in roles suggests an increase in power. The life history narratives include many examples of pre- and postmigration roles and memories of roles performed by parents and grandparents in the past.

Male and female roles in the family and community generally increase in quantity and importance throughout adulthood. The oldest males control family and community resources and can be powerful figures of authority in traditional Southeast Asian families. Greater gender equality may emerge for women living in Southeast Asia in old age after the death of a spouse. In an early study of Vietnamese villages along the Mekong River, Hickey (1964) found that after the husband's death, it would not be unusual for a widow to relocate near siblings. Although a widow is likely to live under the authority of the oldest son, the respect accorded to her lineal position often means that she is treated as head of the family (Baker 1979).

When the most senior male head of the household in Hmong families is very old or frail, leadership and authority is passed on to the next most senior male, typically the oldest son (Geddes 1976). In rural farm families, when the older father is less able to manage the farming responsibilities, many roles are assumed by his sons to ensure the continued prosperity of the family (Geddes 1976; Yang 1968). Elderly Vietnamese in rural villages do not always live in the same household with their adult children, especially if there are many young grandchildren underfoot, but they often live in close proximity. Most individuals live in an extended kin network surrounded by family members (Hickey 1964). Very few households consist of someone living alone and almost everyone has relatives in the village.

The traditional village and family life of the past has been changing across

Asia as the forces of modernization permeate even remote villages. There is evidence of change in elders' roles and the decline of filial piety during the past few decades in the rapidly developing countries of Asia, including China, Japan, Korea, and Hong Kong (Bengston et al. 2000). Similar trends in less-developed Asian countries are also beginning to appear (Kosberg 1992). The migration experience of the elders in our study undoubtedly speeded up the change in their roles, power, and authority; however, it was a process that was already underway at the time of migration. Kibria (1993) discovered that the Vietnamese families she studied in Philadelphia were walking an emotional tightrope as they attempted to balance the desire for role and family continuity with the inevitability of change that surrounded them.

Elderly Southeast Asian men and women are strongly attached to home, family, village, and culture. The birthplace of the household head is an important location to the larger extended family because it represents the place where a branch of the family tree began and it is often the place where ancestors are buried (Liu and Fernandez 1988). In their homelands, the oldest men are the patriarchs, with high-status roles that include responsibilities such as moral leader, teacher, counselor, decision maker, and family head. In the United States, Southeast Asian men typically lose this dominant position as the number and importance of their roles decline; however, women's roles and power tend to increase (Rottman and Meredith 1982).

The life history interviews included several questions about changing roles and responsibilities in the family. Vietnamese and Cambodian elders were selected for closer scrutiny because they represent comparatively high and low levels of social and economic integration. A total of twenty-four different role behaviors were identified in the narratives, and they were grouped according to the type of role and the primary recipient associated with the behavior. For example, roles can be categorized according to whether they were performed for the benefit of the entire family, such as protection/security, breadwinning, housework, and food preparation roles. Some roles were performed for the benefit of the youth and grandchildren, such as teaching/advising, authority/discipline, and child care roles. Others were performed for the parents and grandparents, such as caregiving and serving elder roles. Roles performed for the cultural group and community included participation in religious ceremonies and maintaining tradition. We tried to categorize roles according to the meanings or context ascribed to them by informants in the narratives.

Twenty of the twenty-four role behaviors can be generally described as family roles, including some performed for youth or elders and others for the entire family, while four can be described as different types of community-related roles.

Table 1.   Roles Performed by Vietnamese and Cambodian Elders in the United States

	Vietnamese		Cambodian	
	Male	Female	Male	Female
Roles				
General family				
Family head	1	0	1	3
Protection	2	0	0	0
Shelter	0	0	1	1
Support	1	3	0	3
Outside work	0	2	0	3
Breadwinner	2	0	0	2
Finance affairs	1	1	0	1
Housework	0	3	0	3
Food preparation	0	6	0	4
Shopping	0	1	0	1
Sewing	0	2	0	0
Conflict resolution	1	1	0	0
Children/grandchildren				
Role model	1	1	1	2
Teacher/adviser	3	2	1	2
Disciplinarian	2	1	0	0
Arrange wedding	0	0	0	2
Child care	3	3	1	3
Foster parent	0	1	0	1
Parent/grandparent				
Caregiving	0	1	0	2
Serve elders	0	3	1	0
Community				
Keep tradition	1	4	0	2
Religious	1	3	0	3
Organizer	0	1	0	2
Retiree	0	0	0	0
Totals	19	39	6	40

The preponderance of family roles is evidence of the continuing centrality of the family to elders and the continuing importance of elders within their family systems. Even the roles performed for the benefit of the community, such as maintaining traditions and performing religious ceremonies, are discussed by informants as important to family well-being. For example, the Vietnamese father's performance of the ancestor worship rituals at the new year's *Tet* celebration is designed to teach the young respect for Confucian traditions and to reinforce the link between living and deceased family members.

The number of roles that were discussed in the life histories varied significantly for men (twenty-five) and women (seventy-nine) when summed for both cultural groups. It appears that male roles are more specialized and gender specific than female roles. For example, Vietnamese men performed twelve different roles while Vietnamese women performed eighteen different roles. The contrast for Cambodians was even greater, with males performing only six roles while women performed eighteen of twenty-four potential roles.

The roles most frequently discussed by elders are associated with the important family functions of child care and food preparation. The importance of these unpaid contributions to extended families should not be underemphasized; however, they are not roles that carry high status. Female elders appear to serve important instrumental functions by performing these roles within families; however, male elders have less clear functional roles. Since many roles these women perform in their reconstituted families are roles performed by women in their home country, their functional importance in the family suggests more role continuity for women compared to men. The very limited number of roles performed by Cambodian men suggests that their expressed feelings of uselessness in this context are not exaggerated. On the other hand, the proliferation of Vietnamese women's roles suggests that they have assumed more responsibilities than any other subgroup and may be overloaded or even overwhelmed.

Although elders continue to play important roles within families, they know that they are not as important in the American context as they were in their homelands. Often their roles here are primarily instrumental in nature, helpful to the family system, but not highly prestigious. The elders' capacity to maintain traditional roles and the values that support them is diminished by the all-consuming nature of survival in the new environment. When all the family energy is expended on outside work and education, there is little energy or time left for the younger generations to express their filial piety in the proper ways. Although adult children and grandchildren continue to respect their elders, the absence of many traditional daily practices of respect is a recurring reminder to elders of their loss of authority and status within the family in the new context.

Table 2 provides data that compare the roles currently performed by the elder informants to those performed by their parents and grandparents in the past. Two patterns are noteworthy across generations and cultures. In both the Vietnamese and Cambodian groups, the number of roles performed increases from the earlier generations to the current generation of elders. This pattern may be interpreted as evidence of the growing importance of elders in families, the persistence of traditional roles, an increase in the responsibilities of the informants in the new context, or simply the fading memories of elderly informants. A second pattern is the larger number of role performances reported by Vietnamese informants compared to the Cambodians across all three generations. Since memories about the earlier generations are limited and they are not the focus of this study, no interpretations of the change over time will be suggested here. For the informant generation, at least three interpretations are possible. The larger number and variety of roles performed by Vietnamese elders may be evidence of their integration into family and community and a greater degree of adaptation. The smaller number and variety of roles performed by Cambodian elders may be evidence of the continuing impact of the traumatic stresses they experienced before and during their flight from persecution. It may also be a reflection of differences between cultures with respect to the roles and functions of elders in families.

Table 2.   Roles Performed by Three Generations of Vietnamese and Cambodian Elders

	Grandparents		Parents		Informants	
	Viet-namese	Cam-bodian	Viet-namese	Cam-bodian	Viet-namese	Cam-bodian
Roles						
General family						
Family head	4	1	2	2	1	4
Protection	1	4	2	0	2	0
Shelter	0	0	2	7	0	2
Support	1	1	2	0	4	3
Outside work	3	0	2	0	2	3
Breadwinner	1	1	2	3	2	2
Finance affairs	0	1	1	0	2	1
Housework	1	1	3	0	3	3
Food preparation	0	0	1	1	6	4
Shopping	0	0	0	0	1	1
Sewing	0	0	0	0	2	0
Conflict resolution	1	0	0	0	2	0
Children/grandchildren						
Role model	2	3	2	2	2	3
Teacher/advice	2	1	1	5	5	3
Disciplinarian	3	0	5	3	3	0
Arrange wedding	0	2	2	0	0	2
Child care	5	0	3	4	6	4
Foster parent	2	0	0	0	1	1
Parent/grandparent						
Caregiving	0	0	0	0	1	2
Serve elders	0	0	0	0	3	1
Community						
Keep tradition	1	5	1	6	5	2
Religious	4	3	2	2	4	3
Organizer	1	0	1	0	0	0
Retiree	2	0	2	0	0	0
Totals	34	23	36	35	57	44

The types of roles performed in the family, children, parent, and community categories suggest several preliminary observations regarding the status of elders in families and the community. The most frequently mentioned general family role is food preparation. The acquisition and preparation of appropriate food is an important concern in virtually all the households and an important component of cultural continuity. Since very little Western food is appealing to the elders, the adult children typically purchase traditional Asian foods, and the elders are responsible for preparation. This is a time-consuming task, often taking several hours per day. Typically, the adult children and grandchildren do not have time for elaborate cooking preparations, since they are working outside the home and/ or attending school. The food preparation role indicates the functional value of the elders to their larger kin network and the continuity that comes with traditional foods and aromas in the household. Food can also be a source of conflict between generations, according to elders, as some adolescents prefer American fast foods.

Roles related to children and grandchildren are an important component of elders' responsibilities in the United States, as they often were in the homeland. The most frequently mentioned current role that elders perform in this category is child care. Since middle-generation parents are so often outside the home, grandchildren become the daily responsibility of their grandparents, who often serve as coparents for the children. It was not unusual for the life history interviews to be interrupted several times by child care responsibilities. In one case, an eighty-three-year-old Vietnamese woman we interviewed was taking care of three toddlers during the day and several additional older children after school hours. In addition to child care, several informants also mentioned responsibilities to care for or serve elders in the family or community.

The most frequently mentioned community roles of elders are maintaining traditions and performing religious ceremonies. Often these roles are merged into the ancestor worship rituals performed annually on the birthday of deceased family members or during the new year celebrations. Activities at the Buddhist temples and service to the monks were two of the most frequently mentioned religious activities. Maintaining traditions is a general category in which several activities were discussed, including teaching the native language to the young, telling folk stories, and practicing important rituals. These community roles are important to elders in Southeast Asia and our informants considered them important to their own cultural and personal identities in the United States. Many elders were concerned that the younger generation would not learn or continue these ceremonies, rituals, and traditions in the future. An important motivation for many elders to participate in the life history interviews was the hope that their stories, experiences, and histories would be preserved for future generations.

Gender Roles

In the Confucian orientation, the primary responsibility for elders and the success of the family lineage was largely determined by gender. The sons' responsibility was to secure the future for their parents, the extended family, and the ancestors by continuing the family lineage (Baker 1979). Men married for the benefit of the family, with the highest priority being to provide male descendents and continuation of the family line. Among Chinese populations living in Southeast Asia, the patrilineal line was made continuous through the sons' marriage and coresidence with the parents during the early years after marriage (Hirschman and Rindfuss 1982). Documenting traditional courtship and marriage practices in a Hmong village, Lee (1981) found that most young men married between the ages of sixteen and twenty-one to girls who were thirteen to twenty-one years old and who began childbearing soon after. Thus, the family lineage was preserved and the elders had daughters-in-law who were committed to caring for them for the rest of their lives.

In some Southeast Asian families, it was the oldest son who assumed the primary responsibility for elder parents. In Vietnamese families before the war, it was usually the youngest son who assumed these responsibilities; however, the older male siblings sometime remained in the household to help parents until they had growing families of their own (Hickey 1964). If enough land were available, the older sons would establish residence nearby. The youngest son was expected to remain in the parents' home, marry according to the wishes of the parents, and provide care for parents in old age.

Women's roles were primarily centered on the needs of the family. Marriage was the most important adult role for women. After marriage, it was the wife's duty to produce sons for the husband's family line and become the caretaker of his parents. She was expected to be part of her husband's family and attentive to the "comfort and satisfaction" of her mother-in-law (Hickey 1964). The strong preference for male children occurred because girls were viewed as a financial burden, since their adult lives and most productive years were spent contributing to the husband's family rather than the family of origin (Geddes 1976). A young woman's status in the new family was often tenuous until she was able to provide a son for the husband's family, as in Ngo's story in the previous chapter. If there was conflict within the marriage, the wife's negotiating position was difficult, since she was separated from her own lineage (Dunnigan 1982). Although marriages were arranged and not founded on Western notions of romantic love, affection between spouses was expected to grow (Yang 1968). Divorce was rare, however; some men with resources were married to more than one wife.

If gender is a socially constructed collection of mores, cultural behaviors, and prescriptions for how males and females are expected to interact in the world, then it is easy to understand the dramatic impact of migration on gender roles inside and outside the family. Patterns of gender-specific behaviors were developed over many generations until forced migration disrupted all normative family processes and the structures that surrounded them. Boys and girls learned how to be men and women, husbands and wives, and grandparents by observing role behaviors within the family. They learned to replicate important elements of these gender-constructed realities as they grew up and had children of their own. As parents and grandparents, they taught children how to live in the world and get along with others by their example.

In the new context, women's and men's roles within the family, and their places within the larger community, often became the subject of disagreement. Some male elders continued to hold on to powerful images of themselves as head of the household even while they stayed at home every day to care for grandchildren and wait for their spouse to return home from work with a paycheck. The life histories reveal that many of the older women continued to conform to most of the expectations for their gender, even while they assumed new roles and responsibilities in their resettled families. The adolescent women in our studies strained mightily against tightly regimented family restrictions—especially those applied unevenly to them and their brothers.

With elder and gender roles in a state of change and positions of authority shifting, it follows naturally that family relationships would also be in a state of flux. Whether we examine parent-child, in-law, sibling, or marital relationships we see change in the traditional patterns of deference. Although filial piety expectations remain an ever-present reminder of how relationships should be governed, they are not always practiced fully and are seldom practiced to the satisfaction of elders, especially the men.

Although table 2 reveals that elders continue to perform many family and community roles after arrival in the United States, the older men appear to be engaged in significantly fewer roles than the women, and the Cambodian men are engaged in fewer substantive roles than the Vietnamese men. The number and range of roles in the family and community indicates the continuing importance of elders; however, the types of roles that are performed do not include many examples of the high-status or honorific roles. It appears that men are more limited in the range of roles permitted by their group and family traditions or available to them in the new context. When the actual roles performed by men are compared to those performed by women, it is clear that men are rarely involved in housework, food preparation, or shopping. However traditional this may appear, it is moderated by the nontraditional roles performed by women, including providing shelter and protection for the family, teaching/advising, and performing religious ceremonies. The wide range of women's roles in both cultural groups is an indication that women continue to perform their traditional roles and have taken on typically male roles as well. Part of the disparity may be explained by the fact that there were twelve widows in the sample and it became necessary for them to assume a greater number of nontraditional roles; however, it is also apparent that the married women were engaged in many more functional roles within the family than men. This is not unlike the situation in the home country; however, male elders often mention the loss of status in the family and community as a major difficulty in their adjustment.

The reconstructions of filial piety, gender, and elder roles are closely connected elements of the family's structure that reveal insights into the changing nature of power, authority, and control in families. Socialization into established gender roles is learned from parents, grandparents, and other adults through early and frequent contact. The memories of male and female roles at home are vivid to many of the elders we interviewed. The men, in particular, were quick to explain how the gendered world was ordered in their native lands. It was those memories against which the startling changes occurring in the United States were measured.

The memory of how gender roles and relationships were organized in Vietnam is quite clear to Doan. He explains that his family was unusual because his father, for political reasons, did not work outside the home, while his mother did. Doan's father did all the cooking for the family even though this was considered women's work. Doan is quick to explain, however, that his father never did the cleanup after cooking, since that was a level of women's work to which he would not stoop. Despite having a somewhat nontraditional father, Doan outlines the difference between men's and women's roles in his family: "When I am in the kitchen my father tells me to go out because it's not my duty over there. It's for women. So when I married, everything in my home would belong to my wife. I don't do anything in the kitchen. My duty include provide a steady income. I take care of the education of the family. That's typical for normal family." Doan follows his father's example in family decision making. He explains how his father controlled his mother and how he controls his wife: "My father made the latest decision. My mother must obey him. No quarrel, no questions. Like my wife, if

I say 'Do it,' just do it, no questions. In my family, if there is a disagreement, my father decided it."

Lan remembers the high respect that her grandparents commanded in Vietnam and the fear she had of her very strict and distant grandfather. Within her household when she was a child, Lan's father was the primary authority. When he was gone, the mother was in charge. Lan remembers her father as a powerful man who was steadfast in making and keeping family rules. "My father was very strict. For example, everything we did must be according to the schedule; we had to eat at a certain time and to study at a certain time. If we didn't listen to our father, he would punish us by hitting us with a stick. . . . My mother was very indulgent, she didn't give out orders; she only helped around the house with chores."

Phoune recalls the different roles of boys and girls when she was growing up in rural lowland Laos. As a small child she worked with her grandparents on their farm. In describing them she said: "[T]hey were so old when I remember and their backs were hunched." Like other elders who could no longer do the heaviest farming work, Phoune's grandparents stayed behind to take care of the younger children while the stronger middle-aged men and women worked the farm. It was the girl's job to "go get the water from the lake, not like here." Girls were expected to wear the long traditional skirts and to learn how to weave, while "the boys worked in the fields and raised buffaloes."

Mao recalls the shared responsibility among family members for child care and other household chores when she was living in the mountains of Laos. "Our Hmong never give to one person to do it. Whoever is free and doesn't have a lot of kids does it. One person does one thing and the other person does one thing to help each other." The current situation of Xi Chao contrasts sharply with this traditional image of cooperative child care and male elders being the family breadwinners. He lives in a Minneapolis home with his wife, five adult children, and many grandchildren. While his wife has a part-time job that she goes to every day, Xi Chao has little to do except baby-sit for his grandchildren. Dependency on his wife for financial support and his low-status role as a baby-sitter causes him to "describe myself like a bird that was in a cage and it depends on the feeder."

Thavone offers an example of collaborative decision making and conflict resolution by his parents when he was young man in Laos: "If brother and sisters had a fight, my mom and dad made the decision. Dad talks and Mom talks that this one was wrong and has to change. They listen and were good to each other again." Despite his early experience of cooperative parenting, women's roles are seen by Thavone as kitchen and family related, while the primary male role is to earn income to support the family. When it is not possible to economically support the family in this country because of health or language barriers, men like Thavone often do not move beyond their traditional beliefs. Many sit at home and do almost nothing every day. Without knowing how to drive and not having the language skills to obtain a license, Thavone is completely dependent on his sons and son-in-law for transportation. At the time of the interview, he was worried because his son-in-law had just bought a house in another part of the city and he feared that it would be even harder for him to get around. This example illustrates how dependency in the new context can erode the authority of elders and the traditional gender roles of males.

Zoua recalls that her brothers were granted authority from her Hmong parents to run the household. Girls were expected to obey their brothers: "[W]hatever they tell us to do we have to do it. If we have visitors in a full house they would tell us to find enough drink and food for them to eat so that we won't be embarrassed. We want to keep our face and not be ashamed." Girls were expected to rise very early in the morning to prepare food for brothers and parents going off to work in the fields. When Zoua was growing up: "The son, if he is the one who goes out and cuts the hay to feed the cows and horses or if he is the one to provide wood for the fire, when he gets up from bed, he will tell you to cook breakfast and that he is on his way to collect firewood." Zoua's life as a young girl was filled with an endless routine of work: "Then in the morning you wake up to cook breakfast, then the elders tell you to eat breakfast and bag lunch and go to the fields to work and that's all you do." Often, a day in the fields did not end until dusk, when the women walked some distance back to the village, often with harvested crops, wood for the fire, tools, and children in tow.

> Cooking and cleaning is your job, so you do it all. When you come back to the house from the fields we have many visitors, you cook, and the grandparents keep them company. They sit and chat with the guests. Then after you finish cooking you say, "Let's eat, Mom and Dad." Then you eat. . . . [W]hen you're done cooking there are always a couple of relatives where you have to serve them. Like they say, "No matter what we eat, the men eat before the women." If there is nothing left, then the women eat plain rice.

After Sally's father died during the Pol Pot terrors, she stayed behind in the village to care for her mother, who was sick and too frail to return with her husband and children to Phnom Penh. During that time her husband made a major decision without consulting her, demonstrating both his ability to make important decisions on his own and his sensitivity to the legitimate fears of his spouse. He allowed their son and daughter to attempt the dangerous escape into Thailand "without me knowing it. He was afraid that I would not go along with him. . . . It was very dangerous; that is why he kept it secret." Now as an older Cambodian woman living in the United States, Sally once again confronts the lack of power she has to affect the future. Although she has not had problems with her adult children since migrating to the United States, nevertheless, she said:

> [T]he feeling of insecurity is always in me. I'm afraid that they might not be what I want them to be. Because in this country the children are very different and unpredictable. . . . I just pray that my children will study hard and be good. I no longer have the authority to tell them what to do. . . . If they do something wrong, I just give them advice. If they listen, then it is good. . . . I don't like to talk too much, because the more you talk the less respect they have towards you.

Luot believed that it was his responsibility as a Cambodian father to arrange for the education and marriages of his sons. Now that he is an older man and his sons have been taken care of, he has limited language skills and little prospect of finding work. He has few responsibilities and little real authority left. Luot's wife pays the bills and, with the help of their children, she fills out the necessary forms. "My wife is the one who does the work. I only tell her what to do. I also help, not just sit and watch."

Several male and female elders discussed trying to use what limited powers they had left. Neou believes that his role as a Cambodian father includes providing for the financial and psychological well-being of the family.

> Whoever the father is, he is connected to all. The worries are all on top of the father. If the wife is weak also, the worries of the wife also go to the husband. . . . The father worries very much of caring for the children. . . . When I lost my eyes, if the children have jobs and are able to care for their spouse, I am glad. . . . I worry within the family. I don't know if our children are good or bad.

With a major disability, he faces the likelihood of a continuing loss of functional ability as he grows older. Neou's loss of health, strength, and mobility in the United States means an inevitable decline in his authority within the family as well: "Now at this age I know myself, I'm weaker, not good at doing anything. The year before, I cut the grass. . . . I've stopped because I see that my strength is getting weak. They said to walk and exercise. I couldn't do it because I'm too lazy." Whether Neou is lazy, weak, or too blind to work he has little motivation or ability to assert his presence as a contributor to the family, even as the cutter of the grass. The inevitable physical decline that normatively occurs as part of the aging process and the loss of power that accompanies it are important dimensions of the structural changes occurring in Southeast Asian families with elders. This decline in the authority of elders is a natural part of the turnover in generational power that is accelerated by modernization, migration, and the resettlement process.

Diminished physical abilities and the absence of real authority are present in many of the women's narratives. Many are resilient fighters who have managed with enormous courage to find a safe haven for remnants of their family in the United States. Others are barely holding on to the hope that their children will care for them as their health and power diminish. They are often fearful of the future and wary of the influence of American culture. They believe that good kids can become bad kids if they are not influenced properly. For example, Mao's life is completely dependent on the fealty of her two sons in her later years. The years she spent working in the fields and the difficult escape took their toll physically: "[W]e run and carry very heavy loads and my head hurts and my back hurts. So I quit school because I can't study." Her current roles involve cooking, taking care of a nine-year-old son, and occasionally doing some handcrafts. She is uncertain about the future and hopeful that her sons will continue to respect and care for her as she grows older. "I want to bring my children here to educate them in the school so they could help me."

Family Roles and Relationships

With the reconstruction of male and female roles occurring at a different pace in each generation, and with secondary migration continuing to bring newcomers into the community, the diversity in roles and relationships within and between families becomes even more apparent. Since many gender roles—such as wife, husband, father, mother, brother, sister, aunt, and uncle—are ascribed at birth as family roles, it is not surprising to see dramatic changes in families when the cultural context no longer supports traditional gender roles. Examining the changing definition of what it means to be an elder, a male, or a female is one way to view role change; however, there are other lenses through which the processes of a family's structural change can be observed.

Nu remembers her Vietnamese grandfather as very strict and severe, a real authority figure, to whom a young girl was answerable. She recalls memories of her grandparents:

They loved their grandchildren very much, but they were very grave. For example, when my grandfather wanted anyone to do anything that person had to do exactly what my grandfather wanted. For me, my grandfather wanted me to study at a certain time; I had to study at exactly that time. If I didn't understand my homework I could ask him or my uncles. I got my studying done. If I failed my test, he would punish me by hitting me with a stick.

Despite the stereotype that Asian families are authoritarian, Nu recalls a more democratic decision-making process when she was a child that included the voices of other adults. She remembers the collaborative way that both grandparents conducted the monthly family meetings.

Every month, my grandparents called everybody to come to the meeting. In the meeting they discussed issues of how to improve the ways of teaching their own children or their own grandchildren. . . . If they disagreed on some issues they would ask my aunts' or uncles' ideas. So it usually depended on the majority's idea. Therefore, if the majority agreed on the issues, then everybody would agree. I looked forward to those meetings. When I did everything that I was supposed to do, then my parents and grandparents would give me good compliments. Also, we had a lot of food to eat before the meeting.

Nevertheless, her grandfather was the head of the family and the lines of authority were clear. "My grandfather told my father what he was supposed to do, and my father told his children what they were supposed to do. In general, the elders teach the younger. I tried to use this method to teach my children."

Duc's current family circumstances and limited roles provide a dramatic contrast to the traditional image of powerful Vietnamese male elders whose word was law. He is home most of the day with his wife and grandchildren and he does not feel very useful. When speaking about his grandchildren, he says:

Actually, I don't have any responsibility for them. In the Western culture, after the children grown up and married, they take care of their own family. The grandparents have no responsibility. But in the Oriental culture, we really want to help. Anyway, the reason I take care of them is because I love them. They are my offspring. Usually, I take them for a walk but I would not walk very far. Because my daughter goes to school, we take care of the two kids.

Several female elders discussed the changed power of in-laws within the family hierarchy, since they were once daughters-in-law and they are now mothers-in-law. Zoua recalls what it was like for her as a very young woman to be living in the household of her in-laws, especially after her new husband left to work away from their small village in northern Laos. She had to ask her mother-in-law for permission to leave the house: "If they don't have anyone to go with you, they won't let you go." Thao recalls having to bow her head before her Vietnamese father-in-law although nobody else in the family was required to do so. She deeply regrets not feeling that she had enough power to defy her mother-in-law when her son was sick.

> My mother-in-law was very superstitious, so when my older son was ill, she refused to take him to the doctor. She would just stay home and pray to god to cure my son. Therefore, my son died of illness. He died at age twelve. . . . My older son died due to my mother-in-law not letting me take my son to the doctor. My husband was so mad; after that he told me not to listen to my mother-in-law. If my son becomes sick, I should take him to the doctor.

The power of mothers-in-law appears to have diminished in the United States with the change in gender and family roles and the decline in authority of the oldest generation, and with the younger women working or going to school.

Kim reports that in Cambodia the role of mothers was clearly focused on the children and the household. "The father is usually for the big problems. The small things like not working, not helping each other, are usually for the mother." Touch reports that her current responsibilities as a mother are similar to those she had in Cambodia. She continues to get up at 4:30 a.m. each day. She cleans the house, washes the dishes, and cooks for the four sons who live with her. "They don't even want me to cook for them in the morning, but it is usually done by the time they get up. They said they're big enough to cook. They even go grocery shopping for me."

Some men point to the external influences of American institutions to explain their loss of power and authority within families. Xi Chao, the man who described himself like "a bird in a cage," points out that the cultural and familial support necessary to maintain power is lacking here: "In my country, I can handle both my children and my wife. If I can't teach or handle them, I still have relatives or friends to help out. Now that the law and system are different . . . the police have more authority than me to my children and wife." Without family members nearby Xi Chao is lonely and sad about his plight. "Some people who have relatives here, when there is a big celebration such as Hmong new year, they call their relatives and friends to go as a group. To me, I don't have relatives, so no one calls me. I just watch them and it makes my tear drop." He contrasts Hmong ways of parenting with American ways: "We Hmong are not like the American that when you're old enough, your parents won't share his or her things with them. Also, kick their sons out of the house. . . . In Hmong custom, however much money or property always divide it to their children to have equally. [In exchange] . . . the parents expect their sons to take care of them until they die."

Thao feels lost in the United States. She complains that there are no longer any clear lines of authority or long-term expectations of family members that can be fully relied upon. Instead of financial and emotional support from her family, this Vietnamese woman is supported at a minimal level by the U.S. government's supplemental security income. The historic generational link of family obligations seems to be broken and the future looks frightening to Thao.

> I think about my parents, I remember them. I had a happy life. They loved me. But now I don't have a husband, I don't have anybody to love me. My sons have grown up, gotten married and established their own families. For me, I'm old. When I am sick, there is nobody there to take care of me. When I am just a little ill, I will be able to take care of myself; but when I become very ill, I can't do anything and nobody comes to take care of me. My son goes to work, he gets paid, but he has to take care of his own family. For me, the U.S. government has provided some funds so that I can base on it for my living expenses. I'd feel much better if I didn't depend on my son for living expenses. In Vietnam, my daughter-in-law used to cook for me before she went to work in the morning. But now, when my sons or daughters-in-law go to work, they don't even bother to greet me. My grandchildren also don't greet me when they go out.

Sibling Relationships

According to Confucian hierarchical family traditions, authority was distributed among siblings according to birth order, with the oldest always being the first and most important. Brothers and sisters were arranged hierarchically; the younger were expected to obey the older. Younger brothers were expected to follow the orders of older sisters. Often the authority of older siblings was feared more than that of the father because older siblings were less forgiving. In Xao's childhood family, Hmong children were expected to obey their older siblings: "My father and mother said that you don't have many brothers and sisters, so be obedient and friendly to everyone. This brother should listen to that brother. . . . The younger brother should listen to the oldest bother. Then our parents said that every younger should listen and be obedient to the oldest. If the oldest go somewhere, he/she should take the younger along with." Tip recalls how her parents reinforced the sibling hierarchy in her Cambodian family: "When I did not respect or listen to my older brothers or sister my parents would tell me that what I did was wrong. 'Don't do that again the next time.' . . . When they said that to me they did it when I was alone because they did not want my older brother or sister to know that they were on their side."

The role of the oldest child, whether male or female, varied between cultural groups, but the oldest sibling was significant in all of them. Male children were often expected to care for old parents or, at least, to have their wives care for them. There were higher expectations by parents for the older siblings. Ngo had a particularly harsh memory of the responsibilities that accompanied being the oldest child. Cited earlier as an example of the power of fathers, here attention is focused on the older sibling role. "One incident, my father bought me a small chick and my brother also had a small chick. But his chick wasn't as nice as mine. So he wanted to exchange his chick for mine; but I refused and he picked up my chick and threw it to the floor. My father got so mad and punished me instead of my brother." The older sibling was expected to be more responsible, to mediate the situation, and to work toward harmony within the family. Instead, an outburst by her younger brother is blamed on her.

Currently, Ngo has a major conflict with her sister, yet as the oldest, her father blames her for the conflict and refuses to contact her, even though they live in the same apartment building. She explains the conflict in these terms:

> I used to take my parents to see a doctor, but now my father doesn't call me anymore. I had a conflict with my younger sister who is living with my parents. . . . [O]ne day I found out that she skipped her English classes many times. She went out with an older man who is married instead. So I yelled at her and she told me to mind my own business. My father doesn't like me to argue with my sister, so he stopped calling me.

Ngo is giving up hope on the relationship. "I told my sister many times and she would not listen to me. Now I don't want to bother her anymore so I won't get a heartache."

Intergenerational Relationships

With elder, gender, and family relationships changing, the interpersonal relationships between generations are changing as well. Some examples are described above and others are discussed more fully in chapter 6. For now, we will examine evidence of the structural changes in Southeast Asian families that influence intergenerational relationships.

Nguyen is particularly upset about the ways that intergenerational relationships have changed, especially the treatment of elders by the younger generation, and he places blame squarely on the negative influences of the American environment.

> In Vietnamese tradition, when the parents are old they live with one of their children's families. The other children may come to visit and help financially. It is a custom and has been popular for many generations. But when we came to the U.S. many people change their way of thinking. They want to be more like Americans; the children don't have as much responsibility for their parents as in Vietnam. Although my daughter would like me to stay, my son-in-law thinks that it's a problem to support his father-in-law. My daughter is married to him; she has to listen to her husband anyway. I have to move out.

The United States–Vietnam contrast is used again later in the interview when the effects of public policy on the family are described from Nguyen's perspective: "In Vietnam, the elders are taken care of by their children no matter if they are rich or poor. The government has no responsibility, but it is contrary to the U.S. The government takes very good care of the elders and their children seldom care about them, even if they are rich." He believes that the traditional intergenerational bonds are being loosened in this country. "Very few people are still polite, have a lot of respect for us. But most of them are no longer. They don't even respect their parents. They treat us like Americans treat the elders."

Like Nguyen, most of the male elders are critical of youth and many hold American society responsible for the negative influences that are so pervasive. Duc criticized Vietnamese parents rather than youth or the United States for the loss of respect between generations.

> I'm very sad and hurt because some of the people in the younger generation turn out to be so terrible. Since we are refugees, we live an exiled life, we must do good things, and we are the minority. Because I am not a ruler or law enforcer I can't do anything about this. I'm sad and kind of wonder why their parents do not teach their kids just like my family. I have thirteen kids and none of them turn out to be a bad person.

In the more traditional Hmong families, the historic responsibilities of the young for the old are still maintained. Elders retain enough power to demand their rights to respect and attention and there are usually enough children to help with the support. Xao contrasts Hmong people's intergenerational reciprocity with the American way of government support to older people. "Our Hmong, even if they have a lot of children, even if it fills up the house, the parents still love all of them." The parents give whatever they have to the sons and in exchange the sons have long-term responsibilities for parent care in old age. "And these boys must love their parents until the parent die. The sons will have to come and carry them to be buried. Plus, they have to kill cows and buffaloes for a proper ceremony."

Power Shifting in Families

The process of forced migration forever alters normative life course development and the extended family's typical patterns of development. As we have seen in chapter 3, migration across international borders, refugee camp life, and resettlement produces elders with family stories emphasizing loss, separation, conflict, and resilience as major themes. With normative life course and family development patterns in ambiguous evolution, family structures, roles, and relationships are disrupted. Elders are embedded in families experiencing a diffusion of shifting roles and relationships that often pit Eastern and Western values against the tensions between tradition and adaptation. Elders in all four groups struggled with the changing structure in the family, the power redistribution between men and women and between the older and younger generations, and their loss of authority. The impact of relocation affects men and women differently, as older males lose power and authority while younger women gain some measure of control over their lives.

Place, location, and the daily context of life in Laos, Vietnam, and Cambodia reinforced the position of the male elders as heads of household, clan leaders, and village chieftains. Confucianism reinforced the hierarchical power structure of the traditional family using the major tenants of filial piety as the spiritual and moral framework to reinforce male authority. Men and women, boys and girls, young and old all knew their place within the highly structured age and gender rules. Although there were variations between cultures in religious practice, spiritual beliefs, and the influence of traditional philosophies, there was widespread agreement among elders that filial piety and respect for the hierarchy were critical to understanding how power, authority, and control were organized in their families. The older males were most likely to discuss the loss of power and the erosion of the traditional practices of respect by the young, while the older women were more likely to discuss how they could be helpful to the younger generation in hopes of future reciprocity.

Elders with loss as the primary theme of their family story have had their position of authority eroded by the death of family members, by economic dependency, and by the necessity for the younger generations to adapt to modern life. Many elders contrast their own native practices of respect and care for the aged with their perception of American indifference to its oldest generation.

When elders were separated from their extended family members during escape and relocation, their place within the family system was undermined. Men whose stories focus on the separation of family members are longing not only for the family members they have not seen but also for their traditional place at the head of the family structure. Women who have been widowed or separated from husbands and children find themselves on their own and sometimes exploited by Americanized children, other relatives, or the unfamiliar system.

When the elders' family stories are filled with conflict it is often the change in gender, generational, and family authority that is at the center of the disagreement. The massive and rapid shift in authority from males to females and from the older to the younger generations is responsible for the upheaval in relationships. In some cases, the men were frustrated, angry, or feeling helpless and they reported the use of physical violence, or the desire to use it, against their spouses, children, and grandchildren. In other cases, women were resigned to their fates, aggressively working to overcome barriers, or fearful of the future, when they expected to need help but would not have any resources to exchange or reciprocate.

In elders' stories like Bich's and Touch's, in which resilience is the primary theme, there is a tendency for significant elements of filial piety to be practiced. Some degree of elder authority is maintained even if only symbolic and inside the household. Resilient families maintain links to the past while continuing to move toward cultural integration. Dividing the world into bicultural inside and outside spheres allows a dual or bicultural identity to develop, blending traditional elder authority and filial respect with a realistic understanding of the skills needed for success in the American world outside the home.

Discussion

These are a few examples of the changing structure of relationships in the families of the elders we interviewed. With change occurring in elder, gender, intergenerational roles and relationships, it is not surprising that the structure of the family has been altered. There is evidence for these changes and for a gradual realignment of power throughout the life histories. Families classified as resilient appear to have accepted the changes as part of their developing bicultural perspective, a blending of cultural traditions, and an acceptance of some modern realities. Ironically, it appears that the men who are able to let go of some traditional powers, entitlements, and expectations are more respected by their families in the new context and more likely to retain elements of their authority. The women appear to be less concerned with maintaining a position of power within the restructured family and more concerned with the success of the family in the new environment and with their own survival.

Divergence in Family Cultures 5

IN EACH OF THE MEN'S FAMILY STORIES highlighted in chapter 3, there is evidence of a divergence in the goals, norms, and expectations of the elders and their family members. Sith is estranged from his spouse and distant from his children. Luot's dislike of youthful frivolity causes him to hit his grandchildren to stop them from playing. Xi Chao's homesickness, longing for the past, and sense of inadequacy are caused by dissatisfaction with the filial behavior of his adult children. Although Bich expresses confusion about the future of his grandchildren, he urges retention of Vietnamese culture while adapting to the American system. The family stories of the older women Dam, Mai, Ngo, and Touch in chapter 3 reveal less cultural divergence, since their energies are focused on maintaining some semblance of their family's culture in the new context. Mai and Touch express fear of the future, anticipating physical and financial dependency on family but less filial obligation of adult children and grandchildren.

The culture of Southeast Asian families is a reflection of historically established values, beliefs, and social norms that are deeply rooted in the larger fabric of Asian cultures. We have already established that hierarchically organized family relationships and the authority of elders are central to the filial piety concept and the values of our informants. Concerns about the diminishing importance of these traditional beliefs and the erosion of family culture as these elders defined it are themes that recur in almost all the life history accounts. According to LaRossa (1984), a family's culture is composed of the shared goals, values, beliefs, and norms of the family members. Because the diversity within and among immigrant families along gender, generational, and acculturation dimensions is significant, multigenerational families often find it difficult to cohesively "share" one common culture. Instead what they share is an evolving ethnic identity that is stratified, segmented, and multidimensional, very different from the unified family culture of the past.

Individuals within families participate in two distinct but related cultures, one inside and one outside the family. Families living in their native land typically find that the two cultures strengthen and reinforce each other. Families living in the West often find conflict between the native and foreign cultures that creates discord. For example, the historically rooted American values associated with individualism are reflected in the self-reliant relationships and socialization processes of mainstream families. When the more group-oriented, family-centered culture of Southeast Asian families is located in the context of the U.S. social system, it is inevitable that increasingly divergent values will develop. Without commonly agreed upon beliefs about how the world should be ordered, family members lack a well-understood framework within which individual and group lives can be constructed. Within this diverse context, the traditional values of the old world are questioned by youth and women while parents and men condemn the foreign values of the new world. Family conflicts inevitably occur.

Despite this caveat about families, the life histories reveal many beliefs commonly shared among the elders about family culture, including powerful statements about their fears of the increasing divergence of the middle and younger generations. Interview questions that asked elders to talk about their hopes for the family's future were particularly rich in revealing their most basic cultural values about family life and their concerns about how it was evolving. In the life histories of these elders and the literature on Southeast Asian families the one recurring theme related to family culture is an emphasis on familism (Boyer 1991). Family life and what has happened to the family is the central focus of the life stories, especially the stories told by women. The men's stories are somewhat less family centered, focusing more often on life outside the household, the men's efforts to fight the war and help the family escape, and their hopes to reunite the family.

The diverse American cultural milieu outside of the elders' households is also a dynamic naturally evolving environment within which immigrant family cultures develop and diverge at different rates. The convergence and divergence of beliefs, norms, and expectations inside and outside the family are not easily measured, since they are continuously evolving phenomena with as many perspectives as there are family members. Multigenerational longitudinal studies would be ideal ways to examine how these overlapping cultural boundaries evolve and interact. Our more modest goal in this chapter is to uncover some of the evidence in the life histories revealing the elders' perceptions of their families' changing culture as a way to better understand the internal and external dynamics occurring in these families.

Five recurring dimensions of family culture are revealed in the life histories showing the multidimensional tensions within and across groups: the home and community environments, beliefs about tradition, normative and Western instrumental and terminal values, core family values, and developing bicultural identities.

The Home and Community Environments

Immigrant family cultures develop within home and community environments that reinforce traditional norms, cause them to be called into question, or both. The family's normative development can either flourish or wither in the new environment. Within each immigrant family, the internal and external cultures will converge and diverge depending on each generation's integration into the family, the ethnic group, and the host society. Since both inside and outside cultures are always changing, and family members' exposure to the outside world is variable, we might expect to see cultural conflicts within families to be a daily reality (Detzner 1992; Xiong 2000).

The destruction of the physical home and native village was a traumatic event that was a sharply painful memory by those who witnessed it directly. Several Hmong elders told harrowing tales of losing their family's supportive near environment, as homes, farms, animals, and economic livelihood were destroyed or left behind. In one example, Lor remembers returning to his home village after an attack only to find: "[The] Vietnamese had already destroyed all our homes. They are all burnt. We have a lot of things in the houses, all kinds of things. The Vietnamese took the good things and burned the rest with the houses. We don't know if the Vietnamese did this or the Americans dropped bombs from airplanes . . . but the houses are burnt."

Mao recalls the interwoven norms of family and community life in the mountains of northern Laos before the war and destruction: "We Hmong, we live together and make our houses very close together so we can share among ourselves." Sharing and cooperation were important cultural norms, as was the self-sufficiency that came from farming and owning livestock and tools. Mao recalls: "We have lots of livestock and when we need food we could provide for our own needs. We don't have to buy anything. We come to this country . . . but we are so sad that we do not have any land. We are sad that we have no land to live in and that we have come to live in their land." Although she currently has other Hmong people living nearby, Mao believes that life is very different in the United States: "Everyone lives in their own house and they don't visit you. . . . You don't want to live here because you are scared, but there is no other house . . . so you have no choice but to live here, lock the door very tight and stay home." Another Hmong informant also named Mao expresses a similar opinion about the change in Hmong families that has occurred. Although she was orphaned at a young age and lived with several different relatives as a child, she remembers feeling that she was part of a larger Hmong community in which "the Hmong always will watch over one another and visit each other." In the new country, these cooperative and supportive cultural traditions that shaped daily life are not as prevalent or easily practiced by elders and their families because the struggle to adapt predominates.

The divergence between generations that arise in the family culture narratives are sometimes related to the elders' loss of self-sufficiency and economic provider roles. The problem is well described by the sixty-five-year-old, widowed Xi Chao, the father of twelve children, who said: "We Hmong never had a history of dependency on welfare or other people. Now . . . most of the older people are dependent on welfare, because we didn't have any education and can't go to work. However, most of the younger people who had little education, they [are] already working and didn't depend on welfare." Normative roles are reversed in the new environment as youth find work roles, economic independence, and a place in the new society while elders are stuck at home with low-status family responsibilities. Dependency and role reversal is especially difficult for males, who view their primary function as the economic provider for the family.

In the new country the home environment and surrounding culture are not only foreign, they are often frightening as well. Ny had many fears about coming from Laos to live in the United States. As her family was driven from the airport after first arriving, she was frightened by what she saw: "When I was in the car, I saw houses and smoke was coming out of the chimneys. I said that the houses were on fire." Ny was particularly concerned about the norms surrounding familiar foods: "that I [would have to] eat bread all the time and there wouldn't be any rice to eat." When she first arrived in North Carolina her well-meaning sponsor prepared meals for the family that seemed to fulfill her most dreaded fears: "It was beef, chicken, and fish, but there was no rice." When Ny first heard the noises coming from the heating unit in the trailer that was her home: "I was scared and I started running and hit the door." When the public utilities man, "this big man with a beard," came to check the gas meter, she was terrified. "My children went to school and I thought it was a ghost."

It was not only women who found the external cultural environment and ways of doing things so different and frightening. Sith could never get very far in his mind from the exploding bombs that were falling all around his family as they made their escape from Laos into Thailand. The celebration of the U.S. 4th of July holiday was not Independence Day for him but rather a frightening reminder of that most traumatic event in Sith's family's history. The fireworks made him fearful: "When I heard the fire each time, I was ready to hide."

Beliefs about Tradition

With the external physical and cultural environment so frightening to the new-comers and their family norms in transition, elders attempted to maintain and preserve the family's traditions inside the family. As kin keepers, storytellers, and wise elders, it was natural for them to emphasize in their stories the importance of continuity with the past. They believed that the family needed to cling to important elements of its cultural tradition even as it was pushed into the fast lane of cultural change. At one extreme is Ton, whose husband was a wealthy medical doctor in Vietnam. She was used to having many servants and an easy life. Although most of the other women we interviewed were less subservient to their husbands in the United States than they had been at home, Ton was serving her husband more here. "When I look at my fingers and hands, I see the wrinkles. I work so hard here compared to Vietnam. Every day I have to clean my house, take care of my family. Now I see so many bad things about my husband, because in Vietnam I didn't need to serve him so I didn't see anything wrong with him." Beyond the changes in her role as a spouse, she is concerned about the loss of cultural traditions by the young after she is no longer here. "Oriental families feel attached to each other. We used to celebrate anniversaries, Tet. Now kids don't remember anniversaries—sometime they don't even remember Tet." She feels responsible for continuing these important celebrations: "On those holidays, I call my relatives and invite them to come to celebrate. I feel if I die no one will remember these days."

Instead of fearing the loss of traditions, Lan has taken action to preserve them by writing a short story that was distributed to members of the Vietnamese elders group to which she belongs. She explains:

> The story I wrote is about one family—husband, wife, and two chil-dren. Both the husband and wife go to work and the children at home don't have a chance to speak their mother's language, Vietnamese. So this couple brings them to their neighbor—a Vietnamese elder woman—to teach the children the Vietnamese language. For the con-clusion, because the children are able to speak Vietnamese, the mother is so happy that is why the title is "The Happiness of a Mother."

Lan is hopeful that Vietnamese youth will continue to maintain important family traditions:

> Since I put all my wish in the younger generation, I wish the younger generation can maintain the Vietnamese civilization, culture, and lan-

guage. Also, continue to follow their ancestor footsteps. Don't let the people look down on the Vietnamese people. The Vietnamese usually work hard, honesty, courage, and clever; so the people will look at Vietnamese people with the eyes of respectfulness.

Nguyen eloquently explains that families have a responsibility to teach cultural traditions to their children even if the children are successfully adapting to life in the United States: "I'm very sure that the children must learn from the parents. They have to work a lot. I just hope that they do not forget, even though they are citizens, that they are Vietnamese is enough. By that time they're all Americanized. They must succeed. They must not forget traditions and customs of the Vietnamese." Among the most important traditions Nguyen believes are those that apply to families:

> I hope the younger generation has more feeling for their family. I have noticed young people nowadays live rather selfishly. . . . I wish the young generation would listen more to their parents. Here, a lot of young Americans seldom listen to their parents, and their parents just let it go. Also, parents here have little love for kids. . . . In America, they don't have attachments, and they send parents to a nursing home. In Vietnam, we do not have nursing homes. Children have to take care of old parents.

Bich, the Chinese-Vietnamese man who is no longer king, teaches Vietnamese songs to his grandchildren and expects them to speak respectfully to him in his native language. Although he is fluent in English and can easily converse with them, he chooses to maintain the inside of his household as a Vietnamese enclave in which the language, aromas from cooking, and children's behavior are similar to what they would be in the traditional home. Outside the door of Bich's household is America, where the children are expected to act differently if they are to succeed.

> I sing a song of Vietnamese history for my children to remind them about Vietnam. And usually the kids that are not very good children at home will later hold better positions since they are more Americanized. So I don't know how I want my children. In order to be successful, you have to be more like American. So I told them at home you must be Vietnamese. But outside, it's okay to be an American.

Bich is resigned that some elements of the culture will be lost: "They may forget their language, but they may not forget the culture. That's why I try hard to maintain our culture."

Kang understands how difficult it is for elderly Cambodian women to teach the young in an environment that does not have supportive cultural institutions, values, and family cultures: "The children are hard to teach because they get a lot of pressure from their peers and the culture they live in. Sometimes my grandchildren don't listen to me. I think the Cambodian children are easier to teach in Cambodia than here." Her message to future generations emphasizes maintaining traditions and achieving an education: " Don't forget our culture and tradition, respect elderly people, know friends and enemies, be loyal to each other, and study as much as possible."

Instrumental and Terminal Values

As we observed in the previous chapter, changes in roles are good indicators of changing structural and value orientations within family systems. Families in which the elderly men perform few traditional roles and elderly women take on a variety of nontraditional roles are experiencing a divergence between what is normative and what is expected in the United States. Similarly, families in which elders have few important functions except child care and food preparation may be experiencing a conflict between what is remembered as traditional and what is now possible in the modern context.

Previous research has established the divergence of values between cultural groups (Tharp et al. 1968). To examine value differences more fully, we utilized Rokeach's (1973) definition of values as an enduring belief that a specific mode of conduct (instrumental values) or end-state of existence (terminal values) is better than some other mode of conduct or end-state of existence. Papajohn and Spiegel (1975) used Rokeach's value scheme and Kluckhohn's (1951) categorization of value orientations to define how families were organized in different cultures. From this research it is clear that individuals and families develop value hierarchies that structure their roles and behavior. The nature of values and the hierarchical way that they are organized can be discerned using the life history interview data. Specific interview questions about conflict resolution within the family; hopes for the future of the family; and the message to future generations proved to be unusually rich in revealing value preferences. The answers to these questions were coded according to the emphasis on specific instrumental or terminal values defined by Rokeach. The data displayed in tables 3 and 4 below indicate the number of times each instrumental or terminal value was expressed in

several value-laden questions. We assume that responses reveal the value preferences or emphases of the informants and that the number and variety of responses
can be compared across cultural groups and genders.

We systematically assessed and compared the value preferences of Vietnamese
and Cambodian elders because they are on opposite ends of the acculturation
continuum and because we used these two groups in our earlier discussion of role
changes. Tables 3 and 4 allow comparisons between male and female informants'
emphasis on specific instrumental and terminal values. In both cultural groups
instrumental values (106) are more frequently emphasized than terminal values
(82) in the value-laden interview questions. Further analysis indicates that this
pattern is true for men and women in both cultural groups. This result might be
expected, since elderly refugees are largely invisible and marginalized subgroups
with limited opportunities to affect the end-state of their existence. Their seldom-
expressed desire for terminal values such as a "comfortable life," "a world at
peace," and "wisdom" may be very distant goals to elderly refugees who are struggling with the instrumental realities of daily life in a foreign land that sometimes
seems frightening or hostile.

The interview data reveal that the most frequently discussed instrumental val-

Table 3.   Instrumental Values of Vietnamese and Cambodian Elders

	Male		Female		
	Vietnamese	Cambodian	Vietnamese	Cambodian	Totals
Instrumental Value					
Ambition	6	2	3	1	12
Broadminded	3	0	1	0	4
Capable	0	1	1	1	3
Cheerful	1	1	1	0	3
Clean	0	0	0	2	2
Courageous	1	0	0	0	1
Forgiving	0	0	0	2	2
Helpful	4	0	1	1	6
Honest	1	2	0	2	5
Imaginative	0	0	1	0	1
Independent	4	2	4	2	12
Intellectual	4	2	4	4	14
Logical	2	0	0	0	2
Loving	1	0	0	0	1
Obedient	3	4	3	4	14
Polite	2	1	1	2	6
Responsible	2	2	2	2	8
Self-controlled	2	1	4	4	11
Totals	36	18	26	27	107

ues of the Vietnamese are ambition, independence, and intellectual. Ambition and independence can be viewed as primarily Western-oriented values, since they promote individual autonomy. Intellectual is a value that includes education, highly prized in both the East and the West, and particularly important to immigrant groups. All three values are critical to successful integration in the new environment and reflective of the economic and social success that the Vietnamese have enjoyed since their arrival. In contrast, the instrumental values most often emphasized by Cambodian informants are intellectual, obedient, and self-controlled. Obedience and self-control are primarily Eastern-oriented values associated with filial piety and respect for authority. Historically, intellectual values were strongly embraced by immigrant and refugee groups as one of the few means for immigrant children to seek upward mobility. One explanation for the difference in values held by the two groups is that the Vietnamese informants are better educated, more urban, and more exposed to Western value systems than Cambodian refugees, who tend to have less education, to be more rural, and to have less previous contact with Western value systems. Since the Vietnamese appear to be making the adjustment to Western life more easily than Cambodians, it may be that the partial adoption of Western values has facilitated this process. If maintaining traditional Eastern values in a Western context is counterproductive to successful integration, then these comparisons support the earlier interpretations concerning the greater difficulty experienced by Cambodian refugees, especially the men.

Comparing instrumental value orientations between men and women is helpful as a way to better understand the differences and similarities between genders in these two cultural groups. A surprising consistency between men and women exists in the instrumental values that are emphasized in both cultures, with ambition the sole exception. The emphasis on obedience and self-control tends to be highest among women; however, Cambodian men emphasize obedience more often than any other value. Although women may express more traditional Eastern value orientations, the previous data on role performance indicates that they are more nontraditional than males in their actual behaviors within the family and community. It may be that it is necessary for women to perform a wide variety of roles previously unavailable to them while, at the same time, they express traditional Eastern value orientations considered appropriate for females.

Values promoting integration into mainstream culture are repeatedly emphasized, but so are the values the elders brought with them from home. The emphasis on instrumental values with a Western orientation, such as ambition and independence, indicates the pragmatic nature of elders in the new environment; however, the emphasis on terminal values with an Eastern orientation, such as inner harmony and family security, indicates their desire to maintain important elements of cultural continuity in their new homeland. The tension between Western instrumental and Eastern terminal values suggests that elders are caught between their desire for maintaining tradition and the need to adapt.

Terminal values tend to be broader, more global, and more ideal states of existence that humans aspire to achieve. Table 4 displays Rokeach's eighteen terminal values and the number of times they were emphasized by male and female informants in the life history narratives of elders. Family security and inner harmony received equally high emphasis by Vietnamese and Cambodian informants. Considering the traumas confronted in their homelands, the danger of the escape, and the disrupted nature of family life, it is not surprising that family security would be so highly valued. Inner harmony can be seen as an Eastern value that may reflect the desire of elders to maintain their cultural traditions while adjusting to the realities of the new world. In this context, inner harmony is an end-state in which members of the elders' family system can achieve a balance between Eastern traditions and Western realities. Terminal values receiving no or very little emphasis in the narratives include an exciting life, a world of beauty, mature love, pleasure, self-respect, and wisdom. Except for a world of beauty, these are all

Table 4. Terminal Values of Vietnamese and Cambodian Elders

	Male		Female		
	Vietnamese	Cambodian	Vietnamese	Cambodian	Totals
Terminal Value					
Comfortable life	0	3	2	2	7
Exciting life	0	1	0	0	1
Accomplishment	1	0	2	1	4
World peace	2	0	0	0	2
World of beauty	0	0	0	0	0
Equality	1	0	3	0	4
Family security	4	1	5	4	14
Freedom	5	3	3	1	12
Happiness	3	2	2	0	7
Inner harmony	6	1	3	4	14
Mature love	0	0	0	0	0
National security	1	0	0	1	2
Pleasure	0	0	0	1	1
Salvation	0	1	0	3	4
Self-respect	1	0	0	0	1
Social recognition	0	0	4	2	6
True friendship	0	0	1	1	2
Wisdom	0	0	0	1	1
Totals	23	12	25	21	82

individually oriented values that enhance the self rather than the family or the group.

There is less agreement about terminal values between cultures than there is about instrumental values. Table 4 shows the similarity between the terminal values emphasized by Vietnamese men and women. Although there are fewer units for comparison in the Cambodian data, almost no similarities are noted. This may be a consequence of the greater disruption that has occurred in Cambodian families and/or the general absence of shared aspirations by Cambodian men and women in this environment. The emphasis on freedom in both cultures and genders is not surprising for groups that have escaped from punitive political systems, although the actual degree of freedom enjoyed by elders who cannot communicate or participate in mainstream life in the United States is questionable. Elders define freedom as freedom *from* persecution and fear rather than freedom *to* express civil and political rights.

Core Family Values

Beyond these broad terminal and instrumental values defined by Rokeach, there are other more specific cultural values discussed in the life history narratives that help to define individual and family norms and the divergence of cultures. Informants from all four cultural groups frequently discuss these core family values, often passionately. These core values include education, hard work, adaptability, freedom, and obedience. Several of them overlap with value preferences expressed by informants using Rokeach's instrumental and terminal paradigm, reflecting the tension between the traditional and modern in families and the realities of adjustment.

Education

Cheam was fond of quoting a traditional Cambodian saying about the importance of studying to his children and grandchildren: "If you study hard you will learn. . . . I[I]f you study, even if you are dumb you will learn." He is pleased that there are so many educational opportunities available for youth in the United States; however, Cheam's inability to learn English causes anguish: "Sometimes when I studied with the teacher, I cried in tears. It was a simple thing and I couldn't learn it. . . . Sometimes if there was a doctor that would give me shot to kill me easily, I wouldn't want to live. . . . I am deaf or dumb and can't understand. I'm mad at that."

Despite his self-reported inability to learn simple lessons, Cheam teaches a profound lesson about adaptability in a new environment when quoting an old

Cambodian saying: "When you enter a river you go in along the water flow, you go into a city according to the country. This saying is a tradition we used to tell our children long ago. It meant wherever you go, you must follow other people's ways. . . . If the river bends, you must bend with it."

The Southeast Asians we interviewed viewed education and schools as a means of learning about the bend in the new river. Education is more accessible to Southeast Asian families in the United States than in their homelands, with both boys and girls having more or less similar opportunities to learn. Success in school demonstrates to the family and community that, in addition to academic talent, the child has developed social skills with peers and authority figures. The accomplishments of the children and grandchildren in school bring pride to the family group or shame if failure or problems occur. There is some ambivalence about success in school because the children bring home Western ways of thinking and viewing the world, often diverging from the more traditional views of elders.

Elders believe that education provides access to higher-paid jobs, material success, and future help to older family members. Bounsou wants his grandchildren to have a good education: "I just want them to have an education if they can. I didn't have enough education. Back then [in Laos], only one or two people out of the whole village had a good education. Here everybody is studying. I think it's more fun to study here." Educational achievement in the United States was associated with getting a good job, buying a house, and having other material goods. It was a way out of poverty. Mai remembers her life before marriage as carefree and happy, and she wishes in her fantasy that she could be young again: "If I can do that, I want to go to school and be someone. That way I can have a light job and earn a lot of money."

Hard Work

Although Mai is looking for a lighter job in her next life, the value placed on hard work in this life by the informants is difficult to underestimate. Hard work was a unique core value because it was valued at home and rewarded outside the home. The informants survived during the war, in the camps, and in the United States because of their ability to work hard and persevere in severe circumstances. Working hard was especially valued when it was related to studying and going to school. Working hard can be viewed as a temporary escape from worry and one of several important adaptation strategies (Lin and Masuda 1983).

By explaining her daily routine, Mai demonstrates what hard work meant to a Hmong woman in a small farming village. The day begins before sunrise, as soon as you "can see enough to walk, then they are already at the field . . . you hear the chickens and the pigs making noise then you have to get up to work." The challenge was to work hard enough to produce enough food to last the family for the year:

> You work all day, every day in the field but afterwards you still have to carry loads of stuff home. If you have a baby with you, you carry the baby on the chest and carry a back load and that's hard on you. . . . [Y]ou don't get any good money out of it, but you get enough food for you to eat in a year. If you have a good crop field, you can harvest a lot of crops so it will last you for a year.

After returning from the fields the women's work of food preparation; serving guests, elders, and children; and cleanup was still left to do before sleep. Almost every day was the same.

Zoua explained that the ability to work hard in the fields affected a young woman's opportunity for marriage. Boys observed the girls to see their work habits, defining those who "work hard at the fields and works very well" as the most desirable for marriage. Despite the memories of endless hard work by those who toiled in the fields, some elders found the pace of life in the United States much more difficult. Prak remembers the pace and rhythms of his life in Cambodia as very different: "It's not like here in America. They worked day and night. At night we slept and during the day we worked. After work, we walked for fun. Here they work day and night. That's why this is a rich country."

Although the work may have been physically challenging and seemingly endless, the spirit of cooperation and community made it seem less onerous, at least to Xao, who recalls: "In Laos, it is not like in America that one person can support the family by working in the company. . . . I still remember how we worked together with another family farm for two or three days, then everyone come to my field and working for me for two or three days too and then move on to the next field. All of this thing, I still remember in my heart always."

Adaptability

"Bending like the river" is an important lesson for newcomers, a critical adaptation strategy, and highly valued by most elders. Managing the transition of a family from one side of world to another requires adaptability. It was one of the most important values taught by elders to the young, especially in the twenty elders' stories we classified as resilient. Adaptability was a central value to Bich, whose bicultural expectations for children meant that when they were leaving the front door of the house they were leaving behind one culture for another. Although bending might be good advice for the young, some elders experienced more than enough change and found themselves unable or unwilling to adapt anymore. They were likely to emphasize boundaries, maintaining traditions, preserving continuity, and embracing the past more often than bending with the river.

Unlike the stereotypical authoritarian male head of the family, Duc's father taught him the importance of adaptability as a young child. His father believed that Vietnamese children should choose what they do with their lives rather than have it arranged by parents. "My parents did not enforce anyone to do anything. The children can choose any career they like as long as it is legal and honest. . . . [M]y father believes that one should have his or her own choice."

In contrast, Nguyen is concerned that families not adapt too much since they may lose important values and practices that help to make them distinctive. He believes of Vietnamese children: "They lack some things but have some other things. They are living in a modern and more civilized society. They are more intelligent. For example, they have many toys and the toys make them smarter than we were, like computer games, since we had nothing. Because of too much freedom, their behavior lacks politeness, so they are less humble than we were."

Freedom

The idea of political freedom is new to almost every one of the elders and the concept has several different meanings to them. Often freedom is discussed from both negative and positive perspectives. Freedom as a political right that can be expressed in voting, speech, and diverse religious practice is foreign to most of the elders, since this type of freedom did not exist in their homelands. Despite their lack of experience in the political arena, Southeast Asians have asserted political power at the local, state, and national levels during the quarter century that they have lived in the United States. The Hmong have been particularly active in expressing their views en masse at the state capitol in St. Paul, at congressional offices in Washington, D.C., and in the voting booth. Several Hmong men and women have been elected to local offices in St. Paul, indicating an understanding of the expression of political freedom at the most basic level. In 2002, Mee Moua was elected to the state Senate, the first Hmong to be elected to a statewide office in the United States. In 2003, Cy Thao was elected to the state House of Representatives. Both of these political leaders are frequent guests on television news programs and outspoken advocates for immigrants and other at-risk families. These elections are important indicators of political integration and a symbol to everyone that the freedom to vote is a powerful tool for cohesive new immigrant groups.

Although most Southeast Asians are fiercely patriotic and grateful to the U.S. government for the freedom they enjoy here, the family values practiced inside the household are not always consistent with the notions of freedom and democratic decision making. Neou overlooks many of the bad things he sees in American life because of the freedom that he experiences here. "I see much freedom, that makes me happy." Sally worries, however, that Cambodian girls are becoming "too wild" with all the freedom that they have in the United States. The definition of how much freedom should be allowed to children, especially girls, is a major topic of conversation and source of disagreement in families. Freedom always comes with many restrictions for Cambodian teenage girls. According to Sally: "[G]irls are not supposed to go out at night and if they do, they must have friends with them, and . . . good ones listen to their parents. Some people don't listen to the parents. They just want their own way."

Lor expresses the belief of many male informants that freedom is something reserved primarily for men. Although attitudes are changing, the elder men in general believe that women hold a subservient place in the natural order of things. The notion of freedom, equal rights, and a balanced exchange between partners were foreign ideas to most of our informants, both male and female. Older Hmong men, in particular, tended to be traditional and conservative concerning the rights of girls and women. The attitude toward the freedom of women in the United States confounds the traditional Hmong view of marriage and the cultural perception of women as property. These traditional views governed how most Hmong men we interviewed viewed freedom. Lor responded to a question about the rights of Hmong women by saying: "I have thought about it and why do you want to give women their rights? And your wives, if they want you, they can stay but if they don't feel like it, they could have another boyfriend. This is it! This rule—women's rights—we don't have."

Obedience

A core value applied particularly to women, children, and those who are younger, obedience can be viewed as the opposite of freedom. This is a good example of the bicultural dilemma confronting families as they attempt to juggle two conflicting value systems. Older men and women want their children and grandchildren to respect elders by obeying elders' wishes and fulfilling the obligations of filial behavior. Obedience in children and wives is viewed as respectful of the old ways and evidence that the child (or spouse) is "good."

Luot is one of the few men who tell a story about themselves and obedience, saying that his desire to obey parents as a youth changed the direction of his life. Although he wanted to study in the temple and become a monk, he obeyed his parents' wishes by staying at home and helping them with the work. He

> had this idea that if I stayed and worked like that I won't learn anything, and wanted to run away. I couldn't leave because I married a wife for me. I was married at eighteen years old. . . . I didn't have any feeling of wanting to have a wife, yet, because my parents had already arranged it, I agreed along with them. I only wanted to study. Because they begged me so hard, so I agreed.

Dam described the respect and obedience she gave to her mother as a child growing up in Laos. Like Luot she married the person chosen for her by her parents as a way of being respectful and obedient to them. Her life as a child was centered around going to school and helping her mother every day: "I didn't go anywhere and I listened to my mother." When her mother felt like it was time for her to get married, she did what she was told. "I did it because I listened to my mom." When the arrangements were made, she felt happy. Her future husband came to the house: "After he saw me, he came over to my house and talked with my mom. Then his elders came over to my house. My mom asked me if I wanted to and I told her that it's up to her. Then we got married."

Banthilone explained what happened in Laos when she was young if children, even adult children, did not obey their parents: "They would warn us and sometimes one of them would spank us even if we were big. I spanked my oldest son even though he was twenty-five years old. I told him that what he did was wrong and I'm going to spank you." The power of parents to control the future of their children in Laos was significant: "If my parents did not approve of letting me marry him then I couldn't marry him even if we loved each other really bad." Banthilone has continued this tradition with her daughters: "I told them if I don't like the guys then you can't marry them. One got married after she was in America for three years because I told her that I liked him and they could get married."

Ngo discusses the erosion of adult authority to illustrate the consequences of disobedience:

> I think the older generations are not that close to the younger generations compared to in Vietnam. For example, I have two nephews who are living in [Minnesota]. They don't listen to my advice. I told them that smoking is bad for their health but they don't listen. I told them not to go out too much and have too many girlfriends, these things

will jeopardize your education, but they don't listen to me. . . . They used to live with me but now they moved out. I took care of them when they were very young [their mother was ill] and I was the one who raised them. You see, I have done all these things for them and they don't even listen to me.

Developing Bicultural Identities

Many of the values needed to be successful in the United States have elements that conflict with the more traditional values of elders and some of the core values we have just discussed. As we have seen, obedience can conflict with freedom. Education and hard work can conflict with filial piety obligations.

There is a natural tension between adaptability and maintaining tradition that can sometimes cause conflicts. The Vietnamese informants were more likely than elders from other groups to have developed a bicultural value system that promoted values from both cultures. Perhaps it was easier for them because many Vietnamese migrated from urban areas and were previously exposed to Western values through the French and American occupations. Two of the Vietnamese male informants were educated in Europe, received training in the United States, and were fluent in English before arrival. As an upper-class woman and the wife of a doctor, Ton spoke good English and understood how children and parents had to adopt new values if they were to thrive in the United States. Speaking of her family's approach to the complexities of adaptation and assimilation, she said: "We're very comprehensive. We try to adopt the lifestyle. We try to keep a balance between Vietnamese culture and American culture, so we don't have many problems living in the U.S. society." Nu wants her children to maintain the best of both value systems. She wants her children to be good citizens and also keep Vietnamese traditions like working hard, living a moral life, and respecting the elders. "I told my children to work hard, obey the law, so they can compensate for what the U.S. has done for them."

When asked to offer his advice to future generations of Vietnamese families living in the United States, Duc gave this bicultural message:

> Be good people and citizens. Keep moral values. Learn about science and technology and don't be afraid to change things that are no longer applicable or valid. Go to school. Learn both English and the Vietnamese languages. Speak Vietnamese to Vietnamese people because of the fellowship, and being the same race, same culture. Eat any kind of foods. Respect all religions. Intermarriage is okay, [since] it is fate that

brings people together. Just don't marry a bad person, no matter their race.

It is not always easy for an elder or a middle-aged parent to make the bicultural adjustment necessary to help his or her children and grandchildren adopt a mixed and sometimes conflicting set of values. Instead of being the "king" of the family with unquestioned authority, elders in bicultural families have to concede to what will work in this country. It is especially difficult for elders to retain their preeminent place in the family because the young have more knowledge and experience than their parents. Nguyen acknowledged what has happened in his bicultural family:

> About my role in the family, now they [the children] are very big. The youngest one is already thirty years old. So if they want anything they only need to ask my opinion. Right now I am just like an advisor, not like when they were small. Also they have lived in the U.S. longer than I have. They know the traditions, customs, and way of life here more than I do. Sometimes they tell me how the customs and way of life are here. For example, if they want to change companies or study more in school, they will ask me, and I only give my opinion.

One Hmong elder discussed his bicultural approach to parenting children. Chong accepts the reality that children today are not as respectful of elders. He wants his grandchildren to become successful in their new culture; however, he still wants them to retain the basic elements of filial piety. He says:

> I would like all my grandchildren to change and adjust to everything. I want them to follow what the American did good, except that if they don't listen to me and become the opposite of what I wish them to be. One thing that I don't want to change is our religion, because it was very helpful for us from generation to generation when someone was sick. In the old days, we didn't have doctors to help the sick people, so our religion is one source of helping the sickness.

Noukeo represents the opposite point of view. He wanted his Lao American children to learn English quickly and become assimilated as fast as possible. Unlike almost every other elder we interviewed, he favored intermarriage with Americans. He wanted his children to know how to speak English "so they could talk and work with Americans. I want them to marry Americans because America is a good place."

Xao recognizes that the American cultural environment and the need to develop a bicultural approach are changing his traditional Hmong family culture. He realizes how dramatically different his life has become here and how many things have changed: "Our attitudes and our minds have been changed a lot. The living conditions have changed and the roles between men and women have also changed too. . . . I think the family is starting to change and might not be very important to people as before." After he dies, he still wants his children to remember important traditional values even as they adjust to life in the world around them:

> The oldest child must listen to their parents. The younger should listen to the older brother or sister. So they can be a brother and sister and can live very close together. So they will get along with other people around them. Another message that I would like to leave everyone, I don't want people to have long hair, wear a shirt and pant that was cut into small pieces. . . . I[I]n other words, don't become punks or thieves.

In other words, the family's culture must diverge enough to fit the context and altered circumstances but not so much that the foundations of family culture are lost.

Conflicted Family Interactions　　6

Introduction

THE INTERACTIONS BETWEEN ELDERS, their adult children, and their grandchildren and the meanings associated with these interactions varies across cultural groups, generations, and genders. LaRossa (1984) defines family interactions as the expressed meanings of the verbal and nonverbal behaviors of family members as interpreted by the informant. The narratives that different generations tell about themselves and one another often reveal important clues about family interactions and meanings, although they are usually indirect clues. The life history interviews reveal the elders' insider view of how the structure and culture of families have changed and how they perceive family interactions. The elders' perspective is the focus of the book; however, in this chapter we want to go beyond their point of view to include the parent and adolescent generations from the Helping Youth Succeed (Detzner, Xiong, and Eliason 1999) studies.

Although we have focused attention on the oldest generation, the definition of "elders" can easily include middle-generation parents as well, since they too are elders from the perspective of the younger generations. Hearing the voices and stories of adolescents as they talk about their interactions with parents and grandparents will add an important cross-generational perspective to the discussion. From an interactive family systems perspective, it is necessary to examine the perceptions and meanings of each generation if we want to understand the dynamics occurring in families. The perspectives of two younger generations will broaden our understanding of the elders' perceptions and deepen our understanding of intergenerational relations in Southeast Asian families.

The immediate context for the elders' perceptions of family interactions is the disruption caused by war, separation, and resettlement and their historic memory of how family interactions are *supposed* to be. Several examples illustrate the complexities surrounding disrupted family interactions and the meanings attached to them by elders in this context. Cheam is a sixty-nine-year-old Cambodian man whose primary concern at this stage in life is his inability to interact with family members who were left behind. Hang is a Cambodian women who has resolved to interact with her adult children and grandchildren in a less authoritarian way than her parents did with her; however, she will not allow as much freedom as American children are allowed. Mai, Xi Chao, and Bane continue to play important roles within their families, especially in caring for grandchildren; however, when divorce or geographic separation occurs elders have little contact with their grandchildren. Xi Chao and many other elders believe that family interactions have changed for the worse as elders have lost traditional roles and power and the practice of filial piety has declined.

Conflicted interactions between elders, adult children, and grandchildren, seldom overtly experienced in Southeast Asia, are more likely to occur in the United States. Mai reports examples of the disobedience of a grandson; Xi Chao reports the loss of control of children to U.S. laws and schools; Nguyen reports the loss of humility of the younger generations; and Cheam reports his anger at the behaviors of youth. Bane, a seventy-two-year-old Laotian woman, expressed concern that disrespect for the elderly is evidence of the loss of the Laotian culture in the United States. She reports negative interactions with her daughter, especially when the daughter does not listen: "She can listen or not, but as long as she doesn't talk back. In my head I love her very much. That's why I discipline her; I don't want her to be a bad person. I want her to be like a Laos lady."

Conflict is a regular and normative interaction pattern in families, and it appears in almost every one of the forty life histories. In an earlier study (Detzner 1992), we found that the primary areas of conflict reported by elders involve the interrelated issues of gender, family, and values. Gender-related conflict in families typically involves power and control, in-laws, and obedience. Questions about who has the power to control family behaviors is often at the center of interactions between husband and wives, mothers and daughters-in-law, parents and children, and elders and grandchildren. Power has shifted from men to women and from elders to the younger generations, and the loss of power or the assertion of new powers inevitably generates conflict between family members.

Conflict is often the result of elders' continuing adherence to traditional Confucian values that favor harmonious family relations. Families that lack harmony are likely to attract bad luck that can be transmitted from families to village and nation (Jordan 1972). Traditional Vietnamese families value harmony more than individual achievements (Liem and Kehmeier 1979). Two common sources of disharmony in Chinese Vietnamese families in the United States concern parents' choice of their children's friends and the selection of marriage partners (Chan and Lam 1987). Among the Laotian Hmong, the goals, needs, and harmonious interactions of the family group or clan have the highest priority, whereas the pursuit of individual goals and interests is viewed as selfish (Vang 1983). Since family harmony is a highly prized, socially desired value, family conflicts were not reported as a problem in an early investigation of Hmong, Laotian, Cambodian, and Vietnamese refugees living in Nebraska (Meredith and Cramer 1982).

Changes in norms, roles, and values within cultural and family groups create a certain amount of ambiguity and fluidity within and among families and clans that once were hierarchical and highly structured. Conflicts in relationships reveal the tensions associated with major role changes and the different acculturation rates among generations (Dinh et al. 1991). Researchers have documented other areas of conflict within Southeast Asian refugee families, including generational tensions from the improved language proficiency of younger generations (Tran 1988; Boyer 1991); role conflict related to household authority and respect (Donnelly 1988); and the degree of freedom allowed children and the appropriate method of disciplining them (Hughes 1990). Family interaction tensions resulting from the changes in family structure were noted as among the greatest difficulties of elderly Vietnamese refugees who were living in the United Kingdom (Refugee Action 1987).

In the new context, the sources of tension and conflict often emanate from outside the family. Differing expectations between schools and elders about what kind of discipline is appropriate may be perceived as undermining parental authority, heightening intergenerational conflict, and altering traditional family values (Minnesota Attorney General 1991). Scott (1986) cites increased tensions within California's Hmong families as children learn new skills, knowledge, and familiarity with American culture in schools. Western behaviors and attitudes children exhibit at home often anger parents and elders. Likewise, parental behavior that is too Asian or "old country" can be an embarrassment to children. Many elders and parents believe that children and grandchildren have too much freedom in the new country and they fear the consequences of their loss of control (Kroll 1989; Hughes 1990).

Parent and Adolescent Perceptions of Family Interactions

As we see from this review of the research on conflict in Southeast Asian families, interactions are often difficult as a consequence of differential migration and acculturation experiences as well as normative developmental stress. Our work in the Helping Youth Succeed project advances our understanding of intergenerational interactions by focusing on the perceptions of parents and adolescents

(Detzner, Xiong, and Eliason 1999; Xiong 1997; Xiong 2000). These studies utilized qualitative methods of analysis and in-depth discussion groups with parents and adolescents from each of the four cultural groups. A major outcome of the research was the first multilingual parent education curriculum in the country to address issues of parenting adolescents in all four Southeast Asian groups. (See www.parenting.umn.edu.)

A brief discussion of the naturalistic methods we used to study parents and adolescents is appropriate here. The National Extension Parent Education Model (NEPEM) (Smith et al. 1994) was used as a conceptual framework for the study; a multidisciplinary research team developed the parenting responsibility categories (guide, nurture, advocate, self-care, understand, and motivate) after an extensive review of the parenting literature. We recruited and trained community leaders and professionals from each cultural group to serve as facilitators and translators for a series of four discussion groups with forty-two adolescents (age twelve to eighteen) and four discussion groups with thirty-six parents (age thirty-six to fifty-five). Each group was composed of either parents (males and females) or adolescents (males and females) and two cofacilitators. Questions, probes, and discussion centered on the perceptions of each generation about the parenting categories outlined in the NEPEM. Each group discussion was tape-recorded, transcribed, and translated. The quotations and composite case studies utilized in this and the next chapter are derived from those discussions. The composite family stories were developed from recurring themes and narratives within the discussion groups to illustrate the dilemmas and conflicts in the perceptions and interactions of parents and adolescents. These family stories are brief case studies of family interactions concerning important daily life issues. A synopsis of each family story is used here to illustrate the complex family interaction dilemmas confronting parents and adolescents from the four cultural groups. In addition, these stories are parallel evidence that helps to validate the experiences and perceptions of elders about conflicted family interactions and identity issues within multigenerational family systems.

Parents want to help their children to succeed in the new context, but their cultural beliefs, inexperience with American customs, and fears make it difficult for them to do so in each case. Adolescents want to look up to and respect their parents and elders, but their own developmental agendas and need to fit into the new context make it difficult for them to do so. Although the conflicted interactions documented in these composite cases are grounded in transcribed and translated words and stories from the group discussions, the names, cultural group, and facts of the cases do not represent actual families or individuals. Each case was written after careful analysis of recurring stories and issues in both parent and adolescent group discussions. More fully developed case study materials and a videotape of six cases are available in the Helping Youth Succeed curriculum (Detzner, Xiong, and Eliason 1999).

Interactions between Generations

Migration to a country with such basic value differences as the United States has been identified as a primary threat to Hmong family interactions and the traditional practice of interdependence (Bliatout 1980; Khoa and Van Deusen 1981). For example, children who have better language skills and more education may override the authority of parents and elders (Bliatout 1980). Because parents are unfamiliar with the educational and social systems, Hmong teenagers have been turning away from clan leaders and elders and toward school counselors, particularly for educational and career guidance (Cohn 1986). The acculturation process varies considerably among family members (Lam and Westermeyer 1987; Lin 1986). Often children adapt to the language and behavior of the host culture more easily and sooner than the older generations, and sometimes a youth must become the reluctant family spokesperson (Lin 1986). These changes in families are often perceived by parents as threats to the traditional values of their culture (Gross 1986; Meredith and Rowe 1986; Van Deusen et al. 1980; Williams and Westermeyer 1983). Adolescents may not receive the parental guidance they need as they adapt and move through the normative stresses of adolescent development because of the parents' own acculturation struggles and unfamiliarity with the host culture (Carpio 1981; Kim, Chu, and Lee 1987; Tobin and Friedman 1984). Consequently, intergenerational problems and conflicts tend to predominate in many family interactions. The following composite case illustrates the difficulties of elder-parent-child interactions around the centrally important issue of language usage.

CASE 1: MY PARENT DON'T SPEAK ENGLISH AFTER ALL THESE YEARS

Chea and her younger brother were born in the United States to Cambodian parents Chum and Chanthan. They have two older siblings. Although their parents have been in the United States for fifteen years, they use English very little. Chum, the father, works in a meatpacking plant with a Cambodian supervisor and his job requires little English. Chanthan, the mother, stays home and is lonely, isolated, and depressed. The children must translate for their parents at school conferences and medical appointments. This is often inconvenient and disruptive if they are pulled from school for these appointments and embarrassing if the information to be translated is too personal.

It is particularly difficult for elders who cannot speak English to maintain credibility in advising the young, transmitting cultural values, and maintaining leadership roles. Family members from the middle or younger generations with better English skills often become the mediators between elders and social institutions such as schools, health clinics, and welfare agencies, thus creating an unpleasant role exchange situation. Children are distraught by their parents' and their own struggles with cultural discontinuity. According to Heinbeck's (1983) interview notes: "The dilemmas for younger children are no easier. The role of translator, interpreter and problem-solver is not a comfortable role when children take care of parents and grandparents" (cited in Hayes 1984, 363). Middle-aged parents with limited English skills are worried that they will lose their children's respect and hence their support in old age.

Parents and elders often find it difficult to achieve a balance between their responsibility to give direction and boundaries to young people and allowing them a degree of freedom to gradually make their own decisions. Xiong (1997) found that parents had difficulties guiding their adolescents when the differing values and prescriptions of two cultures confronted them. Parents were confused and conflicted about the American legal system, schools, and disciplinary practices, and they were unsure how to advise their adolescents in this dualistic environment. A Laotian father expressed the frustration of many parents in his discussion group:

> I have only one child. If I want to put pressure on him, he will suffer too much. On the other hand, if I don't do anything, things are going to break apart. When I scold him, he replies: "In the U.S. you can't scold me. I was born in Laos but I have been raised here. In this country if you scold me, I will call the police." My friend told me that. My son is ready to revolt against me. I believe that in Laos, when parents scold their children that means that they want to teach their children and expect their children to do well. I still follow the path of my parents. I don't know why we cannot scold our children here. Scolding our own children is not lawful. My heart is going to stop pumping now. Even if my son is doing wrong, I can't say anything. I can't find a solution. What should I do? If I let it go as it is, I can't breathe and am very upset. He walks out to his friend's house even though I do not want him to go. If I scold him, he slams the door.

The adolescents perceive their parents' efforts to guide them very differently. In their discussions, they complained about how parents continually repeated themselves in a series of constant "reminders" about what to do, what not to do, who to do it with, and what to be careful about. They saw this as excessive meddling and an unwillingness of parents to allow autonomy or to engage in fruitful communication or problem solving on issues about which they differed. Parental guidance was seen by one of the Vietnamese girls in this way:

> [P]arents should listen to what their teenagers have to say, you know. Sometimes we are right too. But we can't reason with our parents because if we do [parents think] it is impolite to talk back to our parents. Parents should help their teens deal with the practical consequences of every decision in life that they have to make. Not to prosecute their teens every time they run into a problem. Parents are not here to play a role of prosecutor or a judge, but instead a friend and a good counselor or advisor and should treat their teens with dignity and respect.

The following case reveals a Hmong parent's belief that a teenage daughter should stay away from an important school dance even though she is well behaved and responsible. Since the idea of a dance party was foreign to the parent she believed that it was necessary to set a firm boundary and not allow the daughter to attend. From the daughter's perspective, school dances were opportunities to socialize with friends, relax, and have some fun. Since she had proven herself to be a good student and a responsible daughter, Chia was unhappy that she was allowed so little freedom and not trusted by her parents. As a result, interactions between parents and daughter were strained.

CASE 2: I DON'T UNDERSTAND THIS IDEA OF A DANCE PARTY

Chia is a sixteen-year-old Hmong girl living at home with her parents and six siblings. The family has been in the United States for six years. Chia has done very well in school and is an honor student. She is well liked and has many friends. She has always obeyed and respected her parents' wishes until now: she wants to attend the prom dance at her school, but her parents are opposed to it.

In another case, Bopha, a widowed Cambodian mother, struggles with how to interact with Rin, her recalcitrant thirteen-year-old son, who is repeatedly in trouble at school and with the law. Bopha does not understand why Rin is such a "bad" child in this context. If this were Cambodia or his father were still alive, she does not believe he would be so disobedient. When a policeman brings Rin home after a shoplifting incident, Bopha begins yelling and hitting him with a broom handle, but the policeman warns her she could be arrested for maltreat-ment is she continues. She despairs because she does not know any other way to control the child. She believes that U.S. authorities have tied her hands and then blamed her for not controlling an errant teenage son. She blames the schools for not being stricter and the police for usurping her authority. Rin blames his mother for being gone all the time at work and not understanding life in the United States.

CASE 3: WHAT CAN I DO WITH A CHILD WHO IS HARD TO DISCIPLINE?

Bopha is a Cambodian mother with four children ranging in age from thirteen to twenty-five. Their father is no longer living. The family has been in the United States for ten years. The thirteen-year-old son, Rin, has become increasingly dif-ficult to handle. He misses classes or entire days of school, and then lies about it when confronted. He was recently picked up for shoplifting with his friends and released on a three-year probation.

In the following case, a widowed Lao woman is skeptical about a birthday sleepover at her twelve-year-old daughter's friend's house. Although Chanthi's friend lives in the neighborhood, the mother does not know the family and does not believe young girls should sleep at someone else's home. Parents are often reluctant to let girls out of their sight or supervision for very long. They fear that the reputation of their daughter, her chance to be married, and the family's repu-tation will be harmed if the girl is allowed to stray too far from home. These same standards are not applied to boys. From Chanthi's perspective, she is being treated unfairly and her mother is being too restrictive, especially since all of her friends' parents will allow their children to participate.

CASE 4: MOM WON'T LET ME GO ON A SLEEPOVER WITH FRIENDS

Chanthi is a twelve-year-old Lao girl who has lived in the United States for most of her life. She has one older brother. Their father was killed in Laos. Chanthi is in sixth grade and goes to a public elementary school in her neighborhood. She has many friends who live in the neighborhood as well. She wants to sleep over at her friend Latisha's house for a birthday party, but her mother is reluctant.

Dung-Vu rarely spends any time at home, preferring instead to hang out with friends. Some of his friends have been in trouble with the law and Dung-Vu's mother fears that he is being lured into a gang. When his mother finds out that he was involved in a drive-by shooting incident, out of desperation, she turns all of them in to the police. She hopes that the authorities will discipline him severely enough that he will change his ways. Dung-Vu is very angry with his mother for what she did.

CASE 5: MY SON'S FRIENDS ARE ALL GANGSTERS

Dung-Vu is a fifteen-year-old Vietnamese boy who lives with an older brother and his mother. He has recently become involved with gangs. A few weeks ago he shot a gun at another group of Vietnamese boys who were passing by in a car, injuring one boy slightly. His mother found out about the incident and reported his friends to the police. He was charged with assault and illegal discharge of a firearm within the city.

We know that "the rate of adaptation and acculturation often varies among family members" (Lin 1986, 66). Because they have more exposure to the new culture, adolescents are quicker to understand and navigate in it; however, the more acculturated they become the more they risk alienating themselves from the older generations and the ethnic community. Confusion is prevalent in many families because of uncertainties about mutual expectations and family roles. As a result, "Feelings of resentment, anger, and frustration are easily fostered in such a situation" (Lin 1986, 66). All of these composite cases reveal the cultural differences between generations, uncertainties about how to interact in the new environment, and frustrations. The cultural gaps are wider and deeper when the oldest generation is involved in the family as grandparents who still think of themselves as the head of multigenerational families and coparents to the children.

Elders and Middle-Aged Adults as Coparents

In almost three-fourths of the households in which the elders in our study lived (twenty-nine of forty), there were adult children of the elder present; in fifteen of the forty households there were also grandchildren present. Only three of the elders we studied were living alone. As we saw earlier, a primary role of elders in families was childcare, even if the children and elders did not live in the same household. This means that elders were very much involved in coparenting their grandchildren and that they continued to play a role as parents to their own adult children. It is appropriate therefore to discuss the difficulties and complexities of the parenting interactions with adolescents as we seek to understand the conflicted interactions in Southeast Asian families.

There are five basic functions of adults who assume the parenting role across cultures: educate, nurture, guide, problem solve, and model (Swick 1986). The coparent's role as the primary educator of children includes responsibility for their cultural development, and we saw earlier that elders view this important role as one that they could uniquely perform in the new country. Much of this cultural education occurs informally through observation and modeling. The interpersonal and behavioral patterns children observe in parents and grandparent caregivers can have a major impact on the level of their social competence in later years. As the adults assist, guide, and demonstrate what is expected, children begin a process of internalizing the cultural and social skills needed to manage in the complex new world.

Adolescents observed their parents and elders trying to overcome their stressful lives in a variety of ways. They reported that adults would spend time with friends, work in the garden, and get out of the house as ways of caring for themselves. Several adolescents reported that the unrelieved stresses of daily life in a new culture could easily be displaced onto the children or other family members, thus creating even more stress in the family. One of the Vietnamese adolescents spoke eloquently in the discussion group about the importance of parents' modeling appropriate methods of stress reduction:

> Parents that are mentally and emotionally stable have a positive self-image, therefore can relay this image to them, especially their children. In other words, they have learned effective ways to deal with stress and negative experiences and turned stress into positive outcomes, as a lesson in life. Therefore, when parents took care of themselves and could maintain a positive self-image, they presented themselves as positive role models to others.

However, it is clear that "[p]arents who lack a clear understanding of their identity within their cultural context will have difficulty in carrying out parental roles such as modeling. Ineffective parenting . . . has a ripple effect on children, the community" (Swick 1986, 74). The parenting role becomes more difficult when caregiving adults are simultaneously confronted by multiple stresses of resettlement, including transitions in their own identity, their ethnic group, and the dominant majority culture. "In order for parents to be effective in carrying out a multicultural paradigm with their children, they must be secure in their cultural identity. . . . If parents feel inadequate about their cultural context, it is unlikely they will make efforts to understand others" (Swick 1986, 75).

In the following composite case, the father, Chong Yee, is seldom home to parent his children, and his wife, Mao, is overwhelmed by the stress of caring for six children and an elderly father-in-law. She seldom gets out of the house and feels inadequate and uncertain when she does leave the home. As a result, the stresses of daily life make her feel exhausted and hopeless.

CASE 6: I FEEL SO TIRED AND HOPELESS IN THIS COUNTRY

Mao and Chong Yee are Hmong parents living with their six children, ranging in age from nine to twenty-two. The family lives on public assistance; Chong Yee, the father, receives supplemental security income because of a physical disability from the war. Chong Yee is away from home a great deal because he is very involved in Hmong community work and meetings; Mao, the mother, stays home and takes care of the house, children, and Chong Yee's elderly father, who also lives with them. Both Mao and Chong Yee suffer from constant stress in their lives and feel depressed.

It is reasonable to assume that coparenting is a particularly challenging task for adults like Chong Yee, Mao, and the elderly father-in-law, as well as for the other parents and elders in our studies who, on one hand, have lost the continuity of their own cultural identity and who, on the other hand, have to expend enormous energy to reconcile their own conflicting cultural/parental roles. Swick (1985) argues that in a homogeneous society, tradition, stability, and well-defined boundaries in parent-child interactions are encouraged, whereas in a more heterogeneous society, diversity in parenting is more common. He introduces the concept of "cultural security" to explain the importance of stability and confidence that basic cultural values will be maintained in the future. He asserts that "as cultural security is achieved, greater emphasis is placed on advancing human knowledge, thus the encouragement of diversity in many cultural areas. Too much diversity, confusion and instability may require 'cultural closure' to provide more security for parents and children" (Swick 1985, 82). Adults who are confronted with the confusion and instability of conflicting cultural contexts tend to be perplexed, to be apprehensive, and to desire a well-defined traditional cultural environment within their "home." For Southeast Asian adults who are coparenting, cultural security also includes the notion of "intergenerational security" (Swick 1985, 83), which assures them that they will be cared for in old age.

Quoting a middle-generation Hmong parent from another study on this issue helps to clarify the dilemma that many elders have already spoken to in earlier chapters:

> We need our identity, our heritage. All that we have or what we can do now is to hold onto our culture and pass it on to the future generations, so they will know whom their ancestors were, and where they

> were from. It is difficult to get the children to keep the culture, because their daily life is so strongly influenced by their American friends' way of life. Because there is little time for children to be involved with their parents' traditional ways, they do not see the importance of it. Many of the Hmong children cannot cope with two different cultures at the same time, with the American ways at school or outside the home, and with their own. (Yang 1989, 33)

As a result, many children embrace the new culture while rejecting the old way. Cultural conflict not only affects the children (Powell et al. 1983) but it also "threatens parental goals and expectations, disrupts the parent-child relationship, and undermines the parents' sense of competence as a parent" (Serafica 1990, 227). Adults responsible for parenting need some help from outside the home. As one Hmong author stated: "We want someone else other than their parents to tell the young people how important it is to keep their own tradition and culture. We need help to find a better way to ease these transitions" (Yang 1989, 33).

The following composite case represents a situation that appears to be common in many of the Southeast Asian families we studied. While the elders and parents want desperately for the youth to love and cherish the rituals and traditions of their native land, the children are indifferent because they are consumed with trying to fit into the peer culture in school. This is especially problematic for the children who were born in refugee camps or the United States, since they have no memory of their homeland and the culture of the adults in their family.

CASE 7: OUR CHILDREN NEED TO KNOW CAMBODIAN CULTURE

Tha and Sokha arrived in the United States from Cambodia more than fifteen years ago. They have five children: two sons, ages twenty and seventeen, and three daughters, ages fifteen, nine, and five. All the children were born in the United States except the two oldest, and they were very young when they came over. The children are very Americanized and seem uninterested in learning about Cambodian culture.

Parents' interactions with children vary considerably between mothers and fathers. According to Hughes's (1990) informants, a "good" Hmong father is foremost a provider, and secondly a disciplinarian. "A good father provides food and money to take care of the children" (56). A "good mother" takes care of her children as well as her husband. The mother and wife roles seem to be inseparable. Although traditional gender-based family roles define the possibilities for interaction, gender and family roles are changing rapidly.

The need to support the family sometimes makes it difficult for parents to have enough time for frequent interactions with their children, especially if the family is large. Often, the grandparents are called in to fulfill most of the parenting roles, since the parents are working many hours each week to support large families. Serafica (1990) points out that many Southeast Asian immigrants who are not professionally trained have to seek employment in the secondary labor market and service industries. Their limited English proficiency and unfamiliarity with a postindustrial social structure can further exacerbate their sense of discontinuity and cultural incoherence. As pointed out by Glenn (1983), there seems to be a complete segregation of work and family life in many dual worker families engaged in the labor-intensive, low-capital service and small manufacturing sectors. Serafica (1990) argues: "The parents' fatigue, the long hours of separation, and the lack of common experiences weaken family communication and closeness" (224).

The additional responsibilities that the older children have to assume for the younger children, a taken-for-granted reality in everyday life at home, become a great burden to the older children in the United States and a recurring source of conflict.

CASE 8: WE NEED TO BOTH WORK TO MAKE ENDS MEET

Chanpheng, Phanom Sone, and four of their children arrived in the United States from Laos eight years ago. There are now six children in the family, ranging in age from six to seventeen. Both parents have full-time jobs that are physically demanding and leave them little time at home. They have been having some trouble lately with their older children, who are supposed to come home directly from school and take care of the younger ones but sometimes they do not arrive home until much later.

Although the family is the primary socialization agent of children, adults typically receive little formal parenting training, and must rely on their own personal experiences (Serafica 1990). Almost no culturally sensitive parent education materials have been developed to assist Southeast Asian immigrant adults with the complex task of parenting in the new context. Therefore, it is natural that immigrant parents would adhere to their traditional cultures and value systems in parenting interactions with children. As immigrant parents encounter discontinuity in and confusion about cultural identities, their effort to maintain tradition alleviates ambiguity and provides cognitive consistency (Serafica 1990). Similarly, culturally desired social patterns serve as a guideline for parental behavior and familial interactions. In cultures in which continuity and stability are strongly desired, conformity to traditional norms is emphasized. In cultures in which creativity and individuality are important values, parents tend to encourage individual uniqueness in each child (Fantini and Cardenas 1980).

Parents in the United States are expected to interact with each child differently, as a unique individual with his or her own needs and developmental stage (Smith et al. 1994). To do so they must be able to listen to their children's problems and act according to what they hear. Parents in the discussion groups and elders whom we interviewed had some difficulty accepting the notion that understanding was solely their responsibility. Instead, many believed that children had the responsibility to understand *them*. The following composite case illustrates the cultural divide between many parents and children that negatively influences their interactions.

CASE 9: OUR KIDS DON'T KNOW WHAT WE HAVE BEEN THROUGH

King and Khamnpheng came to the United States from Laos fourteen years ago, with three children and Khamnpheng's mother. They have since had three more children. The parents and grandmother regularly go to the temple, where they can associate with other Lao families, speak Laotian, and learn Buddha's teachings as they did back home. Their children, however, don't want to go to the temple with them, and show little interest in Lao culture.

Southeast Asian parents and elders tend to describe two categories of children, "good" and "bad" kids. If parents understood their child to be "bad" based on previous behaviors, then they believed that there was little they could do to influence him or her in a positive way. This was especially true in the United States, given the parents' perceptions of legal restrictions on corporal punishment. A "good" child would listen to the parents, do what he or she was told, and understand that the parents' word was the law. Parents found it much more difficult to understand the teens who were born in the United States—the so-called 1.5 generation (Portes 1996)—compared to those who had lived for some years in their homeland before coming to the United States. American-born adolescents had their own ideas, slang, clothing styles, and difficulties understanding what the parents wanted, in comparison to older brothers and sisters or peers who had had more exposure to their native language and culture. Some of the autonomy-seeking behaviors of adolescents were considered dangerous or shameful to the family and it was difficult for adults to understand why children would act in such ways.

Instead of trying to understand, many adults relied on their traditional authority and power to assert control, often with disastrous results. A Hmong woman explained the difficulty she had trying to understand her child's autonomous behaviors:

> If you have a child who needs friends a lot, you will have conflict with him. He will run away if you tell him not to go out too much. Teenagers like to date and have boyfriends or girlfriends. Do you know that in this country, girls like to go out and offer a date to boys first? Our girls like to make phone calls to talk to their boyfriends first. It is not good. It is against our culture. We end up letting them do what they want anyway and only warn our daughters that their boyfriends will not marry them.

The following composite case illustrates the dilemma confronting adults who try to control their children's interactions inside the home and the conflicts that can occur when parents do not understand normative teen behaviors in the new context. In this case, the parents' lack of understanding and assertion of authority creates resentment and a greater misunderstanding between them and their fifteen-year-old daughter.

CASE 10: WHY IS CALLING A BOY ON THE PHONE A BIG DEAL?

Mai is a fifteen-year-old Hmong girl living at home with her parents and three younger siblings. She gets good grades in school and usually listens to her parents, but she feels that her parents are too strict with her when they insist that she not call boys from school on the telephone, even though, as she tells her parents, the boys are "just friends."

According to the adolescent discussion groups, most parents understood the need for teens to have money of their own, but they had difficulty understanding teens' need to "hang out" with friends away from the pressures of school and family. Because parents had difficulty listening to their teens and had more limited exposure to the world the teens lived in, it was difficult for them to be sympathetic to the teens' desires for greater autonomy. This was especially true concerning the selection of friends, some of whom the parents did not know. Parents were adamantly opposed to their sons or daughters "hanging out" with peers whom they perceived as troubled. This issue was a strong source of contention between parents and teens and it influenced their interactions in negative ways.

One of the Cambodian girls in the discussion group expressed her frustration with her mother's inability to understand:

> She knows my friends were getting into trouble, and she thinks when I go out with them, I get into trouble too. But it's not like that. My friends do something; I am not going to do it unless it is something that I want to do. My mom thinks my friends will make me do something, but it isn't like that. . . . But she doesn't understand because my friends are in trouble and locked up [on probation].

In the following composite case, family interactions are strained by the lack of understanding between a Vietnamese woman and her fourteen-year-old son. Khue wants to spend time with friends after school but he is expected to come home immediately after classes to care for his younger siblings. In addition, Khue thinks he should be able to spend the money he earns on whatever he wants. His lack of understanding of his mother's wishes and her misunderstanding of his autonomous behaviors create tensions in the household.

CASE 11: MY MOTHER DOESN'T LISTEN TO ME

Khue is a fourteen-year-old Vietnamese boy living with his mother, Suong, his mother's boyfriend, two younger sisters ages nine and seven, and a baby half brother. His father had been absent most of the time in Vietnam, either away in the military or in a "reeducation" camp. The family immigrated together, but the father left the family two years later and has not been in contact with them since. Suong's boyfriend moved in with the family several years ago, and he and Suong have a baby boy. Suong and Khue have many disagreements, especially about the expectation that he will take care of his younger siblings after school and about the way Khue spends the money he earns on his job.

The difficulties that some adults have understanding the customs and practices that their children bring home with them are the centerpiece of the previous two interaction cases. Adolescents experience these misunderstandings as a function of their parents' unwillingness to listen to their stories and experiences and inability to learn about the new context. The parents rely on their own experience and their fear of the unknown as they establish what the kids feel are unreasonable rules. In the following case, Ra fails to understand his parents, their cultural values, and their fears of negative influences outside the home. Ra's parents fail to understand their son's need to fit in with his peers at school. In this and the previous case misunderstandings rather than ill will shape the interactions between parents and their adolescent son.

CASE 12: I CAN'T WEAR BAGGY PANTS LIKE EVERYONE ELSE

Ra is a fifteen-year-old Cambodian boy, the oldest in a family of seven children. He attends a large, inner-city high school with a diverse student population, including many kids from Cambodia, Laos, and Vietnam. Wearing baggy pants, or "going sagging," is currently a popular way to dress, but Ra's parents are not happy with his choice of clothes because they think he will be mistaken for a gangster and he will bring shame to his family.

Coparenting Adolescents

Coparenting preschool-age children in the new context is not as difficult for elders and middle-aged adults because the young ones do not yet understand all the complexities that lie beyond the household door. Even elementary-age children are still obedient and compliant in the face of adult authority. Interactions between adults and their preadolescent children begin to change rapidly around the age of ten or eleven. Tobin and Friedman (1984) wrote about the confluence of two tumultuous transitions confronting adolescents from refugee families: the normative physiological, emotional, cognitive, and social upheavals of early adulthood and the family interaction upheavals inherent in the refugee experience. They argue that there are three competing cultures in the lives of immigrant children: the American culture they encounter in school and on TV; the culture of their childhood, which may be vivid in their memories and in their parents' memories; and the refugee culture, "the patchwork, pidgin cultures they have been forced to create out of the rubble of their old ways of life" (40).

In describing Southeast Asian cultures that are different and yet similar, Tobin and Friedman (1984) adopted Ruth Benedict's (1938) concept of a culture "with high continuity." They argued that the discontinuities of culture and developmental stages have compounding, detrimental effects on adolescents, young adults, and the elderly. Coming from cultures that do not recognize the adolescent stage as important, Southeast Asian youth have nonetheless been thrown into the trial-and-error challenges of being adolescents in this culture. Because of this, "The Southeast Asian teenager must be seen as experiencing an adolescence which is quite unlike the adolescence of his American peers" (Tobin and Friedman 1984, 41).

Separation from family plays a central role in the lives of teenagers in the United States, and separation is a major theme in the life stories of most adults who are refugees. Within this context, it is difficult for Southeast Asian adolescents to manage a separation from parents when parents and many of the elders in our study view separation as yet another loss, hurt, and betrayal. These difficulties intensify in cultures that uphold the importance of a large kinship network and extended family. Southeast Asian adolescents who struggle with separation from parents find that their interactions with parents are often conflicted, laden with guilt, and confusing. The next case illustrates the dilemma confronting parents as they try to establish strict boundaries when freedom from constraints is what an adolescent is seeking.

CASE 13: TRIA HAS RUN AWAY FROM HOME

Tria is the fifteen-year-old youngest daughter in a Hmong family of five children. She has lived in the United States since she was five years old and feels very Americanized; however, her mother and father want her to follow more traditional Hmong ways and have set limits on her that she resists. For example, her parents insist that she come home directly after school and they do not allow her to go out of the house without taking a sibling along. After months of arguments Tria has run away from home and is living with her girlfriend.

As a consequence of parental inexperience in the new culture, or what some American experts might call neglect, Southeast Asian adolescents often have very difficult problems with the transition to adulthood. There are many reasons for the behavioral problems attributed to some groups of Southeast Asian youth: "One of the major reasons for children developing these behavioral and identity problems is that for the last many years before they came to the U.S., they have gone through war and the camp experiences, which have led them to develop a sense of insecurity, instability, and distrust" (Battisti n.d., 94). Battisti also contends that children from refugee families suffer from confusion about roles and responsibilities in their families. For example, he writes:

> When they are back in Cambodia and Vietnam, the role of every individual family member is well defined. . . . The roles change in the U.S. due to cultural and psychological factors. If the father has not been killed in the war, he is busy working a number of jobs. He may be physically ill or mentally depressed. The role of the children is not well defined. . . . [T]hey bring the parents to see a doctor, and often they are caretakers for their parents, as well as for the younger children. We see tremendous stress among the eldest daughters, and they present a lot of problems. (95)

In the following composite case, an adolescent girl named Soumaly and her family are forced to confront her transition to a respectable adult life within the Cambodian community. She is confused and upset by her parents' insistence that she marry the boyfriend who is responsible for her pregnancy, when her aspirations are for a college education and a career.

CASE 14: MY PARENTS JUST FOUND OUT THAT I AM PREGNANT

Soumaly is a sixteen-year-old Lao girl; she has two younger siblings and two older siblings. The family has been in the United States for sixteen years. Soumaly is a good student and has had a good relationship with her parents up to now. However, her parents recently discovered that she is five months pregnant, and they are putting pressure on her to marry the father, a seventeen-year-old boy named Bounmy whom they both like. But Soumaly doesn't want to get married now; she wants to keep her baby and perhaps marry the father when she is finished with college.

Goldstein (1985) classified school "as a public institution that is responsible for transmitting the dominant culture to youth at large, and particularly, for the assimilation of immigrant youth to the mainstream economic and cultural patterns" (1). As to how immigrant girls and boys respond to schooling, it is largely influenced by their cultural functioning, including their construction of gender and gender relations. Goldstein emphasized the important role gender plays in the experience and meanings of schooling for adolescents. The educational process can be complicated as immigrant youth proceed to make sense of their own ethnicity while simultaneously confronting both traditional and mainstream gender practices. For girls, the process may be particularly difficult: "The course of the girls' school explorations and goals are shaped in part by their images of the past, present and future" (3).

Elder-parent-adolescent interactions about school in the United States are naturally shaped by the adults' limited experience with mainstream educational systems. As a result: "The adults view American schools as the place where the children can learn English and learn how to cope with the foreign, American environment. Yet they rely on their memories of education in Laos to formulate expectations of their children as students in American schools" (Goldstein 1986, 11). As was the custom in Laos, Hmong parents had different expectations for boys and girls. For example, in the United States:

> adults expect the boys to remain in school to learn the technical skills necessary for employment. But, the girls receive a contradictory mes-

> sage to contribute to the community not only through economic quali-
> fications but also by reproducing the community through internal
> maintenance of the domestic sphere, including early marriage and
> childbearing. (Goldstein 1986, 12)

This expectation causes confusion and heartbreak for many young girls because they are caught between cultural and individual responsibilities and conflicting messages. This confusion about school and family is dramatically illustrated in the previous case.

In the following case the confusion of adults about the lack of discipline and authority on the part of teachers in U.S. schools is briefly illustrated. Because education is highly valued by elders, and teachers are viewed as powerful authorities and surrogate parents, it is baffling to Southeast Asian adults that teachers do not assert their power in the classroom.

CASE 15: WHY DON'T SAYSANA'S TEACHER HAVE MORE CONTROL?

Saysana is a Lao boy who moved to the United States with his family five years ago, when he was nine. He has two older sisters who are doing well in school; he has one older brother who dropped out of school and is not living at home. Saysana has been receiving bad grades and is falling further behind in his classes. He has been suspended once for smoking and has had problems with attendance and truancy.

According to Smith and associates (1994), an important parenting responsibility involves motivating, stimulating, and encouraging the intellectual growth of children. Like most other immigrant parents, Southeast Asian parents view education as a key to success in the new country and they have high expectations for their children to succeed in the school environment. Unfortunately, many parents and most elders have limited education themselves; they lack understanding of the American system; and they have limited English language proficiency. These problems make it difficult for adults to interact with their adolescent children about schoolwork and conflicts in school. In the following case the frustration of parents and their thirteen-year-old son, Toua, is highlighted.

CASE 16: I DON'T KNOW HOW TO HELP TOUA IN SCHOOL

Toua is a thirteen-year-old Hmong boy. His parents and three siblings recently arrived in the United States. Toua was placed in sixth grade in an elementary school. He is in ESL classes for one hour each day, and in regular classes for the rest of the day. Toua has been struggling to keep up with his schoolwork and becoming more and more unhappy, especially since his parents don't know enough to help him.

To overcome their own limitations, parents frequently used other trusted friends, family members, or peers as role models and motivators for their children. In addition, they discussed with adolescents their own lack of education and the consequences of not studying hard in the United States. A Cambodian father explained that he keeps an eye on the progress of his children in school despite his own limited language skills: "If I see that my child is doing well in school, I don't need to advise and guide him or her. He or she knows how to do [well] by him- or herself; therefore, parents don't have to say anything but to keep an eye on him or her. But when he or she goes in the wrong way or behaves in the wrong way, we have to explain to him."

Adolescents agreed that their parents were likely to use other family members and peers as good examples for them to emulate as a strategy for motivation. The problem that many experienced, however, was that parents had such high expectations that the adolescents believed they could never achieve them. They were frequently compared to other, more successful adolescents or to adults, and these comparisons made them feel that their parents did not accept them for who they were. Many felt that they were expected to achieve beyond their capacity. A Vietnamese girl expressed the recurring frustration of other adolescents in the focus groups:

> It's because my parent are always comparing me to other kids at the end of the block. She is always stay home and studying hard and a good student and never goes anywhere. All A's and A's. 'Why can't you be like her?' Well, you know, I have to admit that I am not smart like her, but the point is why can't my parents accept me for who I am. I am not the kid at the end of the block. Even when I tried my best, [it is] still not good enough for my parents. They have too high of expectations for me. They expect too much.

A number of kids reported that parents and elders frequently pointed out their own limited education, low incomes, and economic hardships as examples to motivate their children. Still others believed that adults seldom tried to motivate them by using compliments or positive reinforcements but rather were quick to criticize if they did not perform to expectations. This dilemma is illustrated in the following case.

CASE 17: WHY DO MY PARENTS EXPECT ME TO GET ALL A'S?

Thanh The is a twelve-year-old Vietnamese girl who came to the United States with her older brother more than four years ago. Their parents and two more siblings joined them later. Thanh The is a good student and doing well in school. She always attends classes, pays attention, and does her homework. Still she feels as if her parents are never satisfied. When she brought home her report card she had all A's except for a B in social studies. Her parents are concerned about the B grade and Thanh The is upset at the criticism of her accomplishments.

In these cases parents and other relatives are often frustrated by the difficulty they experience trying to interact with their adolescent children. Parents either do not know how to help kids; they have very high expectations for kids; or they do not understand the cocurricular activities youth want to join. The adolescents negatively react to parents' pressure on them to do well, since parents have little understanding of their situation, fail to listen, and can offer few resources to help them to succeed. The adults want to motivate the youth but they are not sure how, and the kids want their elders to help them but they cannot seem to get the types of help they need.

CASE 18: CHANTHA WANTS TO JOIN AFTER-SCHOOL ACTIVITIES

Chantha is a fourteen-year-old Cambodian boy. He immigrated to the United States with his uncle, aunt, and cousins when he was nine years old and he continues to live with them, since the rest of his family is still in Cambodia. Chanta would like to join his classmates in some after-school groups, but his aunt and uncle don't approve. They would like him to get a job after school instead. Chantha's other uncle, Cheat, has been in the United States longer and is more accepting of his participating in these groups.

Youth were also unable to get the type of nurturing that they wanted in the United States from the important adults in their lives. Southeast Asian parents and elders were criticized by youth when they were compared to the parents of the youth's American peers or to the images of American families that the youth saw on television. Although most Southeast Asian parents, especially mothers, had little difficulty expressing warmth and affection toward younger children, parenting practices within the community generally prohibited a show of overt affection toward adolescents. A certain distance between parents, especially fathers, and their older children was maintained in order to define the boundaries of parental authority. Parents generally believed that they demonstrated their nurturing roles best when they went to work and provided for the basic necessities of everyday life: food, shelter, clothing, and safety. Occasionally, when finances permitted, they would purchase nonnecessity items for their adolescents as a way of demonstrating their love. A Cambodian mother spoke about the conditional nurturing practices that she had brought with her from home:

> I tell my daughter that if she washes the dishes, she has to finish it, then I will love her. When adults come to the house, she has to behave nicely and walk across to them with respect. She has to speak Cambodian to them and to me. She has to do what I tell her or I will not love her. I just say that I do not love her but my heart still loves her. I just say that to scare her. I love her but I will not let her know. But sometimes at night I would go up to her room and tell her that I love her.

This conflict between generations and cultural practices is well illustrated by the following composite case.

CASE 19: MY PARENTS DON'T LOVE ME

Bouavone is a ten-year-old Lao girl who has lived in the United States most of her life. She has two older brothers who are also living at home along with her parents. She has always done well in school. She recently became friends with Kate, who is American. Bouavone has become increasingly unhappy comparing her home situation to Kate's. She is convinced that her parents don't love her because they don't show affection in the same way as Kate's parents. Her unhappiness at home has been affecting her schoolwork and her relationships with her mother and father.

The adolescents agreed that parents nurtured them by providing for basic needs, by purchasing nonbasic items, or by giving them money. A Vietnamese girl explained parental nurturing in the following way:

> As long as I can remember, my mom always gives me everything I ever needed. . . . I know a lot of times my mom gives me more than she is given to herself. . . . She would buy for me first, like clothes, and if there is money left over, then she would buy for herself. Many times she didn't get what she really wanted . . . because we didn't have much to begin with. I didn't know then but I know now that my mom has sacrificed her whole life for me.

The interaction problem that many adolescents believed to be most serious was the inability or unwillingness of parents to be empathetic listeners. The emphasis on one-way communication meant that parents reminded, scolded, yelled, and told their teens what to do but rarely listened to them or tried to understand their problems. A Cambodian girl explained the general feeling in all four adolescent discussion groups about this issue: "Well, I want to be able to talk and say what I want. Like when I talk to my mom, I want to be able to tell her how I feel, but she cuts me off and doesn't let me say it. I want her to respect me and let me say what I want, so she hears my side of the story or my opinion or whatever and not just her opinion."

The difficulties that parents may have hearing what their children want or need is exacerbated by the parents' lack of familiarity with the American parenting practices to which their own parenting is unfavorably compared. As a result, children often feel that their parents are disinterested in their activities and unaware of their successes (or failures) outside of school. The following case represents a number of examples discussed by youth that illustrate the misunderstandings between youth and adults about what is needed in this environment.

CASE 20: I WISH MOM AND DAD WOULD COME TO MY BASEBALL GAMES

Thuan and Hong Van came to the United States from Vietnam twelve years ago with two children; they now have three children, ages ten to seventeen. The children are very Americanized. Thuan and Hong Van both have busy jobs and the children are involved in many after-school activities. The family is rarely all together at one time. Lately, Thuan and Hong Van have noticed that their middle son Huy has been withdrawn and moody. They find out that he feels badly because, unlike the parents of his American friends, his parents never attend his baseball games or other events.

Discussion

These family interaction cases and the words and experiences of elders, parents, and adolescents reveal the real difficulties and conflicts occurring across generations, genders, and cultural groups. It appears that the adults are trying very hard to interact with their children in the ways that are familiar to them and that the children are pushing for new ways of interacting. Many of the adults, especially the elders, see little reason to change age-old parenting practices and expectations, while the children see little reason to hold onto past practices in the new environment. The dual cultural dilemma is present either overtly or covertly in almost every family interaction. As a result, there appears to be a standoff between generations that inhibits and restricts the types of interactions that are possible.

A "bicultural pattern" of family interaction is highly recommended (Khoa and Van Deusen 1981) as the preferred approach to coping with and adapting to the new cultural environment. However, biculturalism is difficult to achieve. One has to reconcile conflicting norms or behaviors; to discern and maintain acceptable values from two very different cultures; and to take actions appropriate to both traditional and American cultures (Khoa and Van Deusen 1981). Achieving a bicultural working relationship in families is a challenging task for elders and parents who are coping with the multiple stresses of resettlement, adjusting to their own developmental tasks of late life, and trying to understand the new world that surrounds them. It is also difficult for youth to understand the more traditional perspectives of their parents or to see much value in old world traditions and parenting practices in the new context. Since most youth have little or no experience of life in the world from which their parents and grandparents came, it is difficult for them to understand or appreciate it. As a result, conflicted family interactions is the recurring theme in the households of the elders, parents, and adolescents who participated in our studies.

Multiple Family Identities 7

Introduction

FAMILY IDENTITY CAN BE DEFINED as how a family perceives and manages the balance between the self-concept of individual members and their identity as a distinctive group (LaRossa 1984). A family's identity may be viewed as the summed total of the individual identities of the members or as a unified cohesive group identity that all share. The experiences of each gender and generation in an immigrant family are different enough that a collective group identity may be difficult to construct in a new cultural context. Even if coherence is possible, individual elders, middle-generation parents, and adolescents are likely to perceive and manage their identities in different ways given the very dissimilar contexts of their daily lives. However problematic the definition and multifaceted the concept, it is constructive to examine the efforts that each generation makes to redefine its identity after immigrating. Since family identity appears to be a subset of ethnic identity and ethnic identity is a subset of social identity, it is useful to examine the very different ways that ethnicity has been conceptualized and operationalized during the past three decades.

In Phinney's (1990) review of seventy research studies on ethnic identity published in refereed journals since 1972, several important conclusions were developed. There were no commonly agreed upon definitions of ethnic identity across the studies. It is difficult to understand or generalize about the concept because each group has its own unique history and different characteristics. Despite the absence of conceptual clarity, everyone seems to agree that ethnic identity is central to an understanding of the self-concept and the psychological functioning of individuals who are members of ethnic groups (Gurin and Epps 1975; Maldonado 1975). There is agreement that ethnicity is a component of an individual's social identity and that feeling one belongs to a group is important. To what degree an individual maintains and cherishes the language, customs, values, and history of the ethnic group may vary among members. It is not necessary to embrace all elements of the culture to maintain a commitment to the group and the identity that derives from it. It is important to recognize the dynamic and evolving nature of ethnic identity across genders, generations, and time. Most studies have focused on childhood and adolescent identities at a point in time; no studies were identified that focused on elders and their family identities. Identification with the group may need to be asserted if negative assaults on the group occur (Weinreich 1983). The most frequently cited definition that Phinney discovered comes from Tajfel (1981), who writes that ethnic identity is: "that part of an individual's self-concept which derives from his knowledge of his membership in a social group (or groups) together with the value and emotional significance attached to that membership." (255)

Perspectives on Identity

Phinney divided the research on ethnic identity into three broad conceptual areas conceived and developed by scholars with different disciplinary agendas. These categories are helpful in examining the different ways that Southeast Asian elders and their families struggle with the issue in the U.S. context.

Social and Ethnic Identities

Social psychologists and others point out that group membership is an important component of an individual's social identity and self-concept. They argue that it is difficult to develop a positive self-concept if one does not have a sense of belonging to one or more social groups. This idea is linked closely to symbolic interaction theory, which argues that individuals' understanding of themselves and the world they live in are derived from interactions with other individuals, intimate family members, and groups. Membership in an ethnic group can be an important source of pride when it is defined as a source of meaning and social capital, or it can become a source of shame and self-hatred when outsiders negatively define the group. In some cases, ethnic group members may deny or avoid members of their ethnic group or try to "pass" as a member of the dominant group to avoid the negative evaluation of nonmembers. This choice is generally not available to Asians because of their distinctive physical features. Members of immigrant families may choose to identify with the ethnic group, the dominant culture, or both, although this bicultural option can be difficult because of competing values.

Sharon Kaufman (1981) argues that the assumptions of symbolic interaction theory help to explain identity development over the life course because individual, family, and group identities are the result of interactions between individuals and groups. Identity is evolving and interactive, rarely fixed or immutable. She proposes that older "people create themes—cognitive areas of meaning—in the construction of their biographies which explain, unify, and give substance to their perceptions of who they are and how they see themselves participating in social life" (55). For the elders we interviewed, the conflict and interactions between their social, ethnic, and family identities were recurring themes.

Acculturation and Identity

Ethnic identity is sometimes conceptualized as an artifact of the acculturation process that follows what is thought to be an inevitable process of ethnic melting and an embrace of the dominant culture. Acculturation is a term that is usually applied to groups rather than to individuals. An important issue in this framework is what happens to the ethnic group over time, rather than what happens to an individual or to each generation within a family at a point in time. This perspective is limited because it is linear and it posits either a strong identification with the ethnic group on one pole or a strong mainstream identification on the other. The melting pot theorists believe that group acculturation occurs over several generations. An individual who resists the process and continues to embrace the ethnic group may be viewed as a marginalized separatist living in the past, while an individual who embraces the mainstream may be viewed as a sellout assimilationist. Individuals who do not identify with either group may have an identity crisis and/or a diminished self-concept because of the absence of any group affiliation. A bicultural identification with both the ethnic group and the mainstream group is also possible within the acculturation model; however, this may be a temporary position of second-, third-, or fourth-generation immigrants who are expected to eventually identify with mainstream society. The acculturation identity model may apply more to white ethnic groups in the United States than it does to the new immigrants from Asia, Africa, and other developing nations outside the European cultural groups.

Camino and Krulfeld's (1994) edited volume provides strong evidence for the fluidity of ethnic identity and the importance of the ecosystem, with each chapter providing a case study of a different cultural group in the throes of transformation. Mortland's (1994) chapter identifies four different perspectives on Cambodian identity taken from four distinct contexts: pre–Khmer Rouge Cambodia, flight, detention camps, and U.S. resettlement. He concludes that no one domain explains Cambodian identity and there are no fixed or immutable images of identity. Instead, identity is based on the situation, depending on the type of social interaction and the persons involved in the interaction. Lerner (1982) also used ecosystems theory to develop a "goodness of fit" model, according to which the diverse environments in which refugee adolescents lived were viewed as potential arenas for promoting self-development and healthy identity formation.

Ethnic Identity Formation

From this perspective, ethnic identity is viewed as dynamic, changing, and evolutionary. It is the result of a series of decisions and commitments made by individuals as they move through different stages of life, from youth to old age, and through the different contexts of their daily lives. This is a social construction model, in which the identity is developed in stages. Although Erik Erickson was not focused on ethnicity when he formulated his stage model of ego identity formation, his model has been adapted to conceptualize the complex processes that occur in ethnic individuals over time. Phinney (1989) proposed a three-stage model in which individuals at first do not examine or question their ethnic group membership; second, they begin to explore their ethnic identity and mainstream alternatives more fully; third, they make a commitment to embrace, reject, or modify the identity to fit their situation and comfort level. Although not writing specifically about ethnic groups, Grotevant (1987) suggests that the exploration stage may be continued in a series of cycles over the life course when individuals revisit their constructed identity as they confront new developmental tasks and contexts. The final stage of achieved or committed identity does not necessarily mean a complete embrace of all elements of the ethnic culture, including language, customs, and rituals, but rather an individual may make a commitment to a hybrid identity in which some elements are embraced while others are not. This formulation of ethnic identity is similar to Portes's (1995) notion of segmented assimilation, according to which an individual commits to certain aspects of mainstream society in some contexts but embraces their ethnic identity in other contexts. This conceptualization is more complex and dynamic than others; it is consistent with the ethnogenesis theory of ethnic group formation and fits well with the findings of our studies.

Several theorists suggest that individuals and perhaps ethnic groups go through a somewhat predictable series of stages in identity development. A popular model utilized by cross-cultural counseling psychologists includes five stages (Atkinson, Morten, and Sue 1989). They argue that individuals and groups move from conformity, dissonance, resistance and immersion, and introspection toward integrative self-awareness. In this model, an individual or a group is hypothesized to evolve from self- and group-deprecating attitudes to self- and group-appreciating attitudes while moving from dissonance to awareness.

A further distinction can be made between ethnic identification, in which an individual identifies with membership in a specific group, and ethnic identity, in which an individual internalizes the values, beliefs, and historical experience of a group (Spencer and Markstrom-Adams 1990). This distinction is consistent with the ways that Southeast Asian elders describe their family members, who are often located at different places along a continuum between reluctant identification with the ethnic group and a fully embraced ethnic identity.

Southeast Asian Family Identities

The values, beliefs, and customs of Southeast Asian elders are composed of the cultural ideas and practices the elders brought with them from their homelands. The beliefs, values, and practices of Confucianism, Buddhism, and familism include assumptions about the way individuals should conduct themselves inside the family and present themselves to the outside world. In the elders' home countries, there was widespread consensus about those assumptions and solidarity between generations about the family's identity. How family members perceive and manage the balance between their individual and group identities in the United States, however, is likely to vary considerably and not be a subject of consensus. In fact, the family's past, present, and future identity is at the center of many family conflicts that we have previously discussed.

The *Harvard Encyclopedia of Ethnic Groups* (Thernstrom 1980) points out that, among other characteristics, ethnic groups share both an internal and an external sense of distinctiveness. An excellent example of the operationalization of internal and external distinctiveness within a family occurred during my fieldwork in the Lao community. I observed a group of Southeast Asian teenage boys departing from a school bus. They were laughing, joking around, and making a bit of noise. Several of the boys wore baggy clothes and others had long streaked hair. One of the boys left the group and entered the first-floor apartment where I was attending a meeting of Lao elders. As soon as the boy entered the family's living room, he recognized immediately the importance of the gathering and his responsibility to show respect. The boy bowed deeply to the gathering of elders as he walked through the living room, while his long, orange-streaked hair fell over his face. This simple example illustrates the multilayered social construction of identity that is continuously being redefined by a group's members depending on the context from moment to moment. As Southeast Asians experience the continuing processes of ethnogenesis, their ethnic and family identities will be continually redefined. Over a period of years and decades, individual family members will be able to assume at different times several of the many possibilities for ethnic identification. Given the diverse locations and experiences of each family member as he or she moves through daily life, identity may be understood as a complex process of adjusting the balance between individual, family, and ethnic identities.

Individual and family identities in the West are based on the values of individualism, self-reliance, and equalitarianism. Individual identities in the East are subsumed under family and cultural identities in which familism and filial piety are the primary values. A tension between individual and group identities is inherent in the Southeast Asian migration to the West. In elder, parent, and adolescent interviews and discussion groups, younger members are pushing for an individually oriented family identity, while elders are seeking to retain the group-centered family identity they brought with them from home.

One useful way to think about family identity is presented in Whitbourne's (1986) model of adult identity processes. He posits that there is a tension between individual identity and the experience of that identity as family, coworkers, friends, and others evaluate it. These tensions are mediated and altered by the individual into a revised identity that accommodates the self-evaluation of others. In this model, the individual's identity is dynamic, as accommodations are made to positive or negative feedback from family and associates. In Southeast Asian families, each generation maintains or modifies its identity based on quite different social, cultural, and environmental influences, as elders stay at home, middle-aged adults go to work, and children go to school. The clash of multiple identities within families occurs when all three generations come together in the home or when the accommodations that the young and old generations are willing or able to make are insufficient to satisfy expectations.

Perceptions of Identity

Given the complex nature of social, ethnic, and family identity, the diversity of experiences within and between cultural groups, and the multitude of voices speaking in the life history interviews and the discussion groups, it seems useful to organize the discussion of identity into the several environmental domains suggested by Camino and Krulfeld (1994). We will discuss perceptions of identity from historical and place-oriented perspectives, including the different places where identity takes root (premigration identities); where individuals and families struggled to develop new identities (resettlement identities); and where identity will continue to emerge in future cohorts (future identities/diaspora). Individual identities will be organized around the perspectives of the three generations: elders, middle-aged parents, and adolescents. Finally, we will briefly discuss how the generations manage the tensions between their individual and group identities.

Premigration Identities

The human ecology theorists suggest that specific geographic places are important to the development of identity. Individuals and groups are physically embedded within a geographic nation-state, region, village, or neighborhood. The cultures of those places are where the roots of identity are formed. A home place is a space where the familiar tools of daily life are used and the sacred objects for special occasions are kept (Hoskins 1998). The home, neighborhood, and village are the primary arenas in which roles are played out over time through interactions with family and community members. Individuals are born into a place where a culture is already rooted, where a view of the world is embraced, and where socialization to the realities of life in that place begins at birth. A family does not so much create the cultural world they inhabit as they coconstruct a view of the world within an already established cultural framework. This worldview may be coherent, consistent, and shared, as might be expected within a small Hmong village in northern Laos, or it may be kaleidoscopic and diverse, as we might expect in a multigenerational family transplanted to St. Paul, Minnesota. A few examples from the life histories are illustrative.

Doan's life history is filled with the theme of "tradition severed" since his wife and daughters were left behind in Vietnam while he escaped to the United States with his sons. He is lonely and feels lost in his new place. He is both sad and proud when he remembers the importance of his family's identity in their home village: "When you come to my town, you don't need to know my address. You can ask somebody . . . and say you've come to see this family and they will bring you here because my father has a good name." Ton remembers a similar cohesiveness of family and friends in her homeland: "In Vietnam we were much closer to friends. We were very attached to each other. We felt like a family. My father was very social. We got along with friends and relatives. So did my mother. At certain times I was very depressed when I came here, I felt very lonely. So did my husband." In contrast to these close-knit Vietnamese family groups, Nu explains that she and her siblings had more of an individual orientation. As adults, "Siblings loved each other, but each had their own ideas and individual lives. They only got together for the holidays or to do ancestor worship."

Many of the elders, especially the men, reported that they frequently talk or think about the past in their home countries when they are with friends. The universal tendency to review life in old age is undoubtedly at work here, but also one can hear in many narratives the desire to return to the more familiar identity of the past in the land of the elders' birth. Lor often dreams about his Hmong village at night: "I have lived in Laos and I have lived in this land. We lived for five years in Thailand and nine years here. Everyday when I sleep, and when I dream, it is always like I live in the old country, old house, and place, eat the old types of food. I can see everything the same way as I was over there. Even those that are dead, I can still see." The nostalgic memories of the past are sometimes tinged with bitterness at the loss of homeland and identity. Mao spoke briefly about the loss of her home and life in the old country: "You are mad because you have no country to live in and you run away and leave a life you have behind for the Vietnamese. And you don't have a life anywhere else."

Like that of many of the female elders, Touch's current identity is directly linked to her role as a mother and grandmother and to the success of her off-spring through education and marriage in the United States. In the future, she hopes they will return to Cambodia, where the family identity they shared in the past can be restored. She explains in stark terms the transition from group to individual identities that seemed to occur as families moved from the camps to the United States: "At the refugee camp, the Cambodians were very loyal and loved each other, but here people changed. They worry more about themselves."

In the Lao parents discussion group there was a consensus that an important dimension of their premigration and resettlement identities was fulfilled by their role as parents. "Everything depends on us," said two Lao parents, with reference to the importance of daily conversations with children. Other Lao parents recognized the importance of accommodation to the prevailing culture; however, they also insisted that children learn and retain Lao ways and practices: "We can't force them to appreciate our culture. It's impossible. But, at least, we want them to behave in Lao ways, respect the adult, elderly, since we raise them. We want them to know Lao culture. If our children want to assimilate to a new culture, it is fine. They must know the high and the low."

Resettlement Identities

The dilemma of trying to maintain dual or bicultural identities within families recurs throughout the life history narratives. Bich created the bicultural metaphor, cited earlier, in which the world is divided into internal (Vietnamese) and external (American) realms. In these two worlds, the task for children is to negotiate and translate contradictory cultural messages simultaneously. Bich laments that the children who are considered "bad" inside the Vietnamese realm are frequently more successful in the outside American realm because they are more assimilated. Lan is one of the many elderly women whose identity is closely linked to her children; however, she feels internal conflict concerning her daughter's newly developing external identity since resettlement. On one hand, she recognizes that her daughter's future must include a strong element of biculturalism and acceptance of the new realities. On the other hand, she fears that the more Americanized her daughter becomes, the less likely she will be to care for her in the future.

One of the Vietnamese middle-aged parents explained that cultural dualism split his children and family into two groups: the two oldest, who were born in Vietnam and maintain the culture, and the youngest son, who shows little interest in his heritage.

> Comparing my three children: two born in Vietnam, one in the U.S. All three received same method of raising, same kind of discipline, same parents. Seems that my youngest son didn't have any influence from Vietnam culture. He doesn't have any desire to learn, to know anything about his root. Sometimes I wonder what I did wrong to make him uninterested in his original.

Ngo explains how the identity dilemma confronting resettled elders is related to their economic dependency in this country: "Before in Vietnam, we worked hard and we're able to build up a business, so when we became old we wouldn't have to worry about money matters. Now we've lost everything. The only wish I have is my son. I wish he will be successful in the future. We escaped Vietnam because of our son's future. Otherwise, we would have stayed in Vietnam." The loss of the economic provider role is translated into a family identity that is often focused on the future success of the children, the traditional model for first-generation immigrants. Thao shared a note of concern about her identity as a dependent in this country and her anger that her children have not assumed their traditional obligations: "If I was in Vietnam, I wouldn't be scared of going hungry, because I could do everything with both of my hands; but not in the U.S. I don't feel secure about myself due to my non-English background. I'm so sad that I raised my children until they grew up, but they don't take care of me back."

The impact of their dependency on others is a recurring issue in the life histories of elders. Nu explains that reliance on supplemental security income allows her to maintain a degree of independence from her son and daughter-in-law—quite a major shift in family identity for a mother and mother-in-law. She said:

> If the government keeps sending me enough money for my living expenses, I will really appreciate it because I want to be independent from my son. If I depend on my son, my daughter-in-law might not like it, and then it might break up their marriage. Thus, I don't want to break up their marriage. The life here is so different from Vietnam.

> In Vietnam, the children were supposed to take care of their old
> parent, but not in the U.S.

In this case, Nu has shifted her dependency in old age from her son and daughter-in-law to a U.S. government income support program.

All of the male Hmong elders grieved their loss of identity in the United States, caused, in part, by their dependency on government welfare programs, adult children, and grandchildren. To these proud men—who had been leaders of the family, parents, and economic providers—this loss was humiliating. Chong and Xi Chao discuss their premigration identities as self-sufficient farmers and their current dependency on welfare; their wives, who have jobs; and their children, who have to translate for them in public settings. Despite these dependencies, Chong retains some of his former identity as a spiritual healer in the Hmong tradition, since he believes that he was selected by god to serve his community in this way. Xao retains his highly respected identity as a soldier and remembers proudly his role in defending the home village. But now he feels useless, frustrated by his lack of English skills, unhappy because he does not have enough money and is unable to drive an automobile. In all cases, the Hmong elderly men lament the loss of previous identities rather than discussing new identities that are emerging in this country.

The Hmong women's identity after resettlement, like those of many of the older women from the other Southeast Asian cultural groups, is closely linked to their children's future success in this country rather than a previous identity from home. Mao, a widowed woman, explained how her identity is linked to the success of her children: "When you have your own children you are happy because you tie your life on your children. You are happy although you don't have your husband. You are happy to live because your children are good students and they are successful." In this case and many others like it, there is more continuity in women's resettled family identity than in that of the men.

One of the middle-aged fathers in the Cambodian discussion group explained how difficult it was for some parents to bridge two identities; however, he offered a bicultural solution that blends cultures inside and outside the home. "Cambodian culture is different from American culture. Parents think that if their children act different from the Cambodian culture, you are bad. It doesn't mean that way. To us, children are good when they're at home they must behave and speak according to the Cambodian culture. But not 100 percent Cambodian culture, maybe 70 percent. When they are at school, they can behave and speak according to American culture 100 percent."

One of the Hmong parents in the focus group talked about the confusion experienced when contrasting how American and Hmong families identify themselves. For the Hmong, the role of parent is a lifelong responsibility:

> I want to criticize American people. When children turn eighteen years old, parents want them to move out and be independent. I see that parents don't care about their children after they are eighteen years old. But Hmong parents help their children forever as long as they need help. Hmong parents always consider their married children as child and family members. We don't live in the same house but we support our children financially and spiritually. We cannot adopt American ways. A lot of American children don't even care to visit their parents.

In the Hmong youth focus group an exchange between two adolescent participants explained how the mutually constructed family identity gets developed after resettlement:

> Participant 2: "I mean the son or daughter get a good reputation and then the parents are happy that the world does see them that they have a good son/daughter in their family."
> Participant 3: "And parents get a good name and so does the teenager. And parents get a good name for having a good daughter/son."

One of the Hmong youth explained how difficult it is to actually be a good son or daughter given the dual identities of both parents and youth: "[S]ee the parents wanted to follow the Hmong tradition and because kids live in the U.S. they feel more comfortable following the American way, like hang around with friends and do more things with friends, and the parents don't like and they just want us to stay home all the time, and it feels like we don't get the freedom to do anything."

Future Identities

Although the future is difficult to predict, there is evidence that new bicultural identities are developing for individuals and families. We mentioned earlier the new hybrid identities that are emerging among some younger Asian Americans. Many of the elders were happy that their families were safe in the United States, encouraged by the new opportunities for education, and resigned to the changes in family identity. Neou expressed an unusual degree of happiness for a Cambodian male at his life in the United States: "It's good enough to trust my life on. Until now, I have not worried about anything. It is happy every day." His happiness may be the result of his own diminished needs and an acceptance of the new realities. Speaking about his life now and in the future, Neou said: "Today I am old and don't want to strive for riches anymore. All my stomach is full. The children are the way they are."

There is evidence in the discussion groups that Southeast Asian youth are now creating successful future identities by blending materials from two or more cultures. The "model minority" stereotype is a problematic identity for them since it generalizes far beyond the realities of many Asian American youth; however, the existence of the stereotype also reveals how parents' high expectations have paid off in school achievement for some adolescents. Parents and elders see education as the key to a successful future and many of the adolescents in the focus groups embraced its importance as well. The Vietnamese youth discussed how some parents motivated them to succeed. One youth explained that his parents' words and examples motivated him to move beyond the identity of victimized refugee: "[My] eyes witnessing the parents who have to work so hard and bring home very little, some of them are words like, 'It is your choice'; 'It is you who will create your future'; 'We don't want to see you like us now'; 'There will be no fortune to leave behind when we [parents] leave this world'; 'It is up to you how you want your future will be.'" Another Vietnamese adolescent revealed the bicultural dilemma that confronts parents as their children develop identities that will sustain them in the future. In a lengthy discussion of what makes a good parent, one youth said in frustration: "This is America, we are no longer in Vietnam. Some of the things may not apply here! Why can't they just take the best of two cultures and apply it to our life here in the best way that they can?"

Generational Identities

Elders

For many of the male elders, their individual and family identities are rooted in the premigration past, in a home, village, and culture far from the place where they currently live. For the most part they have not adopted a new or revised ethnic cultural identity in the United States. Instead they see themselves as culturally Vietnamese, Cambodian, Lao, or Hmong men and they are unwilling to make accommodations to the new realities for themselves. To keep the past alive, the old men talk about the past with friends; they try to teach family and cultural history to their children and grandchildren; and they dream about what life used to be like when they are asleep. Bounsou speaks for many other men when he says that he thinks about the past "every day." Some are willing to accommodate the new realities for their children and grandchildren and they acknowledge the need for the younger generations to become more bicultural; however, all of them insist on retention of the important elements of the traditional culture in the new context.

A few examples from the elders' life histories offer a glimpse into the complexity involved in identity issues for the oldest generation. Xi Chao reports that he has lost his former identity as a farmer, worker, and provider for his family. His sense of value is diminished because his practical education in the mountainous fields of northern Laos is not marketable in the capital-intensive fields of U.S. agriculture. Sith laments the differences among members of his Cambodian family about how to define the emerging identity; several of his narratives concern behaviors that are identified as "too" American or "too" traditional for one generation or the other. Sith, Nguyen, and Cheam speak about their loss of identity within families during the migration and resettlement processes and their unsuccessful search for new identities in the United States.

Older Southeast Asian males experience a loss of identity and self-esteem when they are unable to maintain their traditional role as provider and household head (Rottman and Meredith 1982). At the same time that males occupy fewer roles and their status is diminished, the expansion of women's roles may lead to conflict within the marriage (Rottman and Meredith 1982; Detzner 1992). The employment of women outside the home was one of the causes of husband-wife conflict in a study of a Vietnamese family in Chicago (Prendergast 1985). Kulig (1991) suggests that since resettlement, the roles and status of Cambodian women have changed so extensively that men are feeling a loss of the "old order." These losses are best understood in the context of the hierarchical family structure and patriarchal values of the old country. The loss of land, home, and possessions experienced by many men is followed by loss of control of the family, diminished authority, and a loss of identity (Bishop 1985; Hayes 1984, 1987; Yeung 1988). The diminishing of male elders' power and high-status identity has an impact on other family members as roles, rules, and values are renegotiated.

The female elders' identities are also linked to the past; however, they retain continuity in their present-day mother and grandmother roles with their adult children and grandchildren. Many of their previous responsibilities as nurturer, child care provider, housekeeper, and cook are intact in the new context, and even though new roles have been assumed, the women are able to retain important elements of their individual and family identities compared to the men in the oldest generation. Many of the older women are happy here because of the increased safety of their families, the educational opportunities for the children, and the enhanced position of women in the family and community. But the happiness is always tinged with sadness due to memories of their lost country, home, way of life, and family members. Some elderly men and women, especially those without children and those who live alone, feel isolated, depressed, and useless in the United States and have completely lost their sense of identity as important contributors to the family.

Parents

Compared to elders, the middle-generation parents have significantly more long-term responsibilities for children and a greater investment in their success, since the younger generations are the caregivers of their future. The parents who participated in the discussion groups had at least one adolescent child living at home and many had large multigenerational family households. The parenting role continued to be central to their individual and family identities; however, what they perceived as their helplessness and inadequacy in this role exasperated them. The frustration of parents with adolescents was confirmed by a parallel frustration of adolescents with their parents. Often adolescents' frustrations revolved around ethnic identity and how traditional or modern they were forced or allowed to be inside and outside the home. Within this conflicted context, it was difficult for parents or adolescents to develop a positive self-concept or a cohesive family identity.

In the Hmong parent group, one participant contrasted a successful parent identity in Laos with the conflicted identity many Hmong parents have in the United States:

> Hmong people lived in the mountains and had no teaching skills but God blessed us. We always loved our children. We growled [at] them, spanked them, but, in Laos, there were no children who died from it. . . . We had disputes and conflict but our children and wives respected us. Our words were meaningful. Hmong people are skillful. In Laos, parents only told children to study, parents couldn't help them, but they succeed. Here, we adjust, we learn more ideas, we help our children, and it seems like they fail. Maybe we are losing our values, our cultures.

One of the Cambodian parents recalled how much easier it had been to parent at home because of the supportive surrounding community with common cultural values: "In Cambodia, physical discipline is okay. The whole community and neighborhood helped discipline children. If parents hit the child and if the child runs away, the neighbor or community will not accept the child. Rather, the community or neighbor will support the parents." In an effort to improve parent-child relationships and because they found it necessary to adapt, many parents were developing bicultural ethnic identities. However reluctantly, most parents recognized that if they were to understand their children and successfully manage in this culture they needed to blend their native and adopted cultures. To accomplish this transition they confronted every day the tensions between their own changing individual identity, their perception of an appropriate family identity, and the emerging bicultural identities of their children at different stages of development.

Several of the participants in the Cambodian adolescent group had a highly critical view of their parents' ability to make these adaptations. They believed that parents want their children to be afraid of them. Some showed that they were unafraid by talking back to their parents and by not listening to what they perceived as an endless series of lectures. Others disobeyed by skipping school or staying out late. One Cambodian youth had a contrasting view of the overprotective and overbearing parents described by most of his peers: "Sometimes nobody takes care of you."

There was agreement among the youth that a "good parent" fulfilled his or her responsibilities by providing a safe home environment, preparing food, and listening to what his or her children had to say. One adolescent suggested how confusing and conflictual the bicultural learning process could be for parents and children alike: "I grew up with my mom only. My father wasn't around so she was like trying to tell what was right and wrong and plus she's, what do you call them, Buddhas, you know. So she is trying to show me the Buddha culture and how to do things their way. But I also do it with Americans so I'm Christian so that, you know, we argue a lot."

Adolescents

According to the classic studies by Erik Erickson and associates (1980, 1982), identity formation is a primary task of the adolescent stage of development, although development occurs at each stage in the life course. Identity formation involves the linking of the past, present, and future selves into a coherent narrative that has continuity. Adopting Erikson's (1950) developmental task concept, Tobin and Friedman (1984) emphasize that the critical issues facing adolescents are of trust versus mistrust, and autonomy versus shame and guilt. They write: "The refugee adolescent's experience is one of discontinuity not so much because he comes to America from another culture as because the culture he comes from may seem to him failed, archaic, and irrelevant. . . . [T]he greatest threat to identity in refugee adolescents thus is not the feeling of belonging to two cultures but the feeling of belonging to none." Adolescents from refugee families are undergoing all the normal physical and psychological developmental changes of early adulthood while also managing interior and exterior identity issues within their families. This is why the transition from childhood to adulthood for these uniquely situated youth has been called a "tumultuous transition" (Tobin and Friedman 1984). According to Spencer and Markstrom-Adams (1990):

> Several factors thus complicate the task of identity formation among minority youth. The value conflicts that exist between cultures, the lack of identity-achieved role models, and the lack of culture-focused specific guidance from the family represent ongoing issues. The preponderance of negative stereotypes about minorities in general is also counterproductive to acquiring a solid sense of the self." (303)

Not all the research indicates a direct and linear identification of youth with the host culture. In a large-scale study of teenage youth from seventy-seven nationalities called the Children of Immigrants Longitudinal Study (CILS), Ruben Rumbaut (1999) found that Southeast Asian youth decreased their identification with the "American" category during the three-year interval between the first and second interviews. Contrary to expectations, the teens increased their identification with their national origin category. Despite the fact that more than 70 percent of the informants had experienced some type of discrimination, more than two-thirds of them continued to believe that the United States is the best country in which to live.

Some adolescents and young adults are able to create new identities not directly linked to their current situation or their historical past. As a result, our understanding of complexity in defining family identity is

> further complicated by the emergence of new cosmopolitan and hybridized cultures within the Indochinese diasporas, members of which by necessity find themselves simultaneously negotiating with the triangle of past (homeland), present (country of settlement) and future (diaspora). The new identity to emerge among the Indochinese is most likely one of hybridism, diversity, difference—of multiplicity, not simple duality any more." (Chan and Ong 1995, 87)

In summarizing his simple contrasting view of parent and adolescent identities in the United States, one Cambodian youth said: "They are Khmer and we are Americans."

According to Goldstein (1986): "Girls who accepted the responsibility for ethnic identity maintenance through a commitment to the domestic sphere and child-rearing, saw themselves as choosing their families instead of school. Girls who dropped out of school for domestic reasons received community support for moving into a valued gender role. By strengthening the community through physical and cultural reproduction, they acquire a familiar and respected identity." School exposes Hmong girls to alternative gender roles outside the domestic sphere. As a result, Goldstein contends, Hmong girls will continue to redefine their inherited understandings of gender, and these identity issues will continue to be a presence in their families.

As they struggle with their own mixed bicultural identities and the mixed identities of their siblings and peers, adolescents wish that their parents understood them better so that their parents could be more helpful. One of the Lao youth summarized what kids want from their parents. "What we have learned from each other today, [is that] we all want [parents] to understand us. We want them to be approachable. We want them to be able to do that without fear, scared that they will yell at us, be more understanding." Later the same youth argued for the importance of the two generations' trying to understand each other's mixed identity: "Understanding goes two ways. We have to learn to understand our parents and our parents have to learn to understand us."

In their discussion about how they would define a "good" teenager, the Vietnamese youth had a lot to say about the bicultural identities that they are developing. There is evidence of both cultures in their statements; however, a surprisingly strong element of traditional, family-oriented values appears throughout this discussion of what a model teenager would be like:

> Good teenager should always be honest to themselves and to their parents.
>
> Good teenagers should be respectful to their elders, to their parents, and to themselves. Teenager should understand how much their parents had to sacrifice for [them].
>
> Good teenagers should obey their parent's wishes and not argue with their parent side by side.
>
> Good teenagers should have the same values and beliefs as their parent did. . . .
>
> [G]ood teenagers should not be selfish, only live for themselves. They should be responsible for their own action.
>
> Good teenagers should know what they going to be when they grow up.
>
> Good teenagers should be a good role model for their younger brother and sister.

> Good teenagers should put their education as one of the first priority. Good teenagers should be responsible, not only to the family but the community as well.

Although it would be difficult for any Southeast Asian adolescent to live up to all these expectations, the list indicates that Vietnamese youth identify more closely with their parents' values than we might have expected, given the complaints of elders and parents about the younger generation and the younger generation's criticism of parents and elders.

Reconstructing and Managing Family Identities

In the Lao parent group, the discussion of parenting responsibilities elicited a lively discussion with many points of view that highlighted perspectives of family identity. Parents suggested that to rear their children well they had to provide food for them and teach them knowledge and skills useful in life. Most middle-aged parents advocated an active parenting approach, one element of which is paying close attention to a child's performance in school by monitoring homework and meeting with teachers when performance is not good. They believed that parents should act as role models for children by not drinking, smoking, or gambling in front of their children. There should be firm rules that parents maintain consistently, with one parent serving as the refuge to the child when the other is disciplining. The Hmong parents emphasized awareness of activities going on outside the home and the close monitoring of school performance as important parent responsibilities. Although there was widespread agreement about these responsibilities and the importance of active parenting, not all the parents were able to live up to these high expectations.

The Cambodian parents contributed to the dialogue about the reconstructed identity of parents in the new context. One father said:

> I think good parents or bad parents depend on their responsibilities for their children. What is the degree of their responsibilities? Some parents have very little responsibility for their children. For example, [they might say,] "I gave birth to you, I have done a lot of good for you. I'm your mother or father." They don't have a lot of responsibilities in giving advice, discipline, guide, support, and everything else. The parents go out somewhere, their children left alone. This means that parents are bad.

A mother in the group quickly followed up with her definition of what a good parent does: "For good parents, some families work or stay at home. They guide, advise, and discipline in a variety of ways. It depends on children whether they listen to their parents or not. If the children stay in school, get good education and the parents are good parents." In other words, judgment about whether or not one is successful in parenting awaits the full development of the child into an adult. Only when the outcomes are clear will mothers and fathers believe that they are validated as good parents, in their own minds and by the larger community in which the family's identity is partially defined.

A Hmong parent contrasted her perception of good and bad parents: "Bad parents don't know how to discipline children. They just growl and yell all the time. They don't communicate with their children. This makes children run away from home. Good parents always explain and give reason to their kids why they have to change. They communicate nicely with their kids and praise them." Another Hmong parent offered examples of a bad parent: "One who yells, one who has no communications or family meetings, or one who has no fun with his family." Still another parent defined good and bad parenting in terms of the cleanliness, order, and rules of the household. Good parents are well organized and bad parents are not.

As parents and elders redefine what it means to successfully fulfill their most important responsibilities, they are redefining individual and family identity in the new context. When parents' perceptions of a good parent are compared to adolescents' perceptions, there is remarkable similarity. However, the gap between parents own high expectations for themselves and the reality of their daily lives means that the family's identity is unsettled. As parents seek to balance individual, family, and ethnic identities still in formation they are often walking on a tightrope (Kibria 1993). The balance between perceptions and realities must be managed every day as the family seeks equilibrium in an unstable situation.

It appears that identities must be managed both inside and outside the family home. Adolescents have to be well behaved, respectful, and family oriented when at home, and when away from the parent's gaze, they can be whatever they want to be. Parents and elders have to be willing to listen to children's problems as they struggle in the new culture and to offer gentle guidance and an empathetic ear. Elders have to be cautious not to negatively compare everything in the new culture to the traditional practices in their native lands.

On the outside, family identity must be carefully managed so that its reputation is preserved and enhanced. The success of the children has a lot to do with the identity of the family in the new culture. Successful families with "good" parents have good children who bring honor and accomplishment to the family name. "Bad" parents are having difficulty managing in the new environment for one of many reasons discussed in earlier chapters. Their shame and anger is reflected in this comment by one of the Cambodian parents:

> The most difficult part is the children who were born here. Why? I see children grew up in this country use American culture. They go to school and spend time with parents. They see what the teacher teaches them about the American culture and system. Parents at home only know Cambodian. When we try to advise and discipline them in Cambodian it is very difficult. Children who were born in Cambodia know some about Cambodian culture, traditions, and what are Cambodian. So when we speak advice and try to help them in Cambodian, they listen to us. But the children who were born here don't listen to parents. But Americans say what about their children who were born here also, why don't they have much difficulty with their children? Because it's their culture, their country, they don't have any problems.

Of course, American parents do have many problems parenting their adolescent children as well; however, Southeast Asian parents perceive the system as stacked against them and their ways of defining the family. Because these transitions and changes take many years and several generations to integrate into families, we can anticipate multiple family identities and continuing instability in the family's sense of identity in this environment well into the future.

Critical Perspectives: Elders, Families, and Immigration **8**

Introduction

THE MULTIPLICITY OF IDENTITIES within multigenerational Southeast Asian families is due in part to the stressful nature of forced relocation and what has happened to them before, during, and after resettlement. Elders have documented these difficulties and their success in overcoming them in stories of loss, separation, conflict, and resilience. We have seen the change in family structures as older men lose and women gain power. The clash of Western and Eastern values causes divergence in family cultures that were previously coherent. Disharmony created by loss, change, and divergence promotes conflict between genders and generations and a restructuring of identities.

In the larger context of contemporary worldwide migration and the historic immigration that populated the United States, it may appear that elderly Southeast Asian refugees and their families are a small subgroup of little importance. The quiet voices we have heard throughout this volume speak loudly to many of the broader historical and international forces that affect families and communities. These forty elders embody two of the most important demographic trends of the new century converging at the intersection between the aging of the population and its increasing diversification.

The absolute number and percentage of the older population will steadily increase during the next several decades until it reaches something near 25 percent at midcentury. Led by the retirement of the postwar boom generation, the rapid growth of the population aged eighty-five and older, and decreased fertility, the United States will become one of the two or three oldest nations on earth by the middle of the century. The aging of America's population in the twenty-first century is the background for contemporary policy debates on social security and Medicare reform, long-term care, and prescription drug policies.

The second demographic trend is the growing diversity of the nation's population caused by the dramatically increased immigration from Asia, Africa, and Latin America since 1965 and the relatively high birthrates in nonwhite groups. Already major urban areas such as Miami, Los Angeles, and New York are composed of nonwhite ethnic populations that are now in the majority. California recently became the first state in the country in which non-Caucasian ethnic groups compose more than half the population. Although the flow of immigration may stand still or decrease temporarily as a consequence of the xenophobia created by the 9/11 terrorist attacks, the powerful historical trend toward increasing diversity of the population cannot be reversed.

However distinct these two demographic trends appear to be, they are linked in several important ways. The relatively low fertility rates in most population groups across the United States are generating serious policy discussions about the declining number of young workers who will be available to pay social security taxes and medical insurance costs in support of an increasingly older nation. A rapidly increasing dependency ratio (the number of retirees compared to the number of employed workers) will become the source of increasingly burdensome federal taxes for the young and intergenerational stress for mainstream elders. Without a substantial growth in overall fertility rates, a steady stream of new immigrants, or both, the population base is likely to remain stable or decrease slightly in the twenty-first century, while many more people will live into their eighties and nineties. Some economists and social analysts project pessimistic future scenarios with higher taxes, lower productivity, and long-term economic decline, while some social gerontologists predict diminished human resources, increasing family burden, and a decline in the well-being of elders if these converging trends are not addressed creatively.

Three examples in two neighboring upper-Midwest states reveal several issues and opportunities that arise at the intersections of aging and diversity. Iowa has designed outreach policies to recruit new immigrants into the state to remedy the problems caused by decades of youth out-migration, the aging of the population, and too few workers to promote economic growth. While some of the larger immigrant-receiving states, like California, New York, Texas, and Illinois, consider ways to limit the number and impact of new immigrants, Iowa is seeking to increase the number of employable new immigrants who settle there as a strategy for growth and sustainable development.

A second example occurs just to the north in rural southern Minnesota, where immigrants from Southeast Asia, Latin America, and Africa have helped to revive the economies of several small towns that were on the verge of losing their schools, main street businesses, and vitality (Amato 1996). The third example can be found in almost every extended-care nursing home or facility across the Twin Cities and other cities with large immigrant populations. The homes employ a large number of nurse's aides from Africa, Asia, and Latin America in minimum wage positions that typically have a high turnover rate and no benefits. These new immigrants provide hands-on care to frail elders who often come from immigrant families themselves.

These three examples reflect the historic contributions that immigrants make to the nation and host community by taking low-paying service work others do not want, by spending money in the local economy, and by paying taxes. They shop in the markets, clean houses, send their kids to local schools, and eventually they become police officers, business owners, and state legislators. The low-wage, no-benefit jobs of immigrants working in Minnesota's (and other states') agricultural fields, canning factories, and poultry-/meat-processing industries are one of the most important reasons that food prices in the United States are modest despite the high levels of processing. Immigrants serve the social and economic interests of the global economy and the mainstream host community while they are working to improve the lives of their own children and extended families. Despite immigrants' historic contributions to the nation, the members of each generation of new immigrants are somehow seen as interlopers and scabs seeking to dilute American identity.

Perhaps the most recent wave of anti-immigrant attitudes and policies is a consequence of U.S. policy reform in 1965 that promoted a very different type of immigrant in the United States. Asians, African, and Latinos now compose the largest groups of newcomers to the country and to upper-Midwestern states like Minnesota and Wisconsin. The diversity of these new groups and widespread unfamiliarity with their cultural traditions and family systems is a major challenge facing the nation, the states, and individual communities. Scholars, policy makers, and service providers cannot ignore these newcomers because of their complexity or treat them as monolithic groups following a linear path toward inevitable assimilation. It is time to move beyond simplistic theories emanating from narrow subdisciplinary perspectives toward broader interdisciplinary frameworks that acknowledge that individual immigrants are embedded within complex multigenerational family systems with a history and culture that does not melt away. The goal should not be necessarily to discard bad theories but rather to reconstruct good theories and to combine theories that are inadequate by themselves. We need new multifocal lenses through which to view these individuals and groups after their arrival and a broader perspective to understand the forces that propel them from their homelands.

The Importance of Multidisciplinary Theories

The absence of broad theoretical frameworks that span gerontology, family, and ethnicity research severely limits our understanding of the complexities of immigration. The macro- and microtheories used in this volume reveal elements of the complexity we have observed in individuals, families, ethnic groups, and communities over time, but we need more comprehensive theories that integrate time, place, culture, and generations. Symbolic interaction and life course theories urge us to look developmentally across time as individuals interact with others and change over time. Keeping these theories in mind helps us to understand that being a refugee is not a static one-time experience but rather multiple experiences that evolve and change as an individual develops and interacts with others. Neither of these theories by itself can explain the intergenerational dynamics occurring within families who are forced to migrate since youth, middle-aged, and older refugees all have their own developmental tasks and challenges according to their age and stage of life. As important and broad as these theories are, they cannot encompass the diverse changes that occur in ethnic groups as they evolve and influence individuals and families.

Beyond the absence of broad integrative theories and perhaps because of it, there is limited gerontology and family research on new immigrant populations and little research on families by immigration scholars because of the difficulties conducting these investigations. According to Luborsky and Rubinstein (1990): "The compelling need for cross-cultural research about aging poses extraordinary methodological challenges" (246). Social gerontologists have paid more attention to the increasing diversity of the older population in recent years; however, it is difficult to find research on the unique circumstances of refugee elders and families. Rumbaut (2000) analyzed the focus of research conducted by scholars of immigration and discovered that less than 7 percent of recent immigration research concerns generational issues, with only 4.5 percent of published articles on the children of immigrants and 2.4 percent on families, households, or marriages.

Family scientists have become more interested in diverse families in recent years; however, those interests typically extend to the somewhat easier to study, larger, and more established African American and Hispanic populations, while little attention is paid to recent immigrants and refugees from Africa or Asia. Researchers who seek understanding across the many disciplines, domains, and methodological stumbling blocks of cross-cultural comparative research are confronted by the overlapping historical, psychological, and sociocultural issues of this type of investigation. Language issues pose great difficulties for scholars and service providers who seek to communicate meanings across translated idioms. These limitations and the privileged position of nonethnic researchers are significant barriers that make this type of work time-consuming and difficult. Although there is agreement that naturalistic research within community contexts is needed, developing trust in ethnic communities wary of outsiders is an important hurdle that research grantors and results-driven scholars are seldom willing to leap over.

Naturalistic research methods and interactionist approaches to studying elders and immigrant families often assume that researchers begin their inquiry without preconceived notions about what will be discovered. This openness to understanding the words and constructed meanings of informants is important; however, it does not mean that the research should be conducted outside the realm of theory. Indeed, the absence of theoretical considerations is consistently criticized in social science research as a significant shortcoming of many investigations. Theories and concepts from several disciplines are needed to inform cross-cultural research and serve as a contextual guide to frame the inquiry and interpret the results. Macroscopic theories such as modernization and human ecosystems have been helpful in framing this work within the larger global processes that swirl around and influence individual elders. Also important but lesser in scale are theories of ethnic group formation (ethnogenesis) and individual aging (continuity). Symbolic interaction and life course theories pervade the entire study and are discussed more fully in the appendix. The macro-micro and time and place orientations of all these theories offer multiple lenses through which the experiences of Southeast Asian elders and their families may be viewed. Although it is unlikely that our informants would use academic theories to explain their lives, such theories are helpful to scholars, policy makers, service providers, and informed readers who seek to place these experiences in a larger context. The four theories most useful to this inquiry are briefly discussed below, since each offers a framework for understanding—and a critical perspective that sheds light on—the elders, the families, and immigration.

Modernization Theory

Modernization is a macroscopic-level theory used by sociologists, international development specialists, and others to explain large-scale processes at work as a social system moves gradually from traditional tools, extended family structures, and small-scale undifferentiated systems to more advanced technologies, nuclear families, and highly specialized social-economic systems. Social gerontologists use modernization theory to explain the loss of power and status of elders within families and communities as social systems become increasingly differentiated and economic processes modernized. Donald Cowgill (1986) and others believe that there is an inevitable decline in the status of elders within families and society as modern systems are adopted. When traditional values and practices are replaced by modern thinking, nuclear families do not have the same honorific place for elders as the extended family systems. Modernization theory locates this study within the broad contexts of global time and place, because most of the elderly informants and their families moved from technologically undeveloped villages and primitive refugee camps to a modern urban setting in a technologically advanced state, sometimes within a matter of days or weeks. The processes of modernization are likely to be more difficult for individuals and families when they occur not over a period of decades or centuries but quickly, without time for preparation and gradual adaptation. Elders believe that they have lost a place of high status in the modern setting and their stories reveal this and other consequences of accelerated modernization.

The movement of more than one million persons from less-developed countries such as Cambodia, Vietnam, and Laos to a highly developed, technologically advanced country such as the United States is a case study of the impact of rapid modernization on families. Although it took months for some, and years for many to make their way to the opposite side of the globe, the length of the journey in kilometers is an inadequate measure of the psychological distance and historical time that was traveled. The dramatic differences between Hmong farming life on the mountainsides of northern Laos and everyday life in St. Paul's Frogtown neighborhood cannot be overestimated or easily measured with standardized instruments.

A critical perspective of modernization places the elders and their families within the broader global development processes that created the situation that forced them from their homes in the first place. This is not the place for another rehashing of the tragic U.S. involvement in the affairs of Vietnam, Cambodia, and Laos after the 1954 French defeat at Dien Bien Phu; however, the urge toward colonial domination by modernized developed countries is at the root of both the French and American involvement that led to the forced migration of the elders and families in our study. The political-economic individualist ideology of capitalism was pitted against the communal authoritarian ideology of communism in a futile effort at "containment" by a powerful Western nation. Fearful that the "fall" of Vietnam would create a domino effect throughout the region, the arrogance of American power (Fulbright 1966) instead created a domino that toppled Lyndon Johnson's presidency and the Great Society. From this perspective, it is important that the critics of immigration note that it was not the refugees who first crossed American borders seeking economic or ideological modernization but rather the colonizers who first crossed Southeast Asian borders seeking political hegemony over less-developed countries.

Human Ecology Theory

Many elders and their families were forced to cross several borders in their quest for a safe asylum, each time trying to adapt to new and uncertain environments. Human ecology theorists believe that all humans live within a natural interdependent environment that is both influenced by and influences all other organisms. Humans thrive in natural environments with adequate resources, an extended support network, and a social-cultural milieu that is regenerative. In an ecology that is unsafe, where social and human resources are depleted by war, and support networks are scattered, individual and family energy is focused on survival of the organism.

The entire interdependent ecosystem of every elderly refugee was changed radically during and after the flight to safety. Forced to relocate away from the family's home, village, farmlands, supportive social network, and familiar cultural frameworks, the forty elders in this study are coping with significant changes in their family, near environment, social life, and cultural traditions while simultaneously grieving a lost world and way of life. A human ecosystem perspective encourages researchers, policy makers, and service providers to focus our lens on interactions at the individual, family, and social/cultural levels as we try to understand the impact of war, escape, camp life, and relocation to the United States.

An ecological perspective emphasizes the interactions of humans within a series of concentric environments. Individuals are located in the center, surrounded by family, home, near environment, community, socioeconomic political institutions, and culture (Bronfenbrenner 1979; Bubolz and Sontag 1992). It is necessary to study people within their natural environments to truly understand their lives (Bubolz and Sontag 1992). Ray (1988) argues that individual and family ecologies must be included when constructing a study and analyzing results. By interviewing elders in their apartments and homes, we were able to observe directly the sights, sound, smells, and artifacts of their current homes and near environments. We walked in their neighborhoods, felt the frightening stare reserved for outsiders in someone else's territory, and experienced the friendly welcome of an elderly storyteller. In addition to our observing firsthand where the elders now live, interview questions asked elders to describe the place where they lived as a child and adult, the physical arrangement of the camps, and their first impressions upon arrival in the United States. Their responses helped us to locate them within their previous and current environments and to understand the physical and psychological distance they traveled to find themselves in Minnesota.

One can hardly imagine a more dramatic natural environmental change than the abrupt transition from the subtropical flora and steamy heat of Vietnam, Laos, Cambodia, and Thailand to the leafless trees and cold arctic air of a Minnesota winter. Beyond the often-frightening natural environment that surrounded the newcomers are the individual and family adjustments required to negotiate life in the new environment. The current family life of our informants was fragmented; traditional gender and generational roles were altered; and overwhelming feelings of loss and loneliness became part of everyday life in the new context. Isolation of elders was rampant in the low-income neighborhoods and public housing projects where many Southeast Asians lived after arrival, because they were often high-crime areas with a growing presence of gangster activities. The ethnic community was a significant source of social capital and an important source of cultural and psychological stability; however, the communities and families we studied were sometimes divided by internal conflicts and filled with persons at different stages of adjustment and ethnic identification. Individuals with no conception of themselves as part of a racial or ethnic minority found themselves surrounded by a mainstream community that was often ignorant of their culture, often mystified about what they were doing here, and sometimes hostile or discriminating. Although impatient at the rate of the immigrants' language adaptation and economic independence, the mainstream community also included groups and individuals, educators and service providers who were welcoming and helpful. These confusing and contradictory messages from different segments of the host society often intersected in the household, where family roles, cultural values, and several generations lived within emerging ethnic communities. To study refugees and immigrant individuals and families as if their changed context made no difference is to wrench them once again from their natural environments and to treat them as laboratory subjects rather than expert informants.

Ethnogenesis Theory

People from Asian countries are offended when they are taken out of their contexts and lumped together as if they were a monolithic Oriental group. With Asia's large percentage of the world's population, dozens of nation-states, and hundreds of ethnic groups, heterogeneity is the dominant reality. Despite this reality, the United States Census Bureau did not begin to differentiate between Asian cultural groups until the 1990 census, when it discontinued grouping millions of Asian Americans into one huge "Asian-Pacific Islander" category. Within the four Southeast Asian groups we are studying, there are multiple regional, linguistic, and historical differences. In the Hmong group alone there are green, red, striped, and blue subgroups based on the colors of the clothing worn in different regions of northern Laos. In the Twin Cities metropolitan area there are fourteen major Hmong clan groups and eight smaller clans. We interviewed one highly educated elderly Chinese Vietnamese man who was fluent in the Vietnamese, French, Chinese, and English languages and many other immigrants who could not read or write in their native language. Urban-dwelling Vietnamese elders with education and exposure to Western people are vastly different socially, economically, and culturally from their counterparts who escaped from villages nestled in rural rice fields or mountainside farms. Given the many between- and within-group differences, it is not surprising that there has been so little research on immigrant families in the United States.

Ethnogenesis is the slow course of ethnic identification that new immigrant groups appear to travel as the host and immigrant cultures have repeated contact with each other (Greeley 1974; Hildreth and Sugawara 1993). The theory describes the stages of change that occur as the new group establishes a hyphenated "Asian-American" identity different from that of the recent arrivals and far different from their identity at home. The theory is important because it reminds us of the slow process of adaptation that occurs as the host and the immigrant cultures begin to understand and adapt to each other. It points out the dynamic changes occurring within groups and the complexities within families as each individual and generation is situated at a different stage of adaptation and identity formation. This is where the real complexity within these four cultural groups is revealed and why generalizations about the groups as a whole are fraught with difficulty.

Ethnogenesis helps us to understand and be alert to the significant differentiation in individuals and families caused by time of arrival, gender, and generation. Youth, parents, and elders inhabit very different worlds during the daytime, while living in the same household during the evenings. However difficult it might be for adolescents to live in one culture within their household and another outside their home, this type of bifurcated existence is not unusual. The life histories and the discussion groups reveal these overlapping worlds within Southeast Asian families. Acknowledgment of the complexity and importance of ethnic group identity is an important theme of this study and a lesson to be learned by those who conduct research, create policies and programs, and seek to assist new immigrant populations.

Continuity Theory

Although the daily lives of elderly immigrants are filled with complexity and change, these elders seek ways to mitigate the remarkable transformation of their lives. Social gerontologists have identified a powerful tendency for the elderly to seek stability, order, and predictability in their later years. According to Robert Atchley (1989) and others, elders seek to maintain equilibrium by trying to maintain as much continuity as possible. Both internal (physical well-being) and external (social network and environmental place) states of continuity are important and interdependent (Atchley 1989). Continuity provides normalcy, routine, safety, context, and direction during the normative transitions and nonnormative losses of a long life.

It seems intuitive to suggest that elders (and other adults) whose lives were completely disrupted by forced migration would seek to establish some degree of family continuity as a natural shield against multiple adjustment pressures. In analyzing the life histories, efforts to maintain continuity amidst overwhelming change are frequently noted; the urge to maintain consistent environments appears to be a natural consequence of both aging and forced migration. Efforts by elders to maintain continuity and overcome discontinuities are more clearly understood in the light of this theoretical lens and should be the focus of program developers who seek to assist elders with the transition. Policies and programs that promote rapid assimilation for elders and other members of their extended households ignore the psychological need for stability. Efforts are needed to maintain some degree of sameness in families even as efforts to help them adjust to the many changes in the new context go forward. Policies, programs, and educational efforts to maintain native language and bicultural competence in children will be beneficial to them in the long run and assist elders through the discontinuity of their new lives.

Elders Are a Resource in Immigrant Families

Although elders' need for continuity may create conflict in immigrant families as the young and middle generations adapt to the multilevel changes that surround them, a case can be made that continuity provides roots and stability in families that badly need it. Elders offer not only a link to the past but a guide to the future as well, even though many have little understanding of the world outside their doorway and no sense of what the future might be like for their adult children and grandchildren. Because of elders' small numbers in the population and their invisibility to researchers, policy makers, and many service providers, their contributions to the family are seldom noticed and little understood.

Because of their potential contributions to the service economy and their willingness to take low-paying, low-status jobs, youth and middle-aged adult immigrants receive the most attention. The younger generations are likely to be the most adaptable, teachable, and employable and to achieve economic self-sufficiency in a relatively short period. Job training, education, and language skills are the highest priorities for short-term assistance designed to help them achieve independence. Given these assumptions and the generally negative and ill-informed Western attitudes about the hidden contributions of the aged, it is unlikely that elderly immigrants will be viewed as a valuable resource by anyone in a position to influence immigration policies or practices.

There are other reasons why elderly immigrants may be viewed more as a burden than as a resource. The vast majority are non-English speaking and economically dependent on family and government resources. Like all older adults, they are subject to the natural physical, psychological, and social conditions that occur with advanced age. In contrast to members of Asian cultures, Americans tend to have little patience for the universal human conditions of old age or the frailties of the oldest old (Butler 1975). At some point, low-income elders are likely to need health care and other assistance that their families will not be able to provide without government support. If elders utilize unfamiliar Western health care systems, it is likely that the bills will be paid for by state and federal medical assistance dollars. From this perspective, elderly immigrants can be seen as an economic and social burden to the taxpayers, the host communities, and perhaps to their families as well; however, this is a shortsighted perspective that does not account for what we have learned about elders' importance to multigenerational family systems in the new context.

The contributions of elders to the stability, self-sufficiency, and resiliency of extended immigrant families are usually overlooked, since their unpaid labor as child care providers, housekeepers, educators, counselors, and cultural resources is largely indiscernible to outsiders. These family support contributions come at a great cost to the elders, who, as we have seen, have lost their power and elevated place in resettled families. The low-status unpaid work of older women is not counted toward the tax roles and no social security credits are granted for their labors, although their work is important to extended families that cannot afford child care. The education they provide to their grandchildren about the history, culture, and language of their home country is not accredited by any home schooling authority, but it does make a difference for children entering adolescence who are confused about their ethnic identity in a multicultural society. Elders provide cultural roots and a valuable source of both human and social capital to families that have been uprooted and lost most of their other resources.

A fundamental flaw in the conceptualization of immigration by policy makers is the U.S.- and individualistic-centric perspectives that are assumed but never questioned. Immigrants are viewed as "problems" that need to be fixed. "Give me your tired and poor" and we will fix them by converting them to Christianity; teaching them American history, language, and values; and encouraging them to be entrepreneurial. In short, we will make them just like us. Many federal policies view immigrants as individual units rather than as members of an extended family system. From a narrow individualistic perspective, elders can be seen as nonproductive economic burdens, unable to contribute more than they consume. From a broader family systems perspective, elders can be seen as important human resources that support younger family members engaged in the difficult long-term process of social, economic, and political integration.

We have found in this study that many Southeast Asian elders are resilient contributors to their families despite multiple losses, separations, and conflicts. They serve an especially important role maintaining cultural and historical continuity for younger family members. They are a visible link to younger family members of their cultural past, a frequent reminder of the importance of family, and a source of cultural identity for future generations. Although United States immigration policies have historically favored family reunification, recent policy initiatives emphasizing nuclear over extended families make it more difficult for elderly immigrants to join relatives who are already here. With immigrant families already strapped for external resources, the loss of elders may prove to be a critically important loss of an internally important resource.

Families Build Social Capital that Sustains Integration

National, state, and local policy makers, educators, and service providers have difficulty thinking of refuges and immigrants as anything other than individual cases. Individual-oriented policies and programs that do not account for the importance of the larger family system or the cultural context are the norm for most United States social programs, not just those designated for immigrants. Individuals are more easily understood as discrete "units" that have measurable language, job skill, and adjustment problems. Individual problems seem to be manageable because they can be broken down into smaller subunits and "treated" outside the messy complexities of the multigenerational family and ethnic community contexts.

Family behaviors, especially in large extended families, are more multifaceted and dynamic than the behaviors of individuals and even more difficult to understand. As we have seen in the previous chapters, families are complex, evolving socioeconomic systems composed of several generations at different stages of adaptation and individuals at different stages of the life cycle. Individual behaviors are often directly influenced by individuals' positive or negative reactions to the evolving structure, culture, interactions, and identity of their extended family systems, and we miss the mark when individual immigrants, rather than their extended family systems, are the focus of policies or interventions.

Generally, it is more complicated to design policies, programs, and systems for families than for individuals because of the diverse developmental agendas of each generation and gender. Although family reunification policies enable family members to join relatives already living in the United States, it is unlikely that newcomers are prepared for the dramatic changes in roles and relationships of the families with whom they reunite. Even for families who come to the United States together, within a few years of arrival, the segmented processes of adaptation becomes evident, with each generation, gender, and cohort having very different daily lives inside and outside the family. It is within these dynamic, often resilient, and sometimes chaotic family systems that social adaptation and individual development are fostered and promoted. Often, when successful adaptation does not occur, as in the cases of gang or truancy behaviors in youth and gambling or other addictive behaviors in adults, it is because of the inability of highly stressed families to manage change.

Policy makers and service providers sometimes tend to idealize the extended family life of ethnic groups, which leads to assumptions that families are able and willing to provide for the needs of all of their members, including elders. Unfortunately, this is not always true (Sokolovsky 1990a). Most of the elders in this study reported their concerns about the decline of filial piety in the new context. According to Sokolovsky (1990a), "too much emphasis on the ethnic family would be a grave policy mistake" (210). As we have seen, the willingness or ability of families to provide extended care for elders is limited due to the multiple pressures placed upon the younger and middle generations, the decline of filial piety, and other changes in immigrant families. When gaps in ethnic family care occur, service providers are often unsure how to offer culturally appropriate assistance to families. Despite these realities and cautions, the basic assumption underlying public policies concerning immigrant elders is that reunited families will assume responsibility for them.

Successful policies and programs must respond to the commonly shared realities of individuals who are embedded in families, ethnic communities, and the larger community. The programs should realistically address the positive contributions of elders and family groups as well as the challenges they present to the host community. Host communities have to develop broader perspectives on the economic contributions that immigrants make as they assume low-wage, no-benefit agricultural and service jobs, pay taxes, and contribute to the social security of mainstream elders, even while the immigrants themselves live amidst great social insecurities.

One of the major limitations of many studies now conducted on individual immigrants is that they are guided by the needs of private and public social service agencies. According to Gold (1992): "These policy-making bodies seek answers to fiscal and bureaucratically framed questions, not sociological ones. The predetermined closed-ended questions such studies use to generate 'objective' statistics for agencies' consumption offer respondents few opportunities to give their own interpretations of community formation, adaptation, and solidarity" (236). Policies and programs that arise from these studies are often incomplete because they focus on individuals rather than family systems and they neglect the ethnographic traditions that allow for the explanations and meanings of the informants to emerge.

More than two decades ago, Gelfand (1982) outlined the factors and challenges that must be considered in providing services to ethnic elders. They include the fact that most ethnic elders have little knowledge of other cultures, including the one in which they currently live; little knowledge of available services; low utilization of services; an unwillingness to travel for services beyond defined boundaries; low expectations of services; and a strong desire to maintain the traditions of their own culture. Often those traditions do not include seeking help outside the family. Twenty years later, there is not much evidence that these barriers have been overcome, despite the good intentions of many nonprofit service providers. In a 1999 survey of elderly Asian Minnesotans, the Council on Asian-Pacific Minnesotans identified ten major needs; intergenerational conflicts and other cultural changes were fourth on the list of most pressing issues. Included within these two areas of concern are topics familiar to the readers of this book: the breakdown of the extended family system, cultural expectations that the younger generation will take care of the older generation, and Western versus Eastern ideologies (Council on Asian Pacific Minnesotans 1999).

To attract and retain ethnic elders in social service and educational programs, practitioners and educators must be sensitive to the transportation needs of elders and the accessibility of services. Programs are most well received when they are cosponsored by trusted ethnic organizations that employ members of the cultural group. Staff-to-client ratios are important determinants of success, since personal relationships and continuity are important to developing well-received programs (Gelfand 1982). Beyond programs designed to assist ethnic elders are the larger national policies that provide frameworks and resources for the programs designed to assist elders.

The centerpiece of U.S. immigration policy has been family reunification (Fix and Zimmermann 1997). Individual citizens and permanent residents of the United States can sponsor family members who are living in another country. However, recent policy debates in Congress have focused on severely limiting immigration and restricting the admission of siblings, elders, and other extended family members. Restricting the admission of extended family members further reduces the limited human and social capital of families that are already struggling to adapt. Extended family members who join their kin in the United States provide a steady pool of new labor for self-employed entrepreneurs; the newcomers, in turn, are provided with intense hands-on socialization. As we have seen, elders who rejoin families may not be employed outside the home, but they do provide valuable unpaid child care and household assistance. Recent welfare reform legislation limiting access to public benefits for noncitizens will have long-lasting effects on intergenerational relations in extended families, as elders become more of an economic drain on the family's already limited resources. The absence of productive income can negatively affect family morale if elders consume more than they produce; elders can also affect morale if they are a source of conflict rather than support (Fix and Zimmermann 1997).

We have seen that elders can be a source of both stress and support in immigrant families, yet few programs are designed to improve intergenerational understanding or provide support to these complex relationships. The traditional policy of the federal government toward immigrants and refugees who are legally admitted into the United States has been laissez faire. The government has not assumed responsibility for those who enter via family reunification or through special occupation groups, since they are expected to become self-sufficient with family or employer support. The problem with these policies is that the federal government makes the decisions about who can enter and then collects most of the taxes paid by immigrants, while the primary economic and emotional costs of resettling families are assumed by state and local governments, the local host population, and the families who sponsor the newcomers. For most state and local governments across the country the burdens are not severe; however, three-fourths of all new immigrants live in only six states. A state like Minnesota, which is not in the top tier of recipients, has a relatively small population and tax base and a relatively large number of immigrants per capita. Recent deficits in state budgets across the country have targeted services and programs for low-income persons as a major area for elimination and reduction.

With popular anti-immigrant attitudes becoming stronger in recent years, especially in California and the other high-recipient states, there is less support for legal immigrants and refugees in government at all levels. The prospects for the period beyond 9/11 are dim. With tax reduction and smaller government the popular ideology of both major political parties, and a rapidly expanding defense and homeland security budget, the federal government's limited support for legal immigrants and refugees is likely to be diminished even further. The federal retreat on refugee support has been particularly severe during the period of rapid increase in new arrivals. For example, between 1984 and 1994 funding for the federal Refugee Resettlement Program declined from $7,400 to $2,100 per refugee. This striking reduction in minimal resettlement support was followed in 1996 by federal welfare reform legislation that limited economic support to five years.

Policies aimed at reducing the number of immigrants and refugees or the support needed to adapt to life in this country, aside from bringing up human rights and moral issues, are fundamentally shortsighted. These policies often have unforeseen consequences for immigrant families. When children are discouraged from learning and using the language of their parents and grandparents, as well as English, they receive a powerfully negative message about developing a bicultural ethnic identity. When support for special language classes taught by bilingual teachers is reduced or eliminated, children adapt less quickly and find it more difficult to become productive students. For example, between 1984 and 1992 the number of children with limited English skills increased by 85 percent in schools across the country, while adjusted federal funding to support those students increased by only 1 percent. The burden on many local school districts, including those in Minneapolis and St. Paul, has been severe. Undoubtedly, the lack of support for limited-English-speaking children is a consequence of the decades-old debate about bilingual immigrants and whether they should be taught only in English. Some anti-immigrant, pro-English legislators have proposed eliminating bilingual educational programs completely. Meanwhile, we have pious statements about the importance of international and cross-cultural understanding, the global economy, and the development of specialized diversity training. With the planet shrinking and the impact of the global economy visible in the small rural towns of Minnesota, the nation has not yet exhibited enough self-confidence or maturity to embrace the enormous opportunities provided by children growing up in families in which they learn more than one language. Reducing the funding for these language acquisition programs ultimately costs the public more due to the decreased ability of immigrant children to move into higher education, mainstream careers, and the global economy. Such reductions also decrease the social capital of individuals and families and inhibit the already difficult communication between generations. The nation is financially and spiritually poorer because our current policies regarding immigrant language usage promote less diversity, decreased international understanding, and less cross-cultural fluency.

Intergenerational Families as Social Capital

There is evidence suggesting that the social capital of immigrant families decreases with time in the United States (Booth, Crouter, and Landale 1997). Social capital refers to the connections among individuals, their social networks, and the norms of reciprocity and trustworthiness that arise from them. Social capital consists of the accumulation of links among people that promote mutual understanding, shared values, community, and cooperation (Fine 2000; Cohen and Prusak 2001). This finding has disturbing implications considering the limited financial and human resources available to immigrant families and the decline in federal and state government support. The social capital that individuals develop and maintain within their ethnic community may be their only tangible resource.

As families acculturate, gender roles change, and divorce increases there are more single-parent families that are poor. Highly stressful intergenerational problems arise that were not present when families first arrived. The isolation of elders and the diminished authority of parents are exacerbated by their lack of understanding of the new context. The decreased identification with the ethnic group by many adolescents makes it difficult for the family to integrate children into their cultural group or mainstream institutions. Portes (1995) discusses segmented assimilation—which occurs when members of families become assimilated to some parts of American life but not to all—as another factor that decreases the cohesiveness of families. Children may find themselves embracing both the middle-class economic values of the larger culture and underclass social norms of their youth subgroups. All these changes in the important interactions between extended family members decrease the social capital available to all generations.

In Amato's (1996) study of rural southwestern Minnesota towns with relatively large populations of new immigrants (and our discussion of ethnic identity in chapter 7), it is clear that social capital provided through identification with the ethnic community is complex: "The newcomers do not see themselves in terms of abstract classifications of race, continent, or even nation. Their primary identities are about families, clans, villages, regions, and work" (103). This finding suggests that service providers and policy makers should take into account the perspective of the immigrants themselves rather than their own more narrow abstract categories and ethnocentric points of view. However difficult it may be to derive them, policies, social service practices, and educational pedagogy must account for the meanings and definitions of those for whom the programs and services are designed. It is important to avoid the idealization of ethnic families while peering more deeply into their changing dynamics from the perspective of each generation and gender. Ultimately, it is critical to promote self-help through social capital development by nurturing intergenerational relationships in extended families and leadership in ethnic community organizations.

For ethnic elders and their families to finally make a local area, state, or nation their home, many transitions must occur within their minds and hearts, and within the host communities as well. According to Amato (1996): "Leaders of the host community should recognize that, however kindly and fairly they treat newcomers, even prolonged residency in one place does not mean the newcomers will consider it home" (103). Immigrants and refugees need time to develop a feeling of self-confidence while they lose their defensiveness about the erosion of native cultures. Like others who have suffered multiple losses, they need time to grieve, to adjust, and to see the world through a bicultural lens. In many cases, it will take several generations for families to make this adjustment, and the social capital they build within families and communities will be the resource that sustains them. Long after they have achieved economic integration and self-sufficiency, social and cultural integration are likely to lag behind. Amato (1996) explains what it takes to call a place home:

> Having lost a homeland, they may strive, above all else, not to lose their children and community to a new land and its new ways. Immigrants work hardest at re-creating a better version of the world they left behind. They seek the advantages of the new world while keeping the values, sentiments, and traditions of the old. In any case, leaders should recognize that the newcomers alone will decide when they finally call a place home. (104)

Whether refugee families adapt or disintegrate in their new homes may depend on their ability to synthesize three competing forces (Gold 1992). First, a large body of research points to the importance of collectivism on the part of new and emerging ethnic groups. Entrepreneurial, religious, and political engagements are important indicators of cooperation, integration, and adaptation. The collective activities of individuals and groups are evidence of cohesive actions over time that promote ethnic solidarity and build social capital in the community. Leadership from within the ethnic community and tangible evidence of success provide role models to the younger generation, demonstrating how to do well in the new setting without losing the cultural roots that sustain identity. Local action is critical, since few newcomers have the political power or resources to confront major problems on an international or national scale. The old saying "think globally, act locally" is great advice for new ethnic communities and new host communities as well.

Second, the diverse backgrounds and experiences of refugees and their host communities create centrifugal forces, which cause disunity, resistance to unification, segmented communities, and a consciousness shaped by personal rather than collectivist histories. Reinforced by the powerful individualism of American society, the segmented assimilation of the generations, and the ethnogenesis processes of community formation, these formidable factors tend to promote individual achievement rather than the success of the group.

Third, whether the individualistic or collectivist factors predominate in a city, state, or nation depends on the nature and nurture of supportive environments. The political, social, and economic structures shape adaptation at the local, state, and national levels, with each geographic level providing different opportunities for employment, receptivity to immigrants, and collectivist opportunities (Gold 1992). The ability to integrate, combine, and interact within and between these three forces will determine, to a large extent, the success or failure of social capital formation and the integration of each generation in the new context.

Policy makers, service providers, educators, and all those concerned about ethnic relations should consider these factors when making decisions about or designing programs for immigrant groups. The forces of individualism are deeply rooted and powerful; they are reinforced by U.S. history, the schools, and the mass media. Given the importance of the collectivist and ecosystemic forces in the building of social capital, it appears that host community investments in developing ethnic organizations and the integration of immigrant families into mainstream organizations may be more important than individual financial investments. When the entire community is enlisted in the effort to maintain ethnic identity, adaptation becomes a community project that provides both restrictions on negative behaviors and support for positive behaviors. This is simply another version of the "it takes a village" proverb that has become familiar in recent years. With the host and ethnic communities working together, children and young adults are discouraged from engaging in social underclass victim behaviors. This is especially important in poor neighborhoods where economic resources are limited and the social capital of family and ethnicity is one of the few available resources. According to Zhou and Bankston (1996),

> ethnic social integration creates a form of capital that enables an immigrant family to receive ongoing support and direction from other fami-

lies and from the religious and social associations of the ethnic group. Consequently, community standards are established and reinforced among group members, especially among younger members who may otherwise assimilate into an underclass subculture. We thus conclude that social capital is crucial and, under certain conditions, more important than traditional human capital for the successful adaptation of younger-generation immigrants. (218)

This is the same message that the elders from all four ethnic Southeast Asian groups want the younger generations to know and remember. Although the vast majority had never lived in another culture before, they seem to know instinctively that retaining cultural identity and building leadership resources within the community are two of the keys to successful adaptation in the new environment. Even if the elders are unable to make the radical adjustment themselves, they understand how important an individual identity rooted in a cultural tradition and family can be to younger generations living in confusing environments. The twenty elders whose life stories were classified as resilient were most likely to advise the younger generation to create a new identity composed of elements of the old and new worlds in which they live. The importance of bicultural identities is one of the most powerful and enduring messages to emerge from their life histories and a message that many elders wanted to be passed on to their grandchildren and succeeding generations.

When ethnicity is viewed as valuable social capital rather than something to be erased, ignored, assimilated, blended in, or melted away, family members from each immigrant generation and gender will benefit. To accomplish the building of social capital, ethnic families and communities should be encouraged to develop their own self-help organizations that increase ethnic identification and support. Schools and communities should offer language classes, ethnic clubs, and cultural activities based on ethnicity and hire members of the community to be teachers, aides, and counselors. Nonprofit social service organizations should build bridges to ethnic communities and develop programs and curricula that promote ethnic pride, intergenerational harmony, and understanding within the host community.

The development of social capital in new ethnic communities is like putting money in the bank. It appreciates over time, it is available in an emergency, and it can be withdrawn when investments are needed. Social capital provides an intergenerational resource that each community member can contribute to or draw upon depending on his or her talents and resources and the larger needs of the family and community.

If the river bends, the family, the ethnic group, and the host community need to cooperatively develop resources and make investments to build new boats that will safely carry them around the bend. Navigating treacherous and unknown waters is dangerous when traveling alone. Without elders who know the way or a supportive family to provide guidance and comfort along the perilous journey, the chances of floundering are great. A sturdy vessel will provide safety in the passage and can be used over and over again. Traveling with others makes the passage more secure, since some may know the way and the more hands that paddle and steer the craft, the more likely it will navigate the river successfully.

APPENDIX: NATURAL HISTORIES OF SOUTHEAST ASIAN FAMILIES

Introduction to the Research Process

THE DIFFICULTIES CONFRONTING OUTSIDERS who seek to hear and understand the voices of elders was evident at the 1987 national conference on elderly refugees when the interpreter narrated a seventy-one-year-old Hmong woman's life story. Although the Hmong interpreter's English was quite fluent, it was necessary to listen with intense concentration to hear him because of his accent and the unfamiliar inflections of his voice. Even with great effort, there were words and phrases that could not be heard, nuances that could not be translated, and meanings that could not be understood.

Since words and their meanings are the primary data for this study, concentrated focus by the researchers and regular collaboration with the ethnic communities was required during the life history interviews and the iterative stages of interpretation. Many co-researchers, community leaders, and research assistants from the four ethnic groups were enlisted in each stage of gathering and interpreting the elder, middle-generation, and adolescent stories. The names and affiliations of the more than one hundred contributors and co-researchers who worked on the projects leading to this book are listed in the acknowledgments; however, the names of the forty elders, thirty-six parents, and forty-two adolescents who served as our primary informants must remain anonymous. The research could not have been conducted without the ongoing cooperation of many leaders in the community who provided access, advice, and assistance.

As a way to begin to understand the words, stories, and meanings, I began this project by engaging in two years (1988–1990) of part-time fieldwork in the Southeast Asian community as a participant-observer. I participated in a variety of social and educational activities with groups that had been established by each ethnic group for its elders. Among other activities, I participated in educational field trips, played bingo with Lao-speaking women who were learning numbers and the alphabet, cotaught ESL classes for Vietnamese men, listened to male Cambodian elders discussing community problems, and fumbled through a knitting class with Hmong women. I attended celebrations at the impressive community-built Vietnamese Buddhist temple, sat in meditative repose before the Buddha, and listened to stories about life in the old country. I listened for many hours to stories, speeches, and conversations in translated English at social gatherings and meetings. I asked a few questions as well, as I worked my way slowly into friendly conversations. My goal during this first phase of research was to develop trust and begin to understand the family lives of Southeast Asian elders living in a northern climate in a Western country surrounded by strangers.

Considering my cultural background as a grandchild of European immigrants, socioeconomic status, and position of privilege, I was an unlikely translator of Southeast Asian family lives as seen through the eyes of their elders. To overcome the inherent limitations of a cultural outsider, I was willing to listen carefully, to preserve the confidentiality of informants, and to ensure that guidance from the four ethnic communities was integrated into the research process. It was important to learn whether sixty-, seventy-, or eighty-year-old men and women from four cultures would be willing to talk openly about their life experiences to me and others involved with the project we named SAFE, Southeast Asian Families with Elders. Several recurring questions called out for answers before any formal interview process could begin. What right did we have to invade the privacy of elderly refugees, to ask them to explain their private lives and family experiences, and then to interpret and synthesize our "findings"? If elders agreed to be interviewed, how much could a Western ear discern and synthesize from multiple voices after translation and interpretation across linguistic, cultural, and privilege boundaries? Would it be possible to integrate insights from four cultural groups and to develop coherent narratives about the processes of family adaptation? These and other questions motivated me during the fieldwork, as I tried to establish myself as a trustworthy listener, a student of the elders' experiences, and a respectful guardian of their stories.

The leaders of the elder groups introduced me to the participants as a professor from the University of Minnesota who was interested in learning more about Southeast families and elders by volunteering to work with and participate in the group. Since most of the participants spoke only a little English and I spoke only a few words of their languages, most participants seemed to find me an interesting curiosity. Many were eager to communicate and to tell stories but I also noticed a few elders on the periphery of the group, who often spoke little to anyone, and who seemed to an outsider to be psychologically absent from the group although physically present. When elders learned about my interests and profession many expressed happiness that someone was interested in them and, over a period of months, several took me aside to tell me what they thought I should know or could understand about being an elder in an immigrant family.

After more than a year of involvement with the groups, the elders knew about my interest in life histories. Several persons volunteered to be interviewed before anyone asked. In each group, I explained what we hoped to learn, assured confidentiality, and made a general request for participation. The formal requests for participation came from the group leaders who helped to select potential informants and asked them individually if they were willing to be called for an in-person meeting. Those who agreed met with two members of the research team to discuss the project and the consent form. If they were willing to participate, the translator set up the first two-hour meeting in the home of the participants.

The importance of age- and status-oriented "respect," as a general approach to all interpersonal relations, is a central value in Asian cultures. Therefore, it was critical that all stages of the research process be respectful of the traditional position of family elders. In this spirit, the research team approached elders and other informants as students of their culture and experiences. We emphasized their insider roles and expertise and our outsider role as researchers seeking to understand and give voice to their words and experiences. We sought to be interpreters who helped other outsiders to "hear" these hidden voices. The field experiences encouraged me to believe that a middle-aged European American male university professor, with the support and assistance of collaborators from the Southeast Asian community, could respectfully approach and learn from elderly Asian men and women despite the many barriers that separated us.

I learned early in the fieldwork that many of the elders wanted to talk about their experiences as testimony and as a way to educate future generations about their struggles seeking a safe haven. As I informally inquired about their early childhood years, their family's experiences during the war years, and their place within the reconstructed family in the United States, it was clear that the urge to share their life stories was a powerful motivating force. This need to remember and speak about the past, to review the life course, and to have their experiences acknowledged as a legacy for the future may be a universal need of older adults. Social gerontologists call this phenomenon the "life review" and there is a growing body of Western literature documenting its importance for mentally healthy adaptation to the normative losses of old age (Birren and Deutchman 1991; Butler 1963; Lieberman and Falk 1971; Kenyon, Clark, and deVries 2001; Myerhoff 1992).

Southeast Asian cultures have a strong oral history tradition and it is usually the elders who are the primary storytellers and the keepers of the past. The life history approach we employed in this research provided a structured forum to promote a naturally occurring phenomenon. While the elders' family members were busy with school, jobs, and language training we were interviewing, tape recording, listening, and observing. Often when family members were at home when the interviews were being conducted, they gathered around to listen and embellish on what was being told. Although some narratives were emotionally difficult, the elders always encouraged us to return; they expressed a desire to continue the interviews; and they seemed to enjoy the attention and high status that accompanied their role as expert informant. To have a professor and students from "the university" come to their home for interviews, to be respectfully approached as an expert informant, and to have their voice recorded and listened to with care was a novel experience in every home we visited. I was the first American inside several of the elders' homes since their resettlement in the United States.

Multiple Ways of Knowing

A natural history approach to the study of families inevitably crosses disciplinary boundaries, relying on research methods and insights from American studies, anthropology, ethnic studies, family science, social gerontology, and women's studies. A natural history study must be rooted in the communities where families live, directly involve members of the community as coresearchers and key informants, and include historical, interaction, and life course frameworks. The approach we propose here utilizes the words and stories from multiple life history accounts of a unique age cohort as the centerpiece of the investigation; other naturalistic methods are used to validate and provide new perspectives on the life histories.

To more fully understand the multiple perspectives of elders and to better understand the intergenerational dynamics within families, the perspectives of middle-aged parents and adolescents from all four cultural groups were sought in the Helping Youth Succeed data gathering effort in 1995 and 1996. Naturalistic discussion groups were conducted separately with parents and teens as part of a larger project to develop a bicultural parent-education curriculum for Southeast Asian families with adolescent children (Detzner, Xiong, and Eliason 1999). The methods used with and data from the middle and younger generations, discussed more fully in chapters 6 and 7, acknowledge and help to validate the major issues and concerns identified by the elders. These voices from two generations with very different perspectives provide additional insights into the inner workings of immigrant families.

Methodological complexities are inherent in the study of families of refugees, since their natural historical, developmental, and environmental frameworks are drastically altered by forced migration. Studying immigrant families that are in a transitory state is even more difficult because individuals and generations within families adapt at differential rates in new environments (Berry 1980, 1982; Higgitt and Horne 1999). Variations between and within cultural groups add to the complexity. The experiences of male and female adults who are transitioning from a previous life and those of boys and girls adapting to new lives in the United States appear to be very different. The complexity of what is occurring within families ensures our caution not to generalize beyond the direct experiences of those we interviewed.

This natural history study utilizes case study and narrative approaches, with life histories as the centerpiece, and other naturalistic methods—including participant observation, key informants, discussion groups, and community analysis—to study elders within their family, home, and cultural contexts. The life history narratives are the focal point for similarly situated elders to reveal their perceptions of how migration has impacted family life. Using multiple life histories from four cultural groups that experienced similar displacement offers many advantages when compared to other available methods for conducting cross-cultural research with difficult-to-reach populations.

Symbolic Interaction

The natural history approach to the cross-cultural study of families is theoretically rooted in symbolic interaction theory, since the words and narrative data of the life histories, discussion groups, and participant observations closely match the premises of interactionism proposed by Blumer (1969) and others. Interactionists assert that individuals act on the basis of the subjective meanings they ascribe to words, events, persons, and things, *not* on the basis of an objective reality outside of their experience. Meanings develop through language, communication with others, and behavioral interactions between individuals and groups. Meanings are interpreted and reinterpreted over time through a changing cultural prism and the unique experiences of each person, so that a life history retold in old age can be seen as the cumulative construction of reality created over the life course (Berger and Luckmann 1966). Similar experiences, family stories, and constructed realities across a number of life histories can illuminate the impact of life-changing events such as war, forced migration, and family relocation, thus providing an insider social history of a large-scale event or process. Analyzing multiple life histories for recurring expressions and perceptions can extend and validate the insights from one life history (Bertaux 1981; Dollard 1935; Langness 1965; Langness and Frank 1981; Cohler 1982; Watson and Watson-Franke 1985). The goal of research conducted within the symbolic interaction perspective is to elucidate and elaborate on the constructed meanings of informants, to analyze underlying patterns, and to reveal processes in ways that promote understanding.

Symbolic interaction is well suited to studying the family life of culturally diverse groups, since it enables their meanings and explanations to emerge from their words and constructs rather than from the preconceived notions of the investigator (Kirk and Miller 1986). These life events, stories, memories, and reconstructions of reality are the foundation on which new interdisciplinary theoretical propositions can be grounded.

Life Course Perspectives

A natural history approach to the study of elders and families from diverse cultures inevitably includes life course theory, since broad sociohistorical-developmental perspectives are necessary if we are to understand long lives in context and across time (Settersten 2003). The normative life course and family development processes of the elders, evolved over millennia and socialized from birth, was forever altered by the war and its aftermath. Men and women who anticipated comfort, respect, and family devotion late in life found themselves in drastically altered circumstances; they were often dependent on the U.S. government for financial support and younger family members for emotional support. Instead of receiving the respect promised by traditional filial piety beliefs, elders' lives were filled with uncertainty, fear, and a drastic alteration of roles.

Research using a life course or developmental approach seeks to understand individuals and families across their life span and within their historical and cultural contexts (Allen 1989; Hareven and Adams 1982; Unruh and Livings 1989). To begin to understand the life course of an individual within the context of a multigenerational family system requires several levels of analysis, the assistance of key informants, and a great deal of humility. Interpreting oral history texts composed of highly personal memories is always a complex undertaking, since memories are faulty, nostalgia impairs hindsight, and the story itself is forever being altered, reinterpreted, and reconstructed by the individual who lived and remembers it.

A life course perspective is useful in framing life history interview questions and analyzing the responses. Given the inevitable limitations of retrospective accounts, it is important to be modest when interpreting the life experiences of elders from four cultural groups. Nevertheless, the detailed life histories of forty Southeast Asian elders are a unique repository of individual and family stories, cases, examples, and recurring patterns, from their early lives in Vietnam, Cambodia, and Laos to the early stages of resettlement in the United States. Although there are limits to life course research using self-reporting methods, there are enough similar narratives across the forty accounts to distinguish some basic family processes, patterns, and themes that might be overlooked in a smaller number of individual accounts or in quantitative studies with a much narrower focus. Although not as methodologically rigorous as longitudinal studies, life histories are nevertheless very good vehicles to study the reconstructed life course of elders, since they allow the meanings, distinctions, and similarities of experience to emerge from the words, stories, and descriptions of family interactions at different periods in the life course. Knowing how informants remember the respectful attitudes of youth toward elders in their childhood is helpful to understanding why the attitudes and actions of contemporary youth may be disappointing.

Life course theory is closely linked to human and family development theories that seek holistic time-oriented perspectives not limited to a single moment or period in life. Major psychosocial theories of individual development have been developed in recent decades that view life course development as a series of fairly predictable stages in which specific tasks must be accomplished before moving on to the next stage. Erik Erickson's (1975) influential stage theory of human development suggests that elderly persons, in the eighth or last stage of development, are confronted by the looming conclusion of life and the question of whether it can be judged worthy by the person who has lived it. The conclusion pits a positive ending filled with integrity against an alternative negative ending in which despair prevails. Although Erickson and other stage theorists are more appropriately linked to Western individualism than Eastern familism, theories of individual and family development informed this study and provided general guidance in collecting and analyzing the life histories.

Naturalistic Methods

After the Fieldwork

I have already discussed the part-time participant-observation fieldwork with social-educational groups organized for elders from each of the four cultural groups. I continued interacting with the groups, sponsored by the Vietnamese Buddhist Association, the Cambodian Buddhist Association (renamed the United Cambodian Association), the Lao Family Organization, the YMCA, and the

American Refugee Committee, while conducting the life history interviews. From 1988 to 1990, I attended as many events, meetings, and field trips of these groups as possible. I became a friendly helper and a willing listener to those who would talk with me through a translator or as a way of practicing their English skills. By participating in these groups and through the many conversations permitted by informal participation, I began to understand how elders viewed their disrupted lives. Among the forty informants who agreed to be interviewed for this study, there were several elders from each group whom I met during this early stage of the research.

After the initial period of concentrated fieldwork, I continued to attend events sponsored by community agencies, to offer workshops on family issues to staff working with refugees, and to make new acquaintances through the research and field-testing activities of the HYS project (Detzner, Xiong, and Eliason 1999). I supervised and coadvised more than a dozen graduate and undergraduate students on research projects focused on Southeast Asian loneliness, loss, family structure, filial piety, and family conflict; the Hmong new year celebration; the life history of a Hmong sewer; Hmong women's roles; and bicultural parenting. Many of those projects involved analysis of the life history data and others involved the new data emerging from the HYS project. Ten students in my Aging, Family, and Society course chose to write term papers on the lives of elderly Southeast Asians living in the Twin Cities area. Several graduate students who were involved in different stages of the SAFE project later integrated the narratives into doctoral or master's theses and course papers (Seabloom 1991; Hagemeister 1994; Lynch, Detzner, and Eicher 1995, 1996; Parker 1996; Bennett and Detzner 1997). In addition to the Asian bicultural parent-education curriculum, the HYS project resulted in a master's and a doctoral thesis (Xiong 1997, 2000). The SAFE and HYS projects were funded by the University of Minnesota's Agricultural Experiment Station, the graduate school, and the University of Minnesota Extension Service.

Between 1994 and 1998, I served as director of the University of Minnesota's Refugee Studies Center (formerly the Southeast Asian Refugee Studies Center). This role brought me into regular contact with many of the leaders of the Southeast Asian community in Minnesota and around the country. Beginning in 1996, the Refugee Studies Center sponsored monthly roundtable discussions. Faculty and students at the University of Minnesota who were interested in refugee issues were linked with community professionals working in the field for a series of highly successful dialogues around critical issues confronting refugees in the community. These experiences and recurring immersions in the Southeast Asian community helped to ground this study in the daily lives and experiences of Southeast

Asian families. The five-year Helping Youth Succeed project to design, field-test, deliver, and evaluate a bicultural education curriculum for parents of Southeast Asian adolescents was particularly helpful in keeping the project grounded in the stories and experiences of more than one generation.

Selecting Informants

The perceptions, experiences, and reconstructed realities of forty Vietnamese, Cambodian, Laotian, and Hmong elders are the focal point of this book. Although the four groups are culturally distinct, with unique languages, customs, and family systems, these elders have in common a unique generational perspective on the family changes brought about by war and its aftermath. The oldest generation has historical perspective, its own subjective view of the family history, and a strong incentive to preserve its side of story. Because of their traditional position in the family and their historical perspective, elders are in a unique position to report an "insider's" perspective on family behaviors. While they are key informants and expert witnesses of their own family's experience, they also share biases and perspectives that are derived from their generational position as elders. Their voices were both confirmed and challenged by middle-generation adults and adolescent informants from other families in the HYS project. These younger voices helped to broaden our understanding of family dynamics by offering the perspectives of two generations with life course experiences very different from those of the elders. The HYS methods and participants are described more fully in chapters 6 and 7.

A representative sample of Southeast Asian elders in the state of Minnesota was not possible because an accurate census count of residents who are refugees does not exist. Formidable barriers such as language, fear, isolation, and posttraumatic stress make the random selection of informants a less-than-desirable sampling technique for this population, even if an accurate count were available (Mollica, Wyshak, and Lavelle 1987; Rogler 1989). The informant group that we selected was purposively composed with the assistance of the leaders of the four elders' groups in which I conducted most of my fieldwork. Ethnic leaders approached elders about participation based on their knowledge of the informant's current situation, prior traumatic stressful events, and potential interest. In constructing the sampling frames we sought balance across several demographic categories and characteristics. Individuals with known traumatic distress or serious mental or physical health problems were considered inappropriate for the study. Ethnic leaders explained the study and their rights to potential informants and asked those who were interested for permission to submit their names. After agreeing to participate in the study, potential informants were contacted by the bilingual interviewer to arrange a meeting in their home or apartment. After arrival, greetings, and introductions, the purpose of the study and the voluntary nature of the informant's participation were discussed. If they were willing to proceed, informants were asked to sign or assent to the consent form. After each of the first two interviews, informants were asked if they were willing to be interviewed again and reminded that their participation was voluntary.

Considerations in the sampling process included decisions to select ten members from each of the four cultural groups, with an equal number of male and female informants from each group. An effort was made to represent the diversity within cultural groups, including attention to age range, time since arrival, previous economic status, and previous urban or rural residence patterns. Table 5 provides the basic demographic information on the elder informants who agreed to participate.

The selection of an equal number of informants from each gender and cultural group was based on the assumption that all four cultural groups and both genders should have an equal voice in the study without regard to their proportionate distribution within the Twin Cities, the state of Minnesota, the Midwest, or the nation. In 1995, the Refugee and Immigrant Services Section of the Minnesota Department of Human Services estimated that there were approximately 35,000 Hmong, 18,000 Vietnamese, 7,600 Cambodians, and 7,200 Lao living in Minnesota. The 1990 national census data indicates that approximately 615,000 Vietnamese, 147,000 Cambodians, 149,000 Lao, and 90,000 Hmong were living in the United States, a total of just over one million persons. The 2000 census

Table 5. Demographic Characteristics

	Gender		
	Males	Females	Total
Cultural group			
Vietnamese	5	5	10
Cambodian	5	5	10
Hmong	5	5	10
Laotian	5	5	10
Totals	20	20	40

	Age	Years living in the United States
Mean	66.3	6.9
Range	48–83	1–13

Table 6.   Family and Household Composition

Marital status	Percent (%)
Married	44.4
Widowed	16.7
Divorced/separated	8.5
Never married	2.8
Other	27.8
Household composition	
Living with spouse	2.6
Living alone	7.7
Living with spouse/children/others	15.4
Living with spouse/children	25.6
Living with others	48.7
Number of living children	
Mean	6.0
Range	1–13

shows that the Vietnamese and Hmong populations grew the fastest of the four Southeast Asian groups between 1990 and 2000. The number of Vietnamese increased by 47 percent to 1,122,528 in 2000, while the number of Hmong grew by 44 percent to 169,428 in 2000. The numbers of Cambodians and Lao grew at a considerably slower rate between 1990 and 2000. The Cambodian population increased by 13 percent to 171,937 during that decade, while the enumerated Lao population increased by 12 percent to 168,707 (Pfeifer 2001).

The age when one is considered to be an "elder" varies across cultural groups; however, being labeled as such is not necessarily the same as being chronologically "old." After decades of hard work in the fields, poor or nonexistent health care, and inadequate nutrition, a "premature" physical aging is not unusual in many Southeast Asians. Often a family event such as the birth of the first grandchild is an important marker on the way toward achieving the status reserved for elders. In Hmong families living in Laos, marriage for girls often occurred at thirteen or fourteen years of age, so that it would not be unusual to become a grandmother by age thirty; however, the elevated social status of elders more often comes in the forties, fifties, and sixties. The mean age of our informants was 66.3 years.

Our informants included an elder who had arrived thirteen years before the interview with the first wave of Vietnamese refugees and several Hmong and Cambodian newcomers who had arrived within the year. To better understand what the Southeast Asian reconstructed family looked like in the United States we asked questions about the elders' current family and household composition. Table 6 reveals the war's impact on the family system and household. Informants reported a mean of six living adult children; however, many family stories revealed early infant deaths, the loss of children in the war, and recurring family separations. The large percentage of "other" in both the marital status and household composition categories reveals the impact of these family disruptions, hurried escapes, and the relocation process. Many informants were uncertain about their current marital status because their spouses were missing and they did not know if they were living or not. Almost half of the informants lived "with others" at the time of the interview. Often these were widows or widowers who were living with adult children or grandchildren. Others were living with extended kin, clan members, or friends.

The Life History Approach

Life history research has been developed and refined during the past six decades by scholars in the humanities and social and behavioral science disciplines. Life history scholars use a variety of approaches to provide an insider perspective on sociohistorical context, and the meaning of everyday life experiences to individuals and groups (Dollard 1935; Langness 1965; Erickson 1975; Bertaux 1981; Langness and Frank 1981; Watson and Watson-Franke 1985; Turner and Bruner 1986). Life history methods are appropriate for studying elderly refugees because Southeast Asian cultures and families have historically placed elders in the prestigious roles of wise person, teacher, advisor, and keeper of the past. Our interviews affirmed these roles. Moreover, the informants repeatedly told the interviewers that they wanted their stories to be told as a means of leaving a family, cultural, and historical legacy for the younger generation, a desire of elders that may transcend cultural boundaries (Lieberman and Falk 1971; Myerhoff 1992).

Social gerontologists emphasize the therapeutic value of the life review process that is encouraged by a progressive recall to consciousness of individual and family experiences (Baum 1980–1981; Butler 1963; Myerhoff 1992). In a review of studies on reminiscence, Merriam (1980) documents the powerful urge of the elderly to review and place in context the experiences of their lives. In fieldwork conversations with elders and the ethnic group leaders who work with them, it was clear that having a chance to tell their stories for descendants was a powerful incentive for the elders to participate. The culturally sensitive and age-appropriate nature of life history interview methods helped a white, middle-aged, male, Western academic to make close connections with members of difficult-to-reach groups who were eager for someone to listen.

An individual's life story is deeply intertwined with his or her family's evolving story throughout the life course. This may be most evident in traditional

Asian cultures, in which individual lives are subsumed under the larger hierarchical extended family, which includes all generations who are living and dead (Rottman and Meredith 1982). The individual and family stories of the Southeast Asian elders occur within the moving saga of war, dangerous escapes, crowded refugee camps, and resettlement in a Western country (Nicassio 1985). The families of elders have been altered, disrupted, separated, and relocated as a consequence of events occurring far beyond their horizon. By examining the lives of individual older refugees within the context of their family, it is possible to develop portraits and case examples that extend our understanding of elders, family life, and ethnicity (Hess and Handel 1959; Yin 1984).

The Interviewing Process

The bicultural interview teams were composed of both cultural outsiders and insiders. Because each of the research teams was gender specific, a female graduate student studying families might be paired with a female Hmong sophomore pre-pharmacy student. Or a male European American graduate student studying families might be paired with a Lao male undergraduate majoring in engineering. The non–Southeast Asian graduate students who were involved were second- or third-year students in the family social science department with previous research and interviewing experience. One female graduate student was from Thailand and spoke Thai, English, and Lao, while the others were European Americans with an interest in cross-cultural research or elders. Four male and four female Southeast Asian undergraduate students from the University of Minnesota were hired to work as cointerviewers, translators, interpreters, and cultural ambassadors. All of the undergraduates were bilingual in English and their native tongue and experienced as translators. Since these student researchers were from the community themselves they were able to draw on their own experiences and insider knowledge to inform and enlighten during the interviewing and interpreting stages.

All the research teams met individually with me and as a group on a regular basis. Every interview was discussed, analyzed, and translated, and the next interview was prepared for and scheduled. For two years (1989–1990), research teams spread out across the newly emerging ethnic communities in the Twin Cities to examine the family lives of an elderly cohort of immigrants. To better understand the family stories of Southeast Asian elders, I enlisted the assistance of a multiethnic team of key informants composed of professionals, community leaders, and students from all four cultural groups. As the project evolved, these cultural insiders offered to be informal cultural guides, advisors, door openers, mentors, interviewers, and assistants.

Three two-hour interviews were conducted in the homes of informants using an informal approach and open-ended questions concerning individual and family experiences during their youth, middle age, and old age. Ethnic leaders from the community told us that it would be more appropriate for women to interview women and men to interview men, so we organized our teams accordingly. Interviewing teams were composed of two males or two females with one member an American interviewer and the other a bilingual undergraduate student from the same cultural group as the interviewee. I participated in a total of thirty-three interviews, including all of the Vietnamese and Cambodian male interviews and one or two Hmong and Lao male interviews. I was not directly involved in any interviews with female informants. The two people on a team worked as cointerviewers, with the bilingual student serving as translator and lead interviewer. As part of their preinterview training, the bilingual members of the eight teams (four male and four female teams) back-translated the interview questions from English to the native language. After discussing any differences between translations, the teams revised the phrasing of questions so that common meanings were established and understood by the interviewers.

Each of the three interviews focused on a general chronological time period roughly covering three major periods of the life course: childhood, adulthood, and old age. Informants were asked to discuss family organization, household composition, and geographic location at each life stage. Although there were specific questions we wanted all informants to answer, we also encouraged them to discuss any other issues that they chose. We sought to establish a conversational dialogue about the life course rather than a formal interview process. The interviews were conducted in the language chosen by the informant (thirty-eight in the elders' native languages and two in English), tape-recorded, translated into an English language manuscript, and typed into Ethnograph (1988) computer files. More than 240 hours of interviews were conducted, and the translated transcriptions ran to more than two thousand pages of narrative text.

The early part of the first interview focused on the construction of a rudimentary family tree. The intention was to immediately establish the elderly informant as expert and to place the multigenerational family at the center of the discussion. The three interviews usually lasted about two hours, although some extended well beyond the allotted time, with conversations continuing after the tape recorder was shut off. At the conclusion of each interview, informants were told the topics for the next interview and asked if they wished to continue. Informants inevitably wished for us to return. Most second and third interviews were scheduled within a week or two of the previous interview, which helped us to maintain interpersonal familiarity and narrative coherence. The cointerviewers discussed and recorded their impressions of the interview immediately after its conclusion and wrote field notes describing the home and near environment.

Analysis

Qualitative analysis of translated words, vignettes, and stories is a dynamic process that combines the systematic investigation techniques of the scientist and the intuitive insights of the artist. In good qualitative research practice, analysis of the data occurs while it is being gathered. Interview questions are altered, added, or subtracted in light of insights gained during the interviews and early readings of transcripts. More insightful follow-up questions are based on what was learned from earlier informants. In this study, the analysis evolved through a series of stages as different questions were asked of the narrative data.

STAGE ONE   The forty life histories were analyzed using an open coding system to search for broad family-oriented recurring themes. Two conceptually related family themes that were developed in preliminary studies were the elders' filial piety expectations and family behaviors (Seabloom 1991) and family, gender, and generational conflicts (Detzner 1992).

STAGE TWO   For the purposes of this study, all forty life histories were analyzed to examine family patterns across cultural groups and genders. The accounts were carefully read and reread by two or more members of the research team, thoroughly discussed, reanalyzed for basic family-level dimensions, and then reconstructed as case studies. The case studies are organized around five broad dimensions of family life: the family's "story," structure, culture, interactions, and identity (LaRossa 1984). The experiences of each elderly informant were summarized across these dimensions and used as the foundation for the comparative discussion of the elders' families that appears in chapters 3 to 7. The family story is the summary of what has happened to the family as perceived and constructed by the older informant. Family structure is defined as the organization of power and role relationships within the family. A family's culture is the shared goals, values, beliefs, and norms of the family. Family interactions are analyzed according to the expressed meanings attached by the informant to the verbal and nonverbal behaviors of other family members. A family's identity is defined by the way its members perceive and manage the balance between individual and group identity.

These dimensions were chosen for theoretical as well as methodological reasons. From a theoretical perspective, broad categories such as these can be used to uncover, contrast, and compare important baseline elements within culturally diverse family systems. From a methodological perspective, an individual life history account can be developed into a family case study using these dimensions as heuristic constructs for coding, analyzed from a family-level perspective, and compared across cases. Comparisons across cases permit empirically based statements to be developed about the family life of Southeast Asian refugees that can be tested against existing theory or be used to develop new theory (Yin 1984, 1993; Abramson 1992).

STAGE THREE Eight elders and their families were selected for in-depth analysis based on the richness of their narratives and the insights they could provide into the family stories identified in chapter 3. The family's tree as reconstructed by the elder was utilized to analyze the family's structure and story and to graphically portray the impact of war and forced migration on a family system. These eight elders are presented as illustrative case examples and referred to in subsequent chapters.

STAGE FOUR To partially overcome the inherent one-generation bias of attending only to the perceptions of elders about their families and themselves, data were included from the HYS in-depth discussion groups, made up of parents and adolescents from all four cultural groups. The accounts from these discussion groups were analyzed separately for additional perspectives on the family's story, interactions, and identity. These systematically gathered group narratives provide alternative insights on intergenerational family dynamics that are used to supplement and challenge the multiple voices of the elders, especially in chapters 6 and 7. The process of gathering these data from middle-aged parents and adolescents and the characteristics of the informants are discussed more fully in chapter 6.

An Approach to Studying Elders, Families, and Ethnicity

The natural history approach proposed and utilized in this research is not composed of any radically new methodologies or techniques. Indeed the approach is not one method or a prescribed set of methods but rather an approach that cultural outsiders might employ to help them develop trust, gain access, and conduct research in culturally sensitive and appropriate ways. Of course, cultural insiders have many advantages and strengths that they bring with them to research such as this, and we look forward to many more studies from them. However, it is possible for cultural outsiders to know something about elders, diverse families, and ethnicity even if they are not themselves old, a member of the family, or an ethnic insider.

If all research were left to persons who themselves were insiders our knowledge base would be even more limited than it is now. We need to encourage our graduate and undergraduate students and have the courage ourselves to step forward to conduct research about individuals, families, and groups about which we have little inside knowledge. To take this step forward, however, we must be prepared for the long-term commitment that is required and the painstakingly slow process of learning that is required. We must also be prepared to utilize a variety of naturalistic methods that encourage dialogue, self-revelation and self-exploration, and new ways of knowing. I hope that this work meets those standards and that it will provide a useful guide to conducting research with the many new groups that are arriving in the United States and elsewhere, about which we know so little and from which we can learn so much.

REFERENCES

Abramson, P. 1992. *A case for case studies: An immigrant's journal.* Newbury Park, Calif.: Sage.

Adams, J. S., and B.J. Van Drasek. 1993. *Minneapolis-St. Paul: People, places, and public life.* Minneapolis: University of Minnesota Press.

Allen, K. 1989. *Single women/family ties: Life histories of older women.* Newbury Park, Calif.: Sage.

Amato, J. 1996. *To call it home: The new immigrants of southwestern Minnesota.* Marshall, Minn.: Crossings Press.

Anderson, D. M. n.d. *Southeast Asian refugee family stress, coping and adaptation.* Program in Health Education, University of Minnesota, Minneapolis.

Apter, T. 1993. Altered views: Fathers' closeness to teenage daughters. In *The narrative study of lives*, ed. R. Josselson and A. Lieblich. Newbury Park, Calif.: Sage.

Atchley, R. 1989. A continuity theory of normal aging. *The Gerontologist* 29:183–190.

Atkinson, D. R., G. Morten, and D. W. Sue. 1989. *Counseling American minorities: A cross-cultural perspective*, 3rd ed. Dubuque, Iowa: Wm. C. Brown.

Baker, H. R. 1979. *Chinese family and kinship.* London: Macmillan.

Battisti, R. n.d. *Preserving the spiritual and cultural heritage of Amerasian and Southeast Asian families.* Utica, N.Y.: Mohawk Valley Resource Center for Refugees.

Baum, W. 1980–1981. The therapeutic value of oral history. *International Journal of Aging and Human Development* 12, no. 1:49–53.

Benedict, R. 1938. Continuities and discontinuities in cultural conditioning. *Psychiatry* 1:161–167.

Bengston, V. L., K-D. Kim, G.C. Myers, and K-S. Eun. 2000. *Aging in east and west: Families, states, and the elderly.* New York: Springer.

Bennett, J., and D. Detzner. 1997. Loneliness in cultural context: Life history narratives of older Southeast Asian refugee women. *The Narrative Study of Lives* 5:113–146.

Benson, J. 1989. Households, migration, and community context. Paper presented at the American Anthropological Association, November 1989, Washington, D.C.

Berger, P., and T. Luckmann. 1966. *The social construction of reality.* New York: Doubleday Anchor.

Berkowitz, S. 1989. Assessing the unmet service needs of elderly homebound Blacks, Hispanics, and Vietnamese in Arlington: Recommendations for improving delivery and overcoming barriers. Final postdoctoral fellowship report, Gerontological Society of America, Washington, D.C.

Berry, J. W. 1980. Acculturation as varieties of adaptation. In *Acculturation: Theory, models, and findings,* ed. A. Padilla. Boulder, Colo.: Westview.

———. 1982. Acculturation and adaptation in a new society. *International Migration Review* 30:69–84.

Bertaux, D., ed. 1981. *Biography and society.* Beverly Hills, Calif.: Sage.

Bertrand, D. 1992. Resettlement project and foreign language learning: The identity of Southeast Asian refugees in a transit camp. Ph.D. diss., Department of Psychology, University of Toulouse, Le Mirail, France.

Bicultural Training Partnership. 1996. *Voices and visions: Snapshots of the Southeast Asian communities in the Twin Cities.* St. Paul: St. Paul Foundation.

Birren, J., and D. Deutchman. 1991. *Guiding autobiography for older adults.* Baltimore: Johns Hopkins University Press.

Birren, J.E., and B.A. Burren. 1996. Autobiography: Exploring the self and encouraging development. In *Aging and Biography: Explorations in Adult Development,* ed. J. E. Birren, G. M. Kenyon, J. E. Ruth, J. J. F. Schnoots, and T. Svensson. New York: Springer Publishing Company.

Bishop, K. 1985. The Hmong of central California: An investigation and analysis of the changing family structure during liminality, acculturation, and transition. Ed.D. diss., University of San Francisco.

Bliatout, B. 1980. The Hmong from Laos. In *People and cultures of Hawaii: A pschocultural profile,* ed. J. F. McDermott Jr., W. T. Tseng, and T. W. Maretzki. Honolulu: University of Hawaii Press.

Blumer, H. 1969. *Symbolic interactionism.* Englewood Cliffs, N.J.: Prentice-Hall.

Boenlien, J. K. 1987. Clinical relevance of grief and mourning among Cambodian refugees. *Social Science Medicine* 25:765–772.

Booth, A., A. C. Crouter, and N. Landale, eds. 1997. *Immigration and the family,* Mahweh, N.J.: Erlbaum.

Boss, P. 1991. Ambiguous loss. In *Living beyond loss: Death and the family,* ed. F. Walsh and M. McGoldrick. New York: Norton.

Boyer, L. M. 1991. *Southeast Asian refugees—the older generation: An annotated bibliography.* Stanislaus: California State University Library.

Brody E., P. Johnsen, and M. Fulcomer. 1984. What should adult children do for elderly parents? Opinions and preferences of three generations of women. *Journal of Gerontology* 39, no. 6:736–746.

Bronfenbrenner, U. 1979. *The ecology of human development.* Cambridge, Mass.: Harvard University Press.

Bubolz, M. M., and M. S. Sontag. 1992. Human ecology theory. In *Sourcebook of family theories and methods: A contextual approach*, ed. P. G. Boss, W. J. Doherty, R. LaRossa, W. R. Schumm, and S. K. Steinmetz. New York: Plenum.

Bureau of the Census. 2000. www.census.gov/prod/2001pubs/statab/sec01.pdf.

Bureau of the Census. 1990/1. *Census of Population and Housing: Summary Tape File 2 and 4—Income Tables PB 108*. Washington, D.C.: The Bureau.

Bureau of the Census. 1990/2. *Census of Population and Housing: Summary Tape File 2 and 4—Income Tables PB 65/65A/66/95A*. Washington, D.C.: The Bureau.

Bureau of the Census. 1990/3. *Census of Population and Housing: Summary Tape File 4 Population Tables, Tables PB 27*. Washington, D.C.: The Bureau.

Bureau of the Census. 1990/4. *Census of Population and Housing: Summary Tape File 4 Population Tables, Tables PB 1/4/5/5A/5B*. Washington, D.C.: The Bureau.

Bureau of the Census. 1990/5. *Census of Population and Housing: Summary Tape File 2 Population Tables, Tables PB 17*. Washington, D.C.: The Bureau.

Bureau of the Census. 1990/6. *Census of Population and Housing: Summary Tape File 2 Population Tables, Tables PB 2*. Washington, D.C.: The Bureau.

Bureau of the Census. 1990/7. *Population Division and Education and Social Stratification Branch, 1990 Census Special Tabulation. CPH-1-133*. Washington, D.C.: The Bureau.

Bureau of the Census. 1990/8. *Census of Population and Housing: Summary Tape File 4 Income Tables, Tables PB 65/65A/66*. Washington, D.C.: The Bureau.

Bureau of the Census. 2000. United States Census [Data file]. Available from the U.S. Census Bureau, at factfinder.census.gov/servlet/BasicFactsServlet.

Burling, R. 1965. Hill farms and padi fields among Cambodian refugees. *Social Science Medicine* 25:765–772.

Butler, R. 1963. An interpretation of life review in the aged. *Psychiatry* 26:65–76.

———. 1975. *Why Survive? Being Old in America*. New York: Harper and Row.

Camino, L. A., and R. M. Krulfeld. 1994. *Reconstructing lives, recapturing meaning: Refugee identity, gender, and culture change*. Amsterdam: Gordon and Breach.

Caplan, N., J. Whitmore, and M. Choy. 1989. *The boat people and achievement in America: A study of family life, hard work, and cultural values*. Ann Arbor: University of Michigan Press.

Carpio, B. 1981. The adolescent immigrant. *Canadian Nurse* 77:27–31.

Carter, B., and M. McGoldrick, eds. 1988. *The changing family life cycle: A framework for family therapy*. New York: Gardner.

Chan, K. B., and K. Christie. 1995. Past, present, and future: The Indochinese refugee experience twenty years later. *Journal of Refugee Studies* 8, no. 2:87–95.

Chan, K., and L. Lam. 1987. Community, kinship and family in the Chinese Vietnamese community: Some enduring values and patterns of interaction. In *Uprooting, loss and adaptation: The resettlement of Indochinese refugees in Canada*, ed. K. Chan and D. Indra. Ottawa, Canada: Canadian Public Health Association.

Chan, K. B., and J. H. Ong. 1995. The many faces of immigrant entrepreneurship. In *Cambridge Survey on World Migration*, ed. R. Cohen. Cambridge: Cambridge University Press.

Chan, S. 1986. Parents of exceptional children. In *Exceptional Asian children and youth*, ed. M. K. Kitano and P. C. Chin. Washington, D.C.: ERIC.

Chase, R. 1990. *Minority elders in Minnesota*. St. Paul, Minn.: Amherst H. Wilder Foundation.

Chhim, Sun-Him. 1987. *Introduction to Cambodian culture*. San Diego: Multifunctional Resource Center, San Diego State University.

Cho, P. J. 1990. Family care of the Asian American elderly: Myth or reality? In *Aging and Old Age in Diverse Populations*, ed. E. Percil Stanford. Washington, D.C.: American Association of Retired Persons.

Cohen, D., and L. Prusak. 2001. *In good company: How social capital makes organizations work*. Boston, Mass.: Harvard Business School Press.

Cohler, B. 1982. Personal narrative and the life course. *Life Span Development and Behavior* 4:205–241.

Cohn, M. 1986. Hmong youth and the Hmong future in America. In *The Hmong in transition*, ed. G. L. Hendricks, B. T. Downing, and A. S. Deinard. New York: Center for Migration Studies.

Coleman, C. 1980. Mental health problems of Indochinese refugees in the United States. *Refugees and Human Rights Newsletter*.

Connor, J. 1974. Acculturation and family continuities in three generations of Japanese Americans. *Journal of Marriage and the Family* 36 (February): 159–165.

Council on Asian Pacific Minnesotans. 1999. Needs of elderly Asian Minnesotans. See website www.state.mn.us/ebranch/capm.

Cowgill, D. 1986. *Aging around the world*. Belmont, Calif.: Wadsworth.

Cox, C., and D. Gelfand. 1987. Familial assistance, exchange, and satisfaction among Hispanic, Portuguese, and Vietnamese ethnic elderly. *Journal of Cross-Cultural Gerontology* 2:241–255.

Das, M. S., and P.D. Bardis, eds. 1979. *The family in Asia*. London: George Allen and Unwin.

Detzner, D. F. 1981. Teaching life review to the introductory student. *Gerontology and Geriatrics Education* 2, no. 2:119–122.

———. 1985. Archbishop John Ireland and the German-National parishes of St. Paul, *Journal of the Minnesota Academy of Sciences* 51, no. 1:19–23.

———. 1992. Conflict in Southeast Asian refugee families: A life history approach. In *Qualitative methods in family research*, ed. J. Gilgun, K. Daly, and G. Handel. Newbury Park, Calif.: Sage.

———. 1993. Transnational families: Immigrants and refugees. In *One world, many families*, ed. K. Altergott. Minneapolis: National Council on Family Relations.

Detzner, D., and J. Bennett. 1993. A typology of Southeast Asian refugee families. Paper presented to the National Council on Family Relations, Baltimore, Md.

Detzner, D. F., C. Elde, P. Koy, R. Light, M. Seabloom, C. Sok, P. Thai, K. Thai, and D. Vechbunyongratana. 1989. Continuity and change in Vietnamese and Cambodian refugee families: Elder roles, family values, and filial piety. Paper presented at the National Council on Family Relations, New Orleans, La.

Detzner, D., B. Xiong, and P. Eliason. 1999. *Helping youth succeed: Bicultural parenting education for Southeast Asian families.* St. Paul, Minn.: University of Minnesota Extension Service.

Die, A., and W. Seelbach. 1988. Problems, sources of assistance, and knowledge of services among elderly Vietnamese immigrants. *Gerontologist* 28:448–452.

Dinh, K., B. Sarason, I. Sarason, E. Mankowski, and G. Pierce. 1991. Long-term impact of immigration on Vietnamese families: The parent-child relationship. Paper presented at the American Psychological Association annual meeting, San Francisco, Calif.

Dollard, John. 1935. *Criteria for the life history.* New Haven: Yale University Press.

Donnelly, N. 1988. Family issues arising after resettlement. Paper presented at the Southeast Asian Communities in the United States conference, Arizona State University, Tempe, Ariz.

Downing, B., E. Egli, and M. O'Connor. 1988. *Evaluation of elderly refugee program: Final report.* Minneapolis: Southeast Asian Refugee Studies Project, CURA, University of Minnesota.

Dunnigan, T. 1982. Segmentary kinship in an urban society: The Hmong of St. Paul-Minneapolis. *Anthropological Quarterly* 55:126–134.

Erickson, E. 1950. *Childhood and society.* New York: Norton.

———. 1975. *Life history and the historical moment.* New York: Norton.

———. 1980. *Identity and the life cycle.* New York: Norton.

———. 1982. *The life cycle completed: A review.* New York: Norton.

Fadiman, A. 1997. *The spirit catches you and you fall down: A Hmong child, her American doctors, and the collison of cultures.* New York: Noonday.

Fantini, M., and R. Cardenas. 1980. *Parenting in a multicultural society.* New York: Longman.

Fine, B. 2000. *Social capital versus social theory: Political economy and social science at the turn of the millennia.* London: Routledge.

Finley, N., D. Roberts, and B. Banahan. 1988. Motivators and inhibitors of attitudes of filial obligation toward aging parents. *The Gerontologist* 28, no. 1:73–78.

Fishman, C. 1986. Vietnamese families in Philadelphia: An analysis of household food decisions and the nutritional status of Vietnamese women and children living in Philadelphia, 1980–1984. Ph.D. diss., University of Pennsylvania, Philadelphia.

Fitzpatrick, M. A. 1977. A typological approach to communication in relationships. *Communication Yearbook*, vol. I, ed. Brent Rubin. New Brunswick, N.J.: Transaction Press.

Fix, M., and W. Zimmermann. 1997. Immigrant families and public policy: A deepening divide: Research and policy on U.S. immigrants. In *Immigration and the family*, ed. A. Booth, A. C. Crouter, and N. Landale. Mahweh, N.J.: Erlbaum.

Foner, N., R. Rumbaut, and S. Gold, eds. 2000. *Immigration research for a new century: Multidisciplinary perspectives.* New York: Russell Sage Foundation.

Fox, R. 1984. The Indochinese: Strategies for health survival. *International Journal of Social Psychiatry* 30:285–291.

Freedman, M., ed. 1970. *Family and kinship in Chinese society.* Stanford, Calif.: Stanford University Press.

Freeman, J. 1989. *Hearts of sorrow: Vietnamese-American lives.* Stanford: Stanford University Press.

Fulbright, J. W. 1966. *The arrogance of power.* New York: Random House.

Garbarino, J. 1982. *Children and families in the social environment.* New York: Aldine.

Garza, A. C., and A. C. Guerrero. 1974. Culture shock: Its mourning and the vicissitudes of identity. *Journal of the American Psychoanalytic Association* 22, no. 2:408–429.

Geddes, W. R. 1976. *Migrants of the mountains: The cultural ecology of the Blue Miao Hmong Njua of Thailand.* London: Oxford University Press.

Gelfand, D. E. 1982. *Aging: The ethnic factor.* Boston: Little, Brown.

George, L. 1980. *Role transitions in later life.* Belmont, Calif.: Wadsworth.

Gleason, J. B., and G. Melzi. 1997. The mutual construction of narrative by mothers and children: Cross cultural observations. *Journal of Narrative and Life History* 7, 1–4, 217–222.

Glenn, E. N. 1983. Split household, small producer, and dual wage earner: An analysis of Chinese-American family strategies. *Journal of Marriage and the Family* 45:35–46.

Gold, S. J. 1992. *Refugee communities: A comparative field study.* Newbury Park, Calif.: Sage.

Goldstein, B. 1985. Schooling for cultural transitions: Hmong girls and boys in American high schools. Ph.D. diss., University of Wisconsin, Madison.

———. 1986. In search of survival: The education and integration of Hmong refugee girls. *Journal of Ethnic Studies* 16, no 2:1–27.

Gozdziak, E. 1988. *Older refugees in the United States: From dignity to despair.* Washington, D.C.: Center for Policy Analysis and Research on Refugee Issues.

———. 1989. New branches . . . distant roots: Older refugees in the United States. *Aging* 359:2–7.

Greeley, A. M. 1974. *Ethnicity in the United States: A preliminary reconnaissance.* New York: Wiley.

Gross, C. S. 1986. The Hmong in Isla Vista: Obstacles and enhancements to adjustment. In *The Hmong in transition,* ed. G. L. Hendricks, B. T. Downing, and A. S. Deinard. New York: Center for Migration Studies.

Grotevant, H. 1987. Toward a process model of identity formation. *Journal of Adolescent Research* 2:203–222.

Gurin, P., and E. Epps. 1975. *Black consciousness, identity, and achievement.* New York: Wiley.

Hagemeister, A. 1994. Gender in Hmong families: Voices from two generations. Master's thesis, University of Minnesota, St. Paul.

Haines, D., D. Rutherford, and P. Thomas. 1981. Family and community among Vietnamese refugees. *International Migration Review* 15:310–319.

Handelman, L. 1991. *Cambodian elderly explanatory models for illness and help-seeking behavior: Final student fellowship report.* Washington, D.C.: Gerontological Society of America.

Harding, R. K., and J. G. Looney. 1977. Problems of Southeast Asian children in a refugee camp. *American Journal of Psychiatry* 134, no. 4:407–411.

Hareven, T., and K. Adams, eds. 1982. *Aging and life course transitions: An interdisciplinary perspective.* New York: Guilford.

Hayes, C. 1984. A study of the older Hmong refugees in the United States. Ph.D. diss., Fielding Institute, Santa Barbara, Calif.

———. 1987. Two worlds in conflict: The elder Hmong in the United States. In *Ethnic Dimensions of Aging*, ed. D. Gelfand. New York: Springer.

Heinbeck, E. 1983. Interview notes cited in Hayes 1984.

Henkin, A. B., and L. T. Nguyen. 1981. *Between two cultures: The Vietnamese in America.* Saratoga, Calif.: Century Twenty-One.

Henkin, N., G. Weinstein-Shr, and E. Gozdziak. 1988. New Branches . . . Distant Roots: A National Symposium on Older Refugees in America. Philadelphia, Temple University.

Hess, R., and G. Handel. 1959. *Family worlds: A psychosocial approach to family life.* Chicago: University of Chicago Press.

Hickey, G. C. 1964. *Village in Vietnam.* New Haven: Yale University Press.

Higgitt, C. C., and L. Horne. 1999. Resettlement experiences: Refugees from Kurdistan and Vietnam. *Canadian Home Economics Journal* 49, no. 1:24–31.

Hildreth, G. J., and A. I. Sugawara. 1993. Ethnicity and diversity in family life education. In *Handbook of family life education*, ed. M. E. Arcus, L. D. Schvaneveldt, and J. J. Moss. Newbury Park, Calif.: Sage.

Hirayama, K., and H. Hirayama. 1988. Stress, social supports, and adaptational patterns in Hmong refugee families. *Amerasia Journal* 14:93–108.

Hirschman, C., P. Kasinitz, J. DeWind, eds. 1999. *The handbook of international migration: The American experience*, New York: Russell Sage Foundation.

Hirschman, C., and R. Rindfuss. 1982. The sequence and timing of family formation events in Asia. *American Sociological Review* 47:660–680.

Hoskins, J. 1998. *Biographical objects: How things tell the stories of people's lives.* New York: Routledge.

Hughes, M. 1990. Hmong concepts of parenthood and family in the United States. Master's thesis, Department of Anthropology, Washington State University.

Jordan, D. K. 1972. *Gods, ghosts, and ancestors: The folk religion of a Taiwanese village.* Berkeley, Calif.: University of California Press.

Kantor, D., and W. Lehr. 1976. *Inside the family.* San Francisco: Jossey-Bass.

Kaufman, S. 1981. Cultural components of identity in old age. *Ethos* 9, no. 1 (spring): 55.

Kenyon, G., P. Clark, and B. deVries, eds. 2001. *Narrative gerontology: Theory, research, and practice.* New York: Springer Publishing Company.

Khoa, L.X., and J. M. Van Deusen. 1981. Social and cultural customs: Their contribution to resettlement. *Journal of Refugee Resettlement* 1:48–51.

Kibria, N. 1993. *Family tightrope: The changing lives of Vietnamese Americans.* Princeton, N.J.: Princeton University Press.

Kim, S. C., K. H. Chu, and S. Lee. 1987. Focus on Korean-American teens. *COTESOL Newsletter* 10:3–4.

Kinzie, J. D. 1989. Therapeutic approaches to traumatized Cambodian refugees. *Journal of Traumatic Stress* 2, no. 1:75–91.

Kinzie, J., W. Sack, R. Angell, S. Manson, and B. Rath. 1986. The psychiatric effects of massive trauma on Cambodian children. *Journal of American Academy of Child Psychiatry* 25:37–376.

Kirk, J., and M. Miller. 1986. *Reliability and validity in qualitative research.* Beverly Hills, Calif.: Sage.

Kivett, V. R., and M. P. Atkinson. 1984. Filial expectations, association, and helping as a function of number of children among older rural-transitional parents. *Journal of Gerontology* 39, no. 4:499–503.

Kleinman, A. 1976. Depression, somatization, and the "new" cross-cultural psychiatry. *Social Sciences and Medicine* 10:1–8.

Kluckhohn, C. 1951. Values and value orientations. In *Toward a general theory of action,* ed. T. Parsons. Cambridge: Harvard University Press.

Kosberg, J. I., ed. 1992. *Family care of the elderly: Social and cultural changes.* Newbury Park, Calif.: Sage.

Kroll, J. 1989. Ongoing treatment of a Hmong widow who suffers from pain and depression. *Hospital and Community Psychiatry* 40:691–693.

Kulig, J. 1991. Role, status changes and family planning use among Cambodian refugee women. Ph.D. diss., University of California, San Francisco.

Lam, L., and J. Westermeyer. 1987. Refugee adolescent and special mental health problems. *Refugee mental health letter* (Refugee Assistance Program, Mental Health, Technical Assistance Center, Minneapolis).

Langness, L. 1965. *The life history in anthropological science.* New York: Holt, Rinehart, and Winston.

Langness, L., and G. Frank. 1981. *Lives: An anthropological approach to biography.* Novato, Calif.: Chandler and Sharp.

LaRossa, R., ed. 1984. *Family case studies: A sociological perspective.* New York: Free Press.

Lazar, G. 1979. In *The family in Asia,* ed. M.S. Das and P. D. Bardis. London: George Allen and Unwin.

Lebra, T. S. 1979. The dilemma and strategies of aging among contemporary Japanese women. *Ethnology* 18:337–353.

Ledgerwood, J. 1989. *Sri Grap Lakkhana: Khmer images of the perfect woman.* Ithaca: Cornell University.

Lee, E., and F. Lu. 1989. Assessment and treatment of Asian-American survivors of mass violence. *Journal of Traumatic Stress* 2, no. 1:93–121.

Lee, G. 1981. The effects of development measures on the socio-economy of the White Hmong. Ph.D. diss., University of Sydney, Australia.

Lee, G. Y. 1986. Culture and adaptation: Hmong refugees in Australia. In *The Hmong in Transition,* ed. G. L. Hendricks, B. T. Downing, A. S. Deinard. New York: Center for Migration Studies.

Lee, S. M. 1998. Asian Americans: Diverse and growing. *Population Bulletin* (Population Reference Bureau, Washington, D.C.) 53: 2.

Lerner, R. M., 1982. Children and adolescents as producers of their own development. *Developmental Review* 2:342–370.

Leslie, L. M. 2002. A Hmong hallmark: Lots of people under one roof. (Minneapolis) *Star/Tribune*, April 10, at www.lib.umn.edu/web–bin/lex.cgi.

Lieberman, M., and J. Falk. 1971. The remembered past as a source of data on the life cycle. *Human Development* 14:132–141.

Liebkind, K. 1993. Self reported ethnic identity, depression, and anxiety among young Vietnamese and their parents, *Journal of Refugee Studies* 6, 1.

Liem, N. D. 1985. The elderly Indochinese. In *Guide to the utilization of family and community support systems by Pacific/Asian elderly*. Washington, D.C.: National Pacific/Asian Resource Center on Aging.

Liem, N., and D. Kehmeier. 1979. The Vietnamese. In *Peoples and cultures of Hawaii*, ed. J. F. McDermott. Honolulu: University Press of Hawaii.

Lin, K-M. 1986. Psychopathology and social disruption in refugees. In *Refugee mental health in resettlement countries*, ed. C. L. Williams and J. Westermeyer. Washington, D.C.: Hemisphere.

Lin, K-M., and M. Masuda. 1983. Impact of the refugee experience: Mental health issues of the Southeast Asians. In *Bridging cultures: Southeast Asian refugees in America*. Corporate authors: Asian American Community Mental Health Training Center; Asian/Pacific Social Work Curriculum Development Project. Los Angeles: Special Services for Groups.

Linton, R. 1936. *A study of man*. New York: Appleton-Century.

Liu, W. T. 1966. Family interactions among local and refugee Chinese families in Hong Kong. *Journal of Marriage and the Family* 28 (August): 314–23.

Liu, W., and M. Fernandez. 1988. Asian immigrant households and strategies for family reunification. In *The Pacific/Asian mental health research center: A decade review*, ed. W. Liu. Chicago: Pacific/Asian American Mental Health Research Center.

Long, L. 1993. *Ban Vinai: The refugee camp*. New York: Columbia University Press.

Looney, J., R. Rahe, R. Harding, H. Ward, and W. Liu. 1979. Consulting to children in crisis. *Child Psychiatry and Human Development* 10:5–14.

Luborsky, M. R., and R. L. Rubinstein. 1990. Ethnic identity and bereavement in later life: The case of older widowers. In *The cultural context of aging: Worldwide perspectives*, ed. J. Sokolovsky. Westport, Conn.: Bergin and Garvey.

Lum, D. 1983. Asian-Americans and their aged. In *Aging in minority groups*, ed. R. L. McNeely and J. L. Colen. Beverly Hills, Calif.: Sage.

Lynch, A., D. F. Detzner, and J. B. Eicher. 1995. Hmong American new year rituals: Generational bonds through dress. *Clothing and Textiles Research Journal* 13, no. 2:111–120.

———. 1996. Hmong American new year rituals: Transmission and reconstruction of gender through dress. *Clothing and Textile Research Journal* 14, no. 1:1–10.

Lynch, E., and H. Do. 1986. Mental distress among aging Vietnamese refugees: A model for services. Master's thesis, California State University, Sacramento.

Maldonado, D., Jr. 1975. Ethnic self-identity and self-understanding. *Social Casework* 56:618–622.

Manis, J., and B. Meltzer, eds. 1967. *Symbolic interaction: A reader in social psychology.* Boston: Allyn and Bacon.

Martin, B. 1987. Unaccompanied minors: A UNHCR view. In *Years of horror, days of hope,* ed. B.S. Levy and D.S. Sustott. New York: Associated Faculty Press.

Martin, P., and E. Midgley. 1994. Immigration to the United States: Journey to an uncertain destination, *Population Bulletin* 49, 2, Washington, D.C.: Population Reference Bureau.

Mason, S. 1981. The Indochinese: Vietnamese, ethnic Chinese, Hmong, Lao, Cambodians. In *They chose Minnesota: A survey of the state's ethnic groups,* ed. J. Holmquist. St. Paul: Minnesota Historical Society Press.

Maxwell, R. J., and P. Silverman. 1970. Information and esteem: Cultural considerations in the treatment of the aged. *Aging and Human Development* 1:361–392.

McAdams, D. P. 1993. *Stories we live by: Personal myths and the making of the self.* New York: Morrow.

McGoldrick, M. 1982. Ethnicity and family therapy: An overview. In *Ethnicity and family therapy,* ed. M. McGoldrick, J. K. Pearce, and J. Giordano. New York: Guilford.

McLoyd, V. C., L. Steinberg, eds. 1998. Studying minority adolescents: Conceptual, methodological, and theoretical issues. Mahwah, N.J.: Erlbaum.

McNall, M., and T. Dunnigan. 1993. Hmong youth in St. Paul's public schools. *CURA Reporter* 23, no. 1:10–14.

Meredith, W. H., and S. Cramer. 1979. Hmong refugees in Nebraska. In *Building family strengths,* ed. N. Stinnett, B. Chesser, and J. DeFrain. Lincoln: University of Nebraska Press.

Meredith, W. H., and G. P. Rowe. 1986. Changes in Hmong refugee marital attitudes in America. In *The Hmong in transition,* ed. G. L. Hendricks, B. T. Downing, and A. S. Deinard. New York: Center for Migration Studies.

Merriam, S. 1980. The concept and function of reminiscence: A review of the research. *The Gerontologist* 20, no. 5:604–609.

Minnesota Attorney General. 1991. The Hmong community's access to government services: A working group report. March.

Minnesota Department of Health and Human Services. 1988. Assessment of refugee mental health needs, part 2. Project report funded by the National Institute of Mental Health, Washington, D.C.

Minnesota Department of Health and Human Services. 1991. *Refugee and immigrant arrivals to Minnesota by year of arrival, 1979 through 1990.* Minneapolis, Minn.: Refugee Health Unit.

Mollica, R., and R. Jalbert. 1989. *Community of confinement: The mental health crisis in site two.* Brighton, Mass.: The World Federation for Mental Health Committees on Refugees and Migrants.

Mollica, R., G. Wyshak, and J. Lavelle. 1987. The psycho-social impact of war trauma and torture on Southeast Asian refugees. *American Journal of Psychiatry* 44, no. 12:1567–1572.

Morgan, S. P., and K. Hirosima. 1983. The persistence of extended family residence in Japan: Anachronism or alternative strategy? *American Sociological Review* 48:269–281.

Mortland, C. A. 1987. Transforming refugees in refugee camps. *Urban Anthropology and Studies of Cultural Systems and World Economic Development* 16:375–404.

———. 1994. Cambodian refugees and identity in the United States. In *Reconstructing lives, recapturing meaning: Refugee identity, gender, and culture change*, ed. L. A. Camino and R. M. Krulfeld. Basel, Switzerland: Gordon and Breach.

Moua, M. N. 2002. *Bamboo among the Oaks: Contemporary writing by Hmong Americans.* St Paul: Minnesota Historical Society Press.

Mouanoutoua, V. L. 1989. Validity and reliability of the Beck depression inventory adapted Hmong version. Master's thesis, California State University, Fresno.

Muir, K. 1988. *The strongest part of the family: A study of Lao refugee women in Columbus, Ohio.* New York: AMS.

Myerhoff, B. 1992. *Remembered lives: The work of ritual, storytelling, and growing older.* Ann Arbor: University of Michigan Press.

Nash, J. 1992. *Vietnamese Catholicism.* Harvey, La.: Art Review Press.

Nicassio, P. 1985. The psycho-social adjustment of the Southeast Asian refugee: An overview of empirical findings and theoretical models. *Journal of Cross Cultural Psychology* 16, no. 2:153–173.

Northwest Educational Cooperative. 1987. Refugee elderly. Office of Refugee Resettlement, Arlington Heights, Ill.

Nydegger, C. 1983. Family ties of the aged in cross-cultural perspective. *The Gerontologist* 23:26–32.

Nye, F. 1976. *Role structure and analysis of the family.* Beverly Hills, Calif.: Sage.

Office of Refugee Resettlement. 1991a. Estimated cumulative state populations including entries from 1975 through 1/31/91. Washington, D.C.

———. 1991b. Refugee population estimates by ethnicity. Washington, D.C.

Okura, K. P. 1981. Indochinese refugees: Families/children in turmoil. Paper presented at American Orthopsychiatric Association annual meeting, New York, N.Y.

Olney, D. 1988. Age and style of leadership in a Hmong community. Paper presented at the American Anthropological Association annual meeting, Phoenix, Ariz.

Olson, D., C. Russell, and D. Sprenkle. 1979. Circumplex model of marital and family systems: Cohesion and adaptability dimensions, family types, and clinical applications. *Family Process* 18:69–84.

Osaka, M. 1979a. Intergenerational relations as an aspect of assimilation: The case of Japanese-Americans. *Sociological Inquiry* 46:67–72.

———. 1979b. Aging and family among Japanese Americans: The role of ethnic tradition in the adjustment to old age. *The Gerontologist* 19:448–455.

Papajohn, J., and J. Spiegel. 1975. *Transaction in families.* San Francisco: Jossey-Bass.

Parker, M. 1996. Loss in the lives of Southeast Asian elders. Ph.D. diss., University of Minnesota, St. Paul.

Pfeifer, M. 2001. 2000 census shows contrasting growth and settlement patterns of four major Southeast Asian origin groups. At www.hmongstudies.org/growandsetpa.htm.

Phinney, J. S. 1989. Stages of ethnic identity in minority group adolescents. *Journal of Early Adolescence* 8:265–277.

———. 1990. Ethnic identity in adolescents and adults: Review of research. *Psychological Bulletin* 108, no. 3:499–514.

Phommasouvanh, B. 1983. Aspects of Lao family and social life. In *Bridging Cultures: Southeast Asian Refugees in America*. Corporate authors: Asian American Community Mental Health Training Center; Asian/Pacific Social Work Curriculum Development Project. Los Angeles: Special Services for Groups.

Plath, D. W. 1964. Where the family of God is the family: The role of the dead in Japanese households. *American Anthropologist* 66:300–317.

Portes, A. 1995. Children of immigrants: Segmented assimilation and its determinants. In *The economic sociology of immigration: Essays on networks, ethnicity, and entrepreneurship*, ed. A. Portes. New York: Russell Sage Foundation.

———, ed. 1996. *The new second generation*. New York: Russell Sage Foundation.

Powell, G. J., J. Yamamoto, A. Romero, and A. Morales, eds. 1983. *The psychosocial development of minority group children*. New York: Brunner/Mazel.

Prendergast, N. 1985. A Vietnamese refugee family in the United States from 1975–1985: A case study in education and culture. Ph.D. diss., Loyola University, Chicago.

Public Housing Agency of the City of St. Paul. 1992. Social service needs in family public housing: An action plan.

Queen, S., R. Habenstein, and J. Quadagno. 1985. *The family in various cultures*. New York: Harper and Row.

Ray, M. P. 1988. An ecological model of the family. *Home Economics Forum* 2, no. 15:9–11.

Refugee Action. 1987. *Last refuge: Elderly people from Vietnam in the U.K.* Derby, England: Refugee Action.

Refugee Reports. 1987. Elderly Southeast Asian refugees: Still strangers in a strange land. *Refugee Reports* 8 (May).

Roberts, B. 1995. Socially expected duration and the economic adjustment of immigrants. In *The economic sociology of immigration: Essays on networks, ethnicity, and entrepreneurship*, ed. A. Portes. New York: Russell Sage Foundation.

Robinson, B. 1987. Social adjustment program for refugees: Evaluation report on 1985–1986 client intakes. Wilder Research Center, Amherst H. Wilder Foundation, St. Paul, Minn.

Rogler, L. 1989. The meaning of culturally sensitive research in mental health. *American Journal of Psychiatry* 146, no. 3:296–303.

Rokeach, M. 1973. *The nature of human values*. New York: Free Press.

Rottman, L. H., and W. H. Meredith, 1982. Indochinese refugee families: Their strengths and needs. In *Family strengths 4: Positive support systems*, ed. Stinnett et al. Lincoln: University of Nebraska Press.

Rozee, P., and G. Van Boemel. 1989. The psychological effects of war trauma and abuse on older Cambodian refugee women. *Women and Therapy* 12:23–50.

Rumbaut, R. 1999. It takes a family and a village: Patterns of incorporation among children of immigrants. Paper presentation at the Sixty-first National Conference on Family Relations, Irvine, Calif.

————. 2000. Immigration research in the United States: Social origins and future orientations. In *Immigration research for a new century: Multidisciplinary perspectives,* ed. N. Foner, R. Rumbaut, S. Gold. New York: Russell Sage Foundation.

Rumbaut, R., and K. Ima. 1987. The adaptation of Southeast Asian refugee youth: A comparative study. Final report prepared for the Office of Refugee Resettlement, Family Support Administration, U.S. Department of Health and Human Services, Washington, D.C.

Rumbaut, R., and J. Weeks. 1986. Fertility and adaptation: Indochinese refugees in the United States. *International Migration Review* 20, no. 2:428–465.

Scott, G. 1986. Migrants without mountains: The politics of sociocultural adjustment among the Lao Hmong refugees in San Diego. Ph.D. diss., University of California, San Diego.

Seabloom, M. 1991. Filial piety in Vietnamese refugee families: Perspectives of the elderly refugees. Master's thesis, University of Minnesota, St. Paul.

Seelbach, W., and A. Die. 1988. Family satisfaction and filial norms among elderly Vietnamese immigrants. *Journal of Aging Studies* 2:267–276.

Seelbach, W. 1977. Gender difference in expectations for filial responsibility. *The Gerontologist* 17, no. 5:421–425.

Seelbach, W., and W. Sauer. 1977. Filial expectations and morale among aged parents. *The Gerontologist* 17, no. 6:492–499.

Seltzer, M., and L. Troll. 1982. Conflicting public attitudes toward filial responsibility. *Journal of the Western Gerontological Society* 6 (Winter): 26–27, 40.

Serafica, F. C. 1990. Counseling Asian-American parents: A cultural-developmental approach. In *Mental health of ethnic minorities,* ed. F. C. Serafica, A. I. Schwebel, R. K. Russell, D. Isaac, and L. B. Myers. New York: Praeger.

Settersten, R. A., Jr., ed. 2003. *Invitation to the life course.* Amityville, N.Y.: Baywood.

Shanas, E. 1973. Family-kin networks and aging in cross-cultural perspective. *Journal of Marriage and the Family* 35 (August):505–511.

Sherlock, D. 1987. *Southeast Asian refugees in Minnesota.* St. Paul: St. Paul Foundation.

Sih, P. K. T. 1961. *The Hsaio Ching.* New York: St. John's University Press.

Simmons, L. W. 1945. *The role of the aged in primitive society.* New Haven, Conn.: Yale University Press.

Simon, R. J. 1997. Refugee women and their daughters: A comparison of Soviet, Vietnamese and native-born American families. In *Immigration and the family,* ed. A. Booth, A. C. Crouter, and N. Landale. Mahweh, N.J.: Erlbaum.

Smith, C. A., D. H. Cudaback, W. Goddard, and J. A. Meyers-Walls. 1994. *The national extension parent education model: Of critical parenting practices.* Manhattan, Ks.: Kansas Cooperative Extension Service.

Sokolovsky, J. 1985. Ethnicity, culture and aging: Do differences really make a difference? *Journal of Applied Gerontology* 4:6–17.

————. 1990a. Bringing culture back home: Aging, ethnicity, and family support. In *The cultural context of aging: Worldwide perspectives*, ed. J. Sokolovsy. Westport, Conn.: Bergin and Garvey.

————. 1990b. *The cultural context of aging: Worldwide perspectives.* Westport, Conn.: Bergin and Garvey.

Spain, D., 1999. America's diversity: On the edge of two centuries. *Reports on America*, 1, 2, Washington, D.C.: Population Reference Bureau.

Spencer, M. B., and Markstrom-Adams. 1990. Identity processes among racial and ethnic minority children in America. *Child Development* 61:290–310.

Spradley, J., and M. Phillips. 1972. Culture and stress. *American Anthropologist* 74:518–529.

Sprey, J. 1979. Conflict theory and the study of marriage and the family. In *Contemporary theories about the family*, vol. 2, ed. W. Burr et al. New York: Free Press.

St. Paul Foundation. 1987. Southeast Asian refugees in Minnesota. Report prepared by Donna L. Sherlock, the St. Paul Foundation.

Stavans, A. 1996. Development of parental narrative input. *Journal of Narrative and Life History* 6, no. 3:253–280.

Stinett, N., B. Chesser, and J. DeFrain, eds. 1980. *Building family strengths.* Lincoln: University of Nebraska Press.

Strauss, A. and J. Corbin. 1990. Basics of qualitative research: grounded theory procedures and techniques. Newbury Park, Calif.: Sage.

Sussman, M., and J. Romeis. 1981. Family supports for the aged: A comparison of U.S. and Japan responses. *Journal of Comparative Family Studies* 6: 475–492.

————. 1982. Willingness to assist one's elderly parents: Responses from United States and Japanese families. *Human Organization* 41:256–259.

Sutherland, J. E., et al. 1983. Indochinese refugee health assessment and treatment. *Journal of Family Practice* 16:61–67.

Swick, K. 1985. Cultural influences on parenting: Implications for parent educators. *Journal of Instructional Psychology* 12:80–85.

————. 1986. Parents as models in children's cultural development. *Clearing House* 60, no. 2:72–75.

Tajfel, H. 1981. Human groups and social categories. Cambridge, England: Cambridge University Press.

Takaki, R. 1993. *A different mirror: A history of multicultural America.* Boston: Little, Brown.

Tharp, R., A. Meadow, S. Leunhoff, and S. Satterfield. 1968. Changes in marriage roles accompanying the acculturation of the Mexican-American wife. *Journal of Marriage and the Family* 30:404–412.

Thernstrom, S., ed. 1980. *Harvard encyclopedia of American ethnic groups.* Cambridge, Mass.: Harvard University Press.

Thomas, W. I., and F. Znaniecki. [1918–1920] 1958. *The Polish peasant in Europe and America.* Reprint, New York: Dover.

Tobin, J. J., and J. Friedman. 1984. Intercultural and developmental stresses confronting Southeast Asian refugee adolescents. *Journal of Operational Psychiatry* 15:39–45.

Tran, T.V. 1977. Some aspects of cultural adjustments of Asian children in American schools. In *Forum of transcultural adaptation: Asian children in American classrooms, proceedings*. Chicago: Illinois State Board of Education.

———. 1988. Sex differences in English language acculturation and learning strategies among Vietnamese adults aged forty and over in the United States. *Sex Roles* 19:747–758.

———. 1991. Family living arrangement and social adjustment among three ethnic groups of elderly Indochinese refugees. *International Journal of Aging and Human Development* 22:91–102.

Tran, T., and R. Wright Jr. 1986. Social support and subjective well-being among Vietnamese refugees. *Social Service Review* 9:449–459.

Turner, V., and E. Bruner, eds. 1986. *The anthropology of experience*. Urbana: University of Illinois Press.

Unruh, D., and G. Livings, eds. 1989. Personal history through the life course. Greenwich, Conn.: JAI Press.

U.S. Committee for Refugees. 1984. *Vietnamese boat people: Pirates' vulnerable prey*. Washington, D.C.: Immigration and Refugee Services of America.

———.1987. *Uncertain harbors: The plight of Vietnamese boat people*. Washington, D.C. : Immigration and Refugee Services of America.

———. 1993. *World Refugee Survey*. New York: American Council for Nationalities Service.

U.S. Department of Health and Human Services, Office of Refugee Resettlement. 1987. *The refugee family: Region V consultation report*. Washington, D.C.: Office of Refugee Resettlement.

Van Arsdale, P., and E. Skartvedt. 1987. Social-psychological adjustments of older refugees in Colorado. Paper presented at the American Anthropological Association annual meeting, Chicago, November.

Van Deusen, J. M., C. M. Coleman, L. X. Khoa, D. Phan, H. H. Doeung, K. Chaw, L. T. Hguyen, P. G. Pham, and T. Bounthinh. 1980. Southeast Asian social and cultural customs: Similarities and differences. *Journal of Refugee Resettlement* 1:20–39.

Vang, T. F. 1983. The Hmong of Laos. In *Bridging cultures: Southeast Asian refugees in America*. Corporate authors: Asian American Community Mental Health Training Center; Asian/Pacific Social Work Curriculum Development Project. Los Angeles: Special Services for Groups.

Watson, L., and M-B. Watson-Franke. 1985. *Interpreting life histories*. New Brunswick, N.J.: Rutgers University Press.

Weinreich, P. 1983. Emerging from threatened identities. In *Threatened Identities*, ed. G. Breakwell. New York: Wiley.

Weinstein-Shr, G., and N. Henkin. 1991. Continuity and change: Intergenerational relations in Southeast Asian refugee families. *Marriage and Family Review* 16:351–367.

Westermeyer, J., J. Neider, and T. F. Vang. 1987. Somatization among refugees: An epidemiologic study. *Psychosomatics* 30:34–43.

Whitbourne, S. K. 1986. *The me I know: A study of adult identity.* New York: Springer-Verlag.

Whyte, W. F. 1943. *Street corner society.* Chicago: University of Chicago Press.

Williams, C. L., and J. Westermeyer. 1983. Psychiatric problems among adolescent Southeast Asian refugees: A descriptive study. *Journal of Nervous and Mental Disease* 171:79–85.

Wolf, M. 1978. Child training and the Chinese family. In *Studies in Chinese society*, ed. A. P. Wolf. Stanford, Calif.: Stanford University Press.

Wong, A. K.1979. A modern Chinese family—Ideology, revolution, and residues. In *The family in Asia*, ed. M. S. Das and P. D. Bardis. London: George Allen and Unwin.

Wooden, W. S. 1995. *Renegade kids, suburban outlaws.* Belmont, Calif.: Wadsworth.

Xiong, Z. B. 1997. Southeast Asian parenting: Conflicts and meanings. Master's thesis, University of Minnesota, St. Paul.

———. 2000. Hmong American parent-adolescent problem-solving interactions: An analytical induction analysis. Ph.D. diss., University of Minnesota.

Xiong, Z. B., D. F. Detzner, and K. D. Rettig. 2001 Southeast Asian immigrant parenting practices and perceptions of parent-adolescent conflicts. *Journal of Teaching Marriage and Family: Innovations in Family Science Education* 1, no. 1:1–10.

Yang, D. 1996. St. Paul Public School District, personal communication.

Yang, D., and D. North. 1988. Profiles of highland Lao communities in the United States. Final report, Family Support Administration and the Office of Refugee Resettlement, U.S. Department of Health and Human Services, Washington, D.C.

Yang, K. 1989. *Reasons for living and hoping: Southeast Asian refugee children's psychological and spiritual needs.* St. Paul: Hmong Catholic National Association.

Yang, M. C. 1968. *A Chinese village: Taitou, Shantung Province.* New York: Columbia University Press.

Yee, B. 1986. Markers of successful aging among Southeast Asian refugees. Paper presented at the annual meeting of the Gerontological Society of America, Chicago.

———. 1989. Impact of immigration and aging policies on adaptation by Southeast Asian refugee elders. Paper presented at the annual meeting of the Gerontological Society of America, Minneapolis.

Yeung, R. 1988. Help-seeking behavior of Cambodian refugees experiencing posttraumatic stress disorder. Master's thesis, California State University, Long Beach.

Yin, R. 1984. *Case study research.* Beverly Hills, Calif.: Sage.

———. 1993. *Applications of case study research.* Newbury Park, Calif.: Sage.

Yu, E., S. Fugita, T. Prohaska, and W. Liu. 1988. Ethnic elderly needs assessment: Final report. Pacific/Asian American Mental Health Research Center, University of Illinois, Chicago.

Yu, L. 1983. Patterns of filial belief and behavior within the contemporary Chinese American family. *International Journal of Sociology of the Family* 13 (Spring): 17–36.

Zane, N., D. Fujino, G. Nakasaki, and K. Yasuda. 1988. *Asian Pacific needs assessment.* Los Angeles: United Way.

Zhou, M., and C. L. Bankston. 1996. Social capital and the adaptation of the second generation: The case of Vietnamese youth in New Orleans. In *The new second generation*, ed. A. Portes. New York: Russell Sage Foundation.

———. 1998. *Growing up American: How Vietnamese children adapt to life in the United States.* New York: Russell Sage Foundation.

INDEX

ABOUT THE AUTHOR

Dan Detzner received his doctorate in American Studies, served as the director of the Refugee Studies Center, and is currently a professor in the Department of Family Social Science, all at the University of Minnesota. His research is located at the intersection of ethnicity, gerontology, and families with a focus on intergenerational relationships in immigrant families. In 1992 he served as a visiting research professor at Sukhothai Thammatirat Open University in Bangkok, Thailand, where he conducted research on families in Hmong and Thai villages. He is coauthor of *Helping Youth Succeed: Bicultural Parenting for Southeast Asian Families*, a multilingual parent education curriculum for parents and adolescents. Currently, he teaches undergraduate courses on global and diverse families, families and aging, and a graduate seminar on narrative family gerontology. Professor Detzner is a member of the University of Minnesota's Academy of Distinguished Teachers.